'Tim Jackson provides a convincing case as to why conventional economic growth has not and cannot deliver prosperity. By showing why this is the case, we have the tools to start to build an economy based on sustainable development.'
Jan Bebbington, Professor of Accounting and Sustainable Development, University of St Andrews

'This might well become as important for sustainable development as the Brundtland Report.'
Paul-Marie Boulanger, Director of IDD

'Tim Jackson's book simply resets the agenda for Western society. It is both radical and timely. The choice is clear – either remake capitalism as he suggests or deal with the consequences of our old ways.'
Bernie Bulkin, SDC commissioner for Climate Change, Energy and Transport, former Chief Scientist of BP

'A vital, much-needed, and timely work that deserves to be widely read, this is more than a brilliant treatise on the difficulties of developing a truly sustainable economy. It is also an important contribution to the increasingly urgent debate over the nature of the good life and the good society.'
Professor Colin Campbell, Emeritus Professor of Sociology, University of York

'Economic growth is both unsustainable on a finite planet and undesirable in its failure to continue to improve real welfare. What we need is true prosperity without growth. Why we must have this and how it can be achieved are compellingly explained in this essential work. It is not sacrifice to adopt the measures advocated. It is a sacrifice of our current and future well-being not to.'
Dr Robert Costanza, Gordon and Lulie Gund Professor of Ecological Economics and Director, Gund Institute for Ecological Economics, University of Vermont

'Provokes official thought on the unthinkable. No small accomplishment! I hope this gets the serious attention it deserves.'
Professor Herman E. Daly, author of *Steady-State Economics* and recipient of the Honorary Right Livelihood Award (Sweden's alternative to the Nobel Prize)

'What makes it unthinkable to stop growth even though it is killing us? Tim Jackson boldly confronts the structural Catch-22 that drives this madness and proposes in this lucid, persuasive, and blessedly readable book how we might begin to get off the fast track to self-destruction. Don't miss it!'
Dianne Dumanoski, author of *The End of the Long Summer* and co-author of *Our Stolen Future*

'A must-read for anyone concerned with issues of climate change and sustainability – bold, original and comprehensive. We have to define prosperity and welfare differently from the past and separate them from economic growth measured as GDP: this work shows how we should set about the task.'
Professor Lord Anthony Giddens, London School of Economics

'Tim Jackson refutes doctrinaire economist's reckless mantra that growth is the panacea. *Prosperity without Growth*'s hugely encouraging and thrilling theme is that humanity can prosper without growth. In fact there is no other way left to us. We have so overfilled our finite planet that the sources of our raw materials and the sinks for our wastes are both damaged. Jackson's clear and practical vision leads the burgeoning De-Growth movement with Jonathon Porritt, Peter Victor, Herman Daly and Roefie Hueting, all in 2009.'
Dr Robert Goodland, former Environmental and Social Adviser to the World Bank Group, winner of International Union for Conservation of Nature's Coolidge Medal of Honor, 2008

'Tim Jackson cuts through the official cant and wishful thinking to tell us what we have refused to admit – we cannot preserve a habitable planet and pursue endless economic growth at the same time. In an era when all ideologies have failed, this book lays out the basis for the only viable political philosophy for the 21st century.'
Clive Hamilton, author of *Growth Fetish* and Professor of Public Ethics, Centre for Applied Philosophy and Public Ethics, Australia

'Zero growth is not only necessary, it is inevitable and will supersede Selfish Capitalism. In this brilliant analysis, Tim Jackson has laid bare a system in crisis and has lit the way forward.'
Oliver James, author of *Affluenza*

'If you want to understand why current growth centric economics is not fit for purpose then read this book. This is the clearest and most important contribution to proving it's time to rethink growth economics in order to live the low carbon, poverty free and one planet life we all need and want.'
Alan Knight, founder of Singleplanetliving

'Endless growth on a finite planet, or endless misery-spreading recession – both represent impossible futures. Here are some very powerful steps towards a possible, indeed a very hopeful, alternate outcome!'
Bill McKibben, author of *Deep Economy*

'We were delighted when Professor Jackson spoke at our July Meeting at Lloyds Banking HQ in London. He endorsed the feelings of many in the BCSD-UK that business as usual is not an option. His clear and concise challenge of what is considered convention is timely and highly appropriate.'
David Middleton, CEO, Business Council for Sustainable Development UK

'This is the best account of the financial crisis and the state of society I have read in a long time. It is honest about the state we are in but is not despairing. It outlines how we can reshape the world so that we live in a sustainable, fairer and better way. And the beauty is that the change that is needed will make us happier.'
Clare Short, MP

'In the teeth of the economic crisis, Tim Jackson has written the most important book that could possibly be written now. Economic growth may be the world's secular religion, but as Jackson eloquently describes, it is a god that is failing today – underperforming for most of the world's people and, for those of us in affluent societies, creating more problems than it is solving. It destroys the environment, fuels a ruthless international search for energy and other resources, and rests on a manufactured consumerism that is not meeting the deepest human needs. Jackson therefore calls upon us not just to restore the economy but to reinvent it, and to realize a true prosperity beyond growth. In this path-breaking book, Jackson offers a bold agenda for system change.'
James Gustave Speth, author of *The Bridge at the Edge of the World: Capitalism, the Environment, and Crossing from Crisis to Sustainability*

'We live in a finite world but with infinite demands. Human wants, political convenience and intellectual inertia trump planetary limits. Tim Jackson makes headway in setting signposts towards a more sustainable future. Will we have the courage to take the less trodden path? And if not now, when?'
Camilla Toulmin, Director of the International Institute for Environment & Development (IIED)

'This is one of the most brilliant analyses I've seen. It is a thoughtful and action-oriented masterpiece, with an eye open to how to overcome resistance to the task ahead.'
Arnold Tukker, Netherlands Organisation for Applied Scientific Research

'Can we achieve prosperity without growth, or even do we need to? This is one of the fundamental questions of our time. Tim Jackson's book clearly demonstrates how our passion for consumption drives unsustainable results and it opens up the potential for a new model of consumerism that delivers a more sustainable world.'
Chris Tuppen, Chief Sustainability Officer, BT

Prosperity without Growth

Prosperity without Growth
Economics for a Finite Planet

Tim Jackson

publishing for a sustainable future

London • Sterling, VA

First published by Earthscan in the UK and USA in 2009
Reprinted 2009

ISBN: 978-1-84407-894-3
eISBN: 978-1-84977-000-2

Typeset by FiSH Books, Enfield
Cover design by Rob Watts

For a full list of publications please contact:

Earthscan
Dunstan House
14a St Cross Street
London EC1N 8XA, UK
Tel: +44 (0)20 7841 1930
Fax: +44 (0)20 7242 1474
Email: earthinfo@earthscan.co.uk
Web: www.earthscan.co.uk

22883 Quicksilver Drive, Sterling, VA 20166-2012, USA

Earthscan publishes in association with the International Institute for Environment and
Development

A catalogue record for this book is available from the British Library

Library of Congress Cataloging-in-Publication Data
Jackson, Tim, 1957–
  Prosperity without growth: economics for a finite planet / Tim Jackson. – 1st ed.
    p. cm.
  Includes bibliographical references and index.
  ISBN 978-1-84407-894-3 (hardback)
  1.. Sustainable development. 2. Wealth. 3. Globalization–Economic aspects. I. Title.
  HC79.E5J298 2009
  338.9'27–dc22   2009023822

At Earthscan we strive to minimize our environmental impacts and carbon footprint
through reducing waste, recycling and offsetting our CO_2 emissions, including those
created through publication of this book. For more details of our environmental policy,
see www.earthscan.co.uk.

This book was printed in the UK by MPG Books,
an ISO 14001 accredited company. The paper used
is FSC certified.

Mixed Sources
Product group from well-managed
forests and other controlled sources
www.fsc.org Cert no. SA-COC-1565
© 1996 Forest Stewardship Council

Contents

Acknowledgements

This book has drawn extensively from a report written in my capacity as Economics Commissioner for the Sustainable Development Commission (SDC, 2009a). That report was written at the personal invitation of the former Chair of the Commission, Jonathon Porritt. Jonathon himself provided the initial impetus for SDC's engagement in this area and has been unreservedly supportive of my own work for many years. For all this I owe him my profound thanks.

The book has also drawn inevitably from my role as Director of the Research group on Lifestyles, Values and Environment (RESOLVE) at the University of Surrey, where I am lucky enough to work with an enthusiastic team dedicated to research in areas that are enormously relevant to this inquiry. Their research forms part of the evidence base on which this book draws and I'm as grateful for their continuing intellectual companionship as I am for the financial support of the Economic and Social Research Council (Grant No: RES-152-25-1004). I owe thanks to Gemma Cook, the administrative coordinator in RESOLVE, who rose to the challenge of managing our mutually increased workload during the writing of the book with unwavering grace and good humour.

Though written as a monograph, this study builds on a huge resource base. Most obviously it draws on work right across the SDC, in particular the work programme on *Redefining Prosperity* (see Appendix 1) which I led for the Commission over the last five years. Throughout that period, my fellow commissioners past and present – Jan Bebbington, Bernie Bulkin, Lindsey Colbourne, Anna Coote, Peter Davies, Stewart Davis, Ann Finlayson, Tess Gill, Alan Knight, Tim Lang, Alice Owen, Anne Power, Hugh Raven, Tim O'Riordan, Waheed Saleem and Becky Willis – have been generous with their time, attending workshops, offering critical commentary and reviewing drafts of various documents.

Special thanks are owed to all those who contributed directly to a series of workshops on prosperity carried out between November 2007 and April 2008. Contributors included: Simone d'Alessandro, Frederic Bouder, Madeleine Bunting, Ian Christie, Herman Daly, Arik Dondi, Paul Ekins, Tim Kasser, Miriam Kennet, Guy Liu, Tommaso Luzzati, Jesse Norman, Avner Offer, John O'Neill, Elke Pirgmaier, Tom Prugh, Hilde Rapp, Jonathan Rutherford, Jill Rutter, Zia Sardar, Kate Soper, Steve Sorrell, Nick Spencer, Peter Victor, Derek Wall, David Woodward and Dimitri Zenghelis.

A number of other colleagues and friends have helped and advised in this endeavour – sometimes without even knowing it! Particular thanks are due to Colin Campbell, Mick Common, Brian Davey, Andy Dobson, Angela Druckman, Ian Gough, Bronwyn Hayward, Colin Hines, Fritz Hinterberger, Lester Hunt, Nic Marks, Frances O'Grady, Ronan Palmer, Miriam Pepper, Ann Pettifor, Alison Pridmore, Rita Trattnig, Chris Tuppen, John Urry and David Wheat.

The SDC secretariat who helped convene the workshops and launch the original report deserve a special mention. Sue Dibb, Sara Eppel, Ian Fenn, Andrew Lee, Andy Long, Rhian Thomas, Jacopo Torriti, Joe Turrent and Kay West were a constant source of advice and support. I owe a debt of gratitude to Victor Anderson whose experience was indispensable throughout the *Redefining Prosperity* project.

Finally, my thanks to the team at Earthscan – in particular Camille Bramall, Gudrun Freese, Alison Kuznets, Veruschka Selbach and Jonathan Sinclair Wilson – for their patience, support and boundless enthusiasm for the project.

Forewords

A Foreword by Herman E. Daly

The fundamental axiom of growth, rigorously stated by Kenneth Boulding, is that 'When something grows, it gets bigger!' When the economy grows it too gets bigger. So, dear economist, when the economy grows, (a) exactly what is it that is getting bigger? (b) How big is it now? (c) How big could it possibly get? (d) How big should it be? Given that economic growth is the top priority for all nations, one would expect that these questions would get major attention in all economics textbooks. In fact (b), (c) and (d) are not raised at all, and (a) is answered unsatisfactorily. *Prosperity Without Growth* makes a large contribution to filling this void. Given academic economists' long track record of mind-numbing irrelevance it should perhaps not be so surprising that this report originated in the government.

Exactly what is growing? One thing is GDP, the annual marketed flow of final goods and services. But there is also the *throughput* – the metabolic flow of useful matter and energy from environmental sources, through the economic subsystem (production and consumption), and back to environmental sinks as waste. Economists have focused on GDP and, until recently, neglected throughput. But throughput is the relevant magnitude for answering the question about how big the economy is – namely how big is the economy's metabolic flow relative to the natural cycles that regenerate the economy's resource depletion and absorb its waste emissions, as well as providing countless other natural services? The answer is that the economic subsystem is now very large relative to the ecosystem that sustains it. How big can the economy possibly be before it overwhelms and destroys the ecosystem in the short run? We have decided apparently to do an experiment to answer that question empirically! How big should the economy be, what is its optimum scale relative to the ecosystem? If we were true econo-mists we would stop throughput growth before the extra environmental and social costs that it causes exceed the extra production benefits that it produces. GDP does not help us discover this point since it is based on conflating costs and benefits into 'economic activity' rather than comparing them at the margin. There is much evidence that some countries have passed this opti-mal scale, and entered an era of uneconomic growth that accumulates illth faster than it adds to wealth. Once growth becomes uneconomic at the margin it begins to make us poorer, not richer. Therefore it can no longer be appealed to as necessary to fight poverty. It makes it harder to fight poverty!

The claim is often made that wealth can continue to grow with no further growth in throughput and its illth-inducing depletion and pollution. This book discusses that exaggeration very well under the heading of 'absolute and relative decoupling'. But suppose, contrary to experience, that absolute decoupling of GDP from throughput becomes possible thanks to technology. Would that not provide all the more reason to limit throughput, since it would apparently no longer be required in order to generate wealth, yet certainly remains environmentally costly? Saving the growth economy by appealing to disembodied or 'angelized GDP' is implicit surrender to the case that Jackson has so cogently made.

But let me stop here – my intention was only to whet the reader's appetite for this important study, not to summarize it!

Herman E. Daly
Professor, University of Maryland, School of Public Policy

A Foreword by Bill McKibben

Spells are hard to break, especially if you've been under one for a long time – any reader of fairy tales knows that. And it's all the harder if they didn't start out as fairy tales.

For a couple of hundred years, economic growth really was enchanting. It brought problems, yes, but they were outweighed by steady improvements in many areas, not just in longevity but in opportunity. That spell threatened to break in the 1960s and early 1970s – once Rachel Carson had taken some of the shine off modernity, environmentalists and economists started producing a series of profound analyses, most notably *Limits to Growth*, by an MIT team, and *Small is Beautiful* from E. F. Schumacher. And these were influential enough that, by the end of the 1970s, polls showed Americans were at least evenly divided on the question of whether more growth was desirable.

But the spell got a new lease on life with Ronald Reagan and Margaret Thatcher, and with the boom that followed – a boom marked by radical inequality, but a boom nonetheless. 'There is no alternative', Mrs Thatcher was fond of saying – which, if true, would be very bad news. Because we now begin to suspect that our relentless economic expansion is causing trouble that makes *Silent Spring* look like a fairy tale of its own. Global warming literally threatens the underpinnings of our civilization, and it's caused, quite directly, by the endless growth of material economies.

Some of that growth, in some form, is still needed – much of the underdeveloping world needs more. But the overdeveloped world clearly needs less, and not just for environmental reasons. One study after another has shown in recent years that the tie between more stuff and more happiness has broken down – that economic growth is now more likely to yield isolation (those vast suburban castles) and disconnection.

So the time has never been better for a sober and clearheaded book like this, which lays out what we know in clear terms – one is tempted to say so clear that even an economist might understand them. But don't bet on that – they've got the most at stake and will be the last to wake up from this spell. Which is why the rest of us had really better pay attention!

Bill McKibben
author of *Deep Economy*

A Foreword by Mary Robinson

On 10 December 2008, the world marked the 60th anniversary of the Universal Declaration of Human Rights. This first international statement of the inherent dignity and equal rights of all people, forged in the aftermath of two world wars and the Holocaust, remains one of the most forward-looking accomplishments in human history. Over the past six decades, the Universal Declaration has provided inspiration for millions of people around the world in the struggle for equality and justice and has set a 'common standard of achievement' to measure the progress of nations.

Tragically, the rights affirmed in the Universal Declaration too often remain unmet in countries around the world. Nowhere is this more true than in the protection of economic and social rights. In spite of notable successes, today's world remains one of stark contrasts. At a time of unparalleled prosperity for some, 54 countries are poorer now than they were a decade ago. Worldwide, the number of people living in chronic poverty and daily insecurity has not changed for more than ten years, with women and children suffering disproportionately.

Perhaps most extraordinary of all is that six decades of economic growth – and a global economy which is now more than five times the size it was in 1948 – has not brought about equivalent progress on fulfilling basic human rights to adequate food, access to health care and education or to decent employment. And the situation for some has worsened.

In a world of nearly 6.7 billion people, 4 billion still live without basic entitlements. By the middle of this century, when the population is expected to rise to over 9 billion, if the distribution of wealth on the planet remains so skewed, many more people will be impoverished.

In this provocative and timely book, Tim Jackson asks what prosperity means in such a world, and whether economic growth can be the sole basis for delivering prosperity. No one denies that economic development is essential to improving access to basic entitlements in the poorest nations, but Jackson's vital contribution here is to challenge the assumption that continued consumption growth, without greater attention to equity and sustainability, can really deliver prosperity for all. The question at the heart of this book is essentially one of social justice.

Jackson invites us to look beyond common conceptions of social progress and face up to the economic challenges of the future. Some of these are long-standing challenges: how to secure the right of everyone to a decent standard of living, to shelter, health, nutrition, employment, family, and economic security. Others are less familiar but are as urgent as any we have faced before. The threats of climate change, rapid deforestation, looming scarcities in water, food and fuel, for example – all these represent urgent threats to people's livelihoods across the world. And inevitably, it will be the poorest and the most vulnerable who will suffer most.

What does prosperity mean in a world of 9 billion people living under the threat of climate change and resource scarcity? One thing is absolutely clear. It cannot mean business as usual. It cannot mean more of the same. Even if the recent global economic crisis 'goes away', the idea that the economic systems and policies we have today can solve the problems of tomorrow does not seem plausible.

Human rights and prosperity are intimately linked. The Universal Declaration remains a vital blueprint for a meaningful prosperity. A new economics fit for purpose is absolutely essential if that promise is to be delivered. It is my hope that the important ideas contained in this book contribute to that task.

Mary Robinson
President, Realizing Rights: The Ethical Globalization Initiative
UN High Commissioner for Human Rights (1997–2002)
President of Ireland (1990–1997)

A Foreword by Pavan Sukhdev

Classical economists including Adam Smith designed our thinking framework for economics in a world in which global capital and trade were measured in millions, not trillions of dollars. But that was two and a quarter centuries ago. Land was plentiful, labour was cheap, energy was not a major factor of production and the scarce input to production was financial capital. The capitalist thus achieved a social purpose and was feted and rewarded, not pilloried for causing the worst financial and economic crises. How times have changed.

Bill McKibben brackets the steam engine and that other 'engine' – economic growth – as the two most significant discoveries of the 18th century. No doubt, both have improved well-being for a significant part of humanity. The engine of economic growth created jobs, avoided recessions and became a ubiquitous yardstick for progress in the 20th century. This was despite the fact that its key measure 'GDP growth' does not capture many vital aspects of national wealth and well-being, such as changes in the quality of health, the extent of education and changes in the quality and quantity of our natural resources. And yet, GDP growth had become the 'mantra' by which governments benchmarked their performance, managed their economies and indeed sought re-election.

The history of post-war economic growth has been one of unsustainable development: unsustainable for the planet's ecosystems, for its species diversity and indeed for the human race. By some recent yardsticks of sustainability, our global ecological footprint has doubled over the last 40 years, now standing at 30 per cent higher than the Earth's biological capacity to produce for our needs, and is poised to go higher. Based on population projections alone, 50 per cent more food than is currently produced will be required to feed the global population by 2050.

Already, 35 per cent of the Earth's surface has been converted for agriculture, limiting the scope for the future productivity of natural systems. The livestock sector represents the world's single largest human use of land and largest sectoral source of water pollutants. Grazing land covers 26 per cent of the Earth's surface, while animal feed crops account for about a third of arable land. Extending agricultural production will have consequences for biodiversity and is also a major factor in rising deforestation: in the tropics, deforestation is occurring at a rate of about 12.5 million hectares per annum, representing not only a serious loss of ecosystems and biodiversity, but also creating one-fifth of anthropogenic CO_2 emissions. Without a 'green carbon' regime in place yet for controlling such emissions, we are at risk of perpetuating a polarized 'brown carbon' regime, requiring extensive conversions of pasture land, cropland and forests into bio-energy crops, in the process emitting more CO_2 than was saved by switching to bio-energy.

There is now an increasing awareness that something is very wrong, and that in fundamental ways, human society needs to change in order to solve any of the capacity constraints described above. From many directions, fingers are being pointed at the ongoing economic crisis, itself a result of crises in fuel, food and finance, and at the parallel crisis in our ecological and climate commons, suggesting that both share a common cause: our failed economic model. The distributional challenge arising from unsustainable growth is particularly difficult because those who have largely caused the problems – rich countries – are not going to suffer the most, at least not in the short term. For instance, if climate change resulted in a drought that halved the income of the poorest of the 28 million Ethiopians, this would barely register on world GDP – it would fall by less than 0.003 per cent.

The Millennium Development Goals (MDGs) represent the world's ambition to attack poverty. The target for these goals was

2015, a date that looks ominously too close to suggest a successful outcome. Social stresses are mounting as a result of wider disparities in living standards, and because poverty is as much about self-respect as it is about food, clothing and shelter. Yet another deep worry.

But perhaps not all is lost. Anecdotal evidence abounds showing that achievement of the MDGs assumes sound environmental practice and governance. Exemplarily, safeguarding tropical forests in developing countries provides exceptional opportunities to link two of the most serious problems threatening human well-being today: poverty and climate change. It also brings side-benefits: food, fibre, fuel wood, freshwater and soil nutrients. It helps control drought, and buffer against natural hazards – which will only increase with climate change. This is an example of making use of 'natural capital' to solve big problems, an avenue not enough explored today because mankind has disconnected itself from the natural world, spiritually and mentally. Human society needs to change – its economics, its accounts, its implicit biases against natural capital (versus man-made capital), against public wealth (versus private wealth) and against logical and less consumption (versus manic and more). And perhaps above all, human society needs to re-examine and change its relationship with nature to one of harmony and co-existence.

In this thought-provoking book, Tim Jackson acknowledges that society faces a profound dilemma: economic growth is unsustainable, but 'de-growth' – or economic contraction – is unstable. The 'escape route' from this dilemma is to try and 'decouple' economic activity from its impacts. But there is no evidence at all that this is working, and global resource consumption is still rising. Meeting climate change targets will require reductions in carbon intensity two orders of magnitude higher than anything achieved historically. Faced with this challenge, the book engages in a critical re-examination of the economic structure and social logic of consumerism.

Prosperity without Growth proposes a new way forward, allowing humankind to survive and to thrive within the finite resources of the planet.

Pavan Sukhdev
Head, Green Economy Initiative, UNEP,
and Study Leader, TEEB

1
Prosperity Lost

I think all of us here today would acknowledge that we've lost that sense of shared prosperity.

Barack Obama, 27 March 2008[1]

Prosperity is about things going well for us: in accordance with our hopes and expectations.[2] 'How's life?' we ask each other. 'How are things?' Everyday exchanges convey more than casual greeting. They reveal a mutual fascination for each other's well-being. Wanting things to go well is a common human concern.

It's understood that this sense of things going well includes some notion of continuity. We aren't inclined to think that life is going swimmingly, if we confidently expect things to fall apart tomorrow. 'Yes, I'm fine, thanks. Filing for bankruptcy tomorrow.' Such a response wouldn't make sense. There is a natural tendency to care about the future.

There is a sense too in which individual prosperity is curtailed in the presence of social calamity. That things are going well for me personally is of little consolation if my family, my friends and my community are all in dire straits. My prosperity and the prosperity of those around me are intertwined. Sometimes inextricably.

Writ large, this shared concern translates itself into a vision of human progress. Prosperity speaks of the elimination of hunger and homelessness, an end to poverty and injustice, hopes for a secure and peaceful world. And this vision is important not just for altruistic reasons but often too as reassurance that our own lives are meaningful. It brings with it a comforting sense that things are getting better on the whole – rather than worse – if not always for us then at least for those who come after us. A better society for our children. A fairer world. A place where those less fortunate will one day thrive. If I cannot believe this prospect is possible, then what can I believe? What sense can I make of my own life?

Prosperity in this sense is a shared vision. Echoes of it inhabit our daily rituals. Deliberations about it inform the political and social world. Hope for it lies at the heart of our lives.

So far so good. But how is this prospect to be attained? Without some realistic way of translating hope into reality, prosperity remains an illusion. The existence of a credible and robust mechanism for achieving prosperity matters. And this is more than just a question of the machinery of doing well. The legitimacy of the means to live well is part of the glue that keeps society together. Collective meaning is extinguished when hope is lost. Morality itself is threatened. Getting the mechanism right is vital.

One of the key messages of this book is that we're failing in that task. Our technologies, our economy and our social aspirations are all mis-aligned with any meaningful expression of prosperity. The vision of social progress that drives us – based on the continual expansion of material wants – is fundamentally untenable. And this failing is not a simple falling short from utopian ideals. It is much more basic. In pursuit of the good life today, we are systematically eroding the basis for well-being tomorrow. We stand in real danger of losing any prospect of a shared and lasting prosperity.

But this book isn't a rant against the failings of modernity. Nor is it a lament on the inevitability of the human condition. There are undoubtedly some immutable constraints on our prospects for a lasting prosperity. The existence of ecological limits to human activity maybe one of these. Aspects of human nature may turn out to be another. Taking heed of these constraints is central to the spirit of this investigation.

The overriding aim of this book is to seek viable responses to the biggest dilemma of our times: reconciling our aspirations for the good life with the constraints of a finite planet. The analysis in the following pages is focused on finding a credible vision of what it means for human society to flourish in the context of ecological limits.

Prosperity as growth

At the heart of the book lies a very simple question. What can prosperity possibly look like in a finite world, with limited resources and a population expected to exceed 9 billion people within decades?[3] Do we have a decent vision of prosperity for such a world? Is this vision credible in the face of the available evidence about ecological limits? How do we go about turning vision into reality?

The prevailing response to these questions is to cast prosperity in economic terms and to call for continuing economic growth as the means to deliver it. Higher incomes mean increased choices, richer lives, an improved quality of life for those who benefit from them. That at least is the conventional wisdom.

This formula is cashed out (almost literally) as an increase in the gross domestic product (GDP) per capita. The GDP is broadly speaking a measure of 'economic activity' in a nation or region.[4] As we shall see later, there are good grounds to question whether such a crude measure is really sufficient. But for now it's a fair reflection of what is meant, in broad terms, by rising income. A rising per capita GDP, in this view, is equivalent to increasing prosperity.[5]

This is undoubtedly one of the reasons why GDP growth has been the single most important policy goal across the world for most of the last century. Such a response clearly still has an appealing logic for the world's poorest nations. A meaningful approach to prosperity must certainly address the plight of the 1 billion people across the world who are living on less than $1 a day – half the price of a small cappuccino in Starbucks.[6]

But does the same logic really hold for the richer nations, where subsistence needs are largely met and further proliferation of consumer goods adds little to material comfort? How is it that with so much stuff already we still hunger for more? Might it not be better to halt the relentless pursuit of growth in the advanced economies and concentrate instead on sharing out the available resources more equitably?

In a world of finite resources, constrained by strict environmental limits, still characterized by 'islands of prosperity' within 'oceans of poverty',[7] are ever-increasing incomes for the already-rich really a legitimate focus for our continued hopes and expectations? Or is there perhaps some other path towards a more sustainable, a more equitable form of prosperity?

We'll come back time and again to this question and explore it from a variety of different perspectives. But it's worth making quite clear here that to many economists the very idea of prosperity without growth is a complete anathema. Growth in the GDP is taken for granted. Reams and reams have been written about what it's based on, who's best at making it happen and what to do when it stops happening. Far less is written about why we might want it in the first place.

But the relentless quest for more that lurks within the conventional view of prosperity is not without some claim to intellectual foundation. In short, the reasoning goes something like this. The GDP counts the economic value of goods and services exchanged on the market. If we're spending our money on more and more commodities it's because we value them. We wouldn't value them if they weren't at the same time improving our lives. Hence a continually increasing per capita GDP is a reasonable proxy for a rising prosperity.

But this conclusion is odd precisely because prosperity isn't obviously synonymous with income or wealth. Rising prosperity isn't self-evidently the same thing as economic growth. More isn't necessarily better. Until quite recently, prosperity was not cast specifically in terms of money at all; it was simply the opposite of adversity or affliction.[8] The concept of economic prosperity – and the elision of rising prosperity with economic growth – is a modern construction. And it's a construction that has already come under considerable criticism.

Amongst the charges against it is that growth has delivered its benefits, at best, unequally. A fifth of the world's population earns just 2 per cent of global income. The richest 20 per cent by contrast earn 74 per cent of the world's income. Huge disparities – real differences in prosperity by anyone's standards – characterize the difference between rich and poor. Such disparities are unacceptable from a humanitarian point of view. They also generate rising social tensions: real hardships in the most disadvantaged communities which have a spill-over effect on society as a whole.[9]

Even within the advanced economies, inequality is higher than it was 20 years ago. While the rich got richer, middle-class incomes in western countries were stagnant in real terms long before the current recession. Far from raising the living standard for those who most needed it, growth let much of the world's population down over the last 50 years. Wealth trickled up to the lucky few.

Fairness (or the lack of it) is only one of the reasons to question the conventional formula for achieving prosperity. Another is the growing recognition that, beyond a certain point at least, continued pursuit of economic growth doesn't appear to advance and may even impede human happiness. Talk of a growing 'social recession' in advanced economies has accompanied the relative economic success of the last decade.[10]

Finally, and perhaps most obviously, any credible vision of prosperity has to address the question of limits. This is particularly true of a vision based on growth. How – and for how long – is contin-ued growth possible without coming up against the ecological limits of a finite planet?

The question of limits

Concern over limits is as old as the hills. But its recent history can be thought of as having three distinct phases. Late in the 18th century, the Parson Thomas Robert Malthus raised it in his enor-mously influential *Essay on Population*. In the 1970s, it was raised again in a different form in the Club of Rome's *Limits to Growth* report. The third phase is the one we find ourselves in now: concerns over climate change and 'peak oil'[11] compete for attention with fears of economic collapse.

Raising the spectre of Malthus is dangerous, of course. He's roundly condemned for all sorts of reasons. Some of them – such as his jaundiced view of poverty and fierce opposition to the Poor Laws – quite valid. It was Malthus, after all, who gave economics the reputation for being a 'dismal science'. So it might as well be said upfront that Malthus was wrong. At least in so far as the partic-ulars of his claims.[12]

His argument (massively condensed) was that growth in popula-tion always runs faster than growth in the resources available to feed and shelter people. So sooner or later the population expands beyond the 'means of subsistence' and some people – the poorest inevitably – will suffer.

That he failed to see (and even defended) the structural inequali-ties that kept people locked into poverty is one of Malthus' failings. But he was also wrong about the maths. The global population is now more than six times the size it was in Malthus' day. And this is partly because the means of subsistence expanded considerably faster than population did – completely counter to Malthus' premise. The global economy is 68 times bigger than it was in 1800.[13]

He missed completely the longer term implications of the massive technological changes already taking place around him. Nor could he have foreseen that with development would come a considerable slowing down of the rate of population increase. Today, increasing affluence is driving resource throughput faster than population growth is.[14] The means of subsistence more than kept pace with people's propensity to reproduce, largely because of the easy availability of cheap fossil fuels. And yet the massive increases in resource use associated with a global economy almost 70 times bigger than the one in his day, might still have given Parson Malthus pause for thought. How could such increases possibly continue?

That was the question asked by a group of scientists commissioned by the Club of Rome in the 1970s to explore the question of ecological limits. Donella and Dennis Meadows and their colleagues looked at exponential growth in resource use, population and economic activity since the industrial revolution and asked themselves a very simple question. How could these kinds of curves (Figure 1.1(a)) possibly continue in the way conventional economic projections supposed they would?

They knew that natural ecosystems obeyed very different kinds of curve (Figure 1.1(b)). Could it be that the massive advances in human progress were after all nothing more than the steep early growth associated with the left hand side of a bell-shaped curve? And that inevitably, just like any other ecosystem that exceeds its resource base, we were heading for collapse?

The Meadows argued that resource scarcities would push prices up and slow down the possibilities for future growth. Eventually, if material throughput wasn't curtailed, the resource base itself would collapse and with it the potential for continued economic activity – at least, at anything like the scale anticipated by the optimists.

Collecting together as much data as they could find on resource extraction rates and available reserves, they set themselves the task

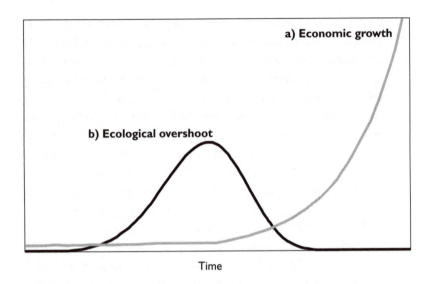

Figure 1.1 Growth curves for economic and ecological systems
Source: Author

of figuring out when the turning points would arrive – the points at which real scarcity might begin to bite.

As it turned out, and as they themselves were later to admit, they also got it wrong. But not by anything like as much as Malthus got it wrong. Back in the 1970s, the Meadows expected to see significant resource scarcities before the new Millennium. That didn't happen. Remember this was almost 40 years ago when basic data on natural resources were even scarcer than they are today. But the prospect of scarcity wasn't far behind their expectations.[15]

Most significantly, the peak oil debate had already emerged as a fiercely contentious issue by the year 2000. The 'peak-ists' argued that the peak in oil production was only a matter of years away, possibly already on us. Their opponents pointed to the massive reserves still lying in the tar sands and oil shales. Getting the oil out might be costly and environmentally damaging, but absolute scarcity was still a long way away, claimed the optimists.

Meanwhile the price of oil rose steadily. Oil price hikes had already shown they have the potential to destabilize the global economy and threaten basic securities. In July 2008 oil prices reached $147 a barrel (Figure 1.2). Though they fell sharply in the following months, the threat of peak oil hasn't gone away. The rising trend had returned by early 2009.

Even the International Energy Agency (IEA) now suggests that the 'peak' could arrive as early as 2020. Other commentators believe it could be even sooner. Oil will not disappear beyond that peak. But it will be scarcer and more costly to extract. The era of cheap oil would to all intents and purposes be gone and the economics of energy would be irrevocably altered as a result.[16]

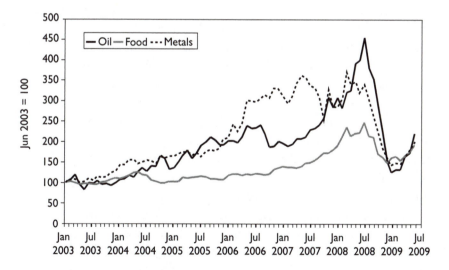

Figure 1.2 Global commodity prices: January 2003–July 2009[17]

Source: Drawn by the author from data in note 17.

Oil is not the only commodity for which resource scarcity will be an issue within decades. Food prices also rose sharply in the year to July 2008, sparking riots on the streets in some countries. Beyond the spike, the underlying trend appears to be rising once again (Figure 1.2). Productive land, as Malthus himself recognized, is the ultimate resource when it comes to basic subsistence. Conflicts over land use, particularly related to the use of land for growing bio-fuels, were certainly one of the factors pushing food prices up through 2008. No-one imagines these conflicts will become easier over time.

The trend in mineral prices has been rising too. This isn't surprising. Demand is growing and even at current extraction rates, a number of important minerals measure their time to exhaustion in decades rather than centuries. As extraction rates increase, the horizon of scarcity shortens.

If the whole world consumed resources at only half the rate the US does, for example, copper, tin, silver, chromium, zinc and a number of other 'strategic minerals' would be depleted in less than four decades. If everyone consumed at the same rate the US does today, the time horizon would be less than 20 years. Some rare earth metals will be exhausted in a decade even at current global consumption rates.[18]

All kinds of factors were at play during the commodity price 'bubble' of 2008. Some of them were just about short-term policy. Everyone agrees that it's difficult to glean much about real scarcity from short-run price fluctuations. This fact is seized on by optimists wanting to downplay the question of resource scarcity. But it's also worrying that commodity prices are just too volatile to offer reliable information about imminent scarcity. The threat of scarcity was enough to send them rocketing. They were equally prone to collapse in the face of recession. Through both peak and trough, the underlying physical resource base moved inexorably towards exhaustion. The market is just too self-obsessed to measure this.

As an economist commented to me in the middle of the credit crisis: 'we didn't get the recession that many economists, looking at the commodity bubble, thought we'd get, the one driven by high resource prices'. But one thing is for sure: that recession is coming. Sooner or later. And when that happens, the price impact will be no less shocking than it was during 2008. Its impact on the economy will be devastating.

This third phase of the limits debate is different from the last two. Resource scarcity – the problem of 'sources' in the language of environmental economists – is only part of the concern. The debate is driven even more strongly by the problem of 'sinks' – the capacity of the planet to 'assimilate' the environmental impacts of economic activity. 'Even before we run out of oil,' explains ecologist Bill McKibben, 'we're running out of planet.'[19]

Climate change is one of these sink problems. It's brought about by the accumulation of greenhouse gases in the atmosphere – accelerated by human activities, especially the burning of fossil fuels. The ability of the climate to assimilate these emissions without incurring 'dangerous' climate change is fast running out.

Brought to the world's attention in the late 1980s by climate scientist James Hansen and others, climate change has risen up the political agenda inexorably over the last two decades. Its visibility was given a massive boost by the influential Stern Review published in 2006. A former World Bank economist, Nicholas Stern was asked to lead a review of the economics of climate change for the UK Treasury. The review concluded that a small early hit on GDP (perhaps as low as 1 per cent of GDP) would allow us to avoid a much bigger hit (perhaps as high as 20 per cent of GDP) later on.[20]

It's telling that it took an economist commissioned by a government treasury to alert the world to things climate scientists – most notably the Intergovernmental Panel on Climate Change (IPCC) – had been saying for years. This is partly a testament to the power of economists in the policy world. But the impact of the Stern report was also due to the seductive nature of its message. Climate change can be fixed, it said, and we'll barely notice the difference. Economic growth can go on more or less as usual.

We'll have occasion to look at that message a bit more closely in what follows. The history of climate policy certainly suggests some caution in believing things will be that easy. The Kyoto Protocol committed the advanced economies to greenhouse gas emission reductions equivalent to about 5 per cent over 1990 levels by 2010. But things haven't worked out that well. Globally, emissions have risen by 40 per cent since 1990.

In the meantime, the science itself has moved on. The Stern Review took as its target the task of stabilizing carbon emissions in the atmosphere at 550 parts per million (ppm).[21] Most scientists – and Stern himself – now accept that that target won't prevent dangerous anthropogenic climate change. The IPCC's Fourth Assessment Report argues that a 450 ppm target will be needed if climate change is to be restricted to an average global temperature increase of 2°C.[22] Achieving that target could mean reducing global emissions by up to 85 per cent over 1990 levels by 2050.[23]

Two articles published in the journal *Nature* in April 2009 challenge even that conclusion. The authors argue that what matters is the total greenhouse gas budget we allow ourselves over the period to 2050. Global atmospheric concentrations are already at 435 ppm. And if we want a 75 per cent chance of staying below 2°C, the global economy can only afford to emit a total of 1 thousand billion tonnes of carbon dioxide (CO_2) between the year 2000 and the year 2050. Crucially, they show that by 2008 we had already used up a third of this budget. Staying within the budget is going to be more demanding even than existing 450 ppm stabilization scenarios suggest.[24]

The message from all this is a profoundly uncomfortable one. Dangerous climate change is a matter of decades away. And we're using up the climate 'slack' too quickly. It may take decades to transform our energy systems. And we have barely started on that task. As the science improves it becomes clearer that a warming world may pose the gravest threat to survival we face. Though it came late to the party, the climate may just turn out to be the mother of all limits.

Beyond the limits

This brief sketch of ecological limits does no justice at all to the accumulating wealth of understanding about resource scarcity or climate change. It hasn't even touched on questions of rapid defor-estation, historically unprecedented biodiversity loss, the collapse of fish stocks, water scarcity or the pollution of soil and water supplies. Interested readers must go elsewhere for detailed discus-sions of these issues.[25]

In a sense, the details are not the point. Nobody seriously disagrees with the assessment of impacts. It's now widely acknowl-edged, for example, that an estimated 60 per cent of the world's ecosystem services have been degraded or over-used since the mid-20th century.[26]

During the same period of time the global economy has grown more than 5 times. If it continues to grow at the same rate, it will be 80 times bigger in 2100 than it was in 1950.[27] This extraordi-nary ramping up of global economic activity has no historical precedent. It's totally at odds with our scientific knowledge of the finite resource base and the fragile ecology on which we depend for survival.

A world in which things simply go on as usual is already incon-ceivable. But what about a world in which an estimated 9 billion people all achieve the level of affluence expected in the OECD nations?[28] Such an economy would need to be 15 times the size of today's economy (75 times what it was in 1950) by 2050 and 40 times bigger than today's economy (200 times bigger than in 1950) by the end of the century.[29] What on earth does such an economy look like? What does it run on? Does it really offer a credible vision for a shared and lasting prosperity?

For the most part, we avoid the stark reality of these numbers. The default assumption is that – financial crises aside – growth will continue indefinitely. Not just for the poorest countries, where a better quality of life is undeniably needed, but even for the richest nations where the cornucopia of material wealth adds little to happiness and is beginning to threaten the foundations of our well-being.

The reasons for this collective blindness are (as we shall see in more detail later) easy enough to find. The modern economy is structurally reliant on economic growth for its stability. When growth falters – as it did dramatically during the latter stages of 2008 – politicians panic. Businesses struggle to survive. People lose their jobs and sometimes their homes. A spiral of recession looms. Questioning growth is deemed to be the act of lunatics, idealists and revolutionaries.

But question it we must. The idea of a non-growing economy may be an anathema to an economist. But the idea of a continually growing economy is an anathema to an ecologist. No subsystem of a finite system can grow indefinitely, in physical terms. Economists have to be able to answer the question of how a continually growing economic system can fit within a finite ecological system.

The only possible response to this challenge is to suggest – as economists do – that growth in dollars is 'decoupled' from growth in physical throughputs and environmental impacts. But as we shall see more clearly in what follows, this hasn't so far achieved what's needed. There are no prospects for it doing so in the immediate future. And the sheer scale of decoupling required to meet the limits set out here (and to stay within them while the economy keeps on growing in perpetuity) staggers the imagination.

In short, we have no alternative but to question growth. The myth of growth has failed us. It has failed the 1 billion people who still attempt to live on half the price of a cup of coffee each day. It has failed the fragile ecological systems on which we depend for survival. It has failed, spectacularly, in its own terms, to provide economic stability and secure people's livelihoods.

Of course, if the current economic crisis really does indicate (as some predict) the end of an era of easy growth, at least for the advanced nations, then the concerns of this book are doubly relevant. Prosperity without growth is a very useful trick to have up your sleeve when the economy is faltering.

The uncomfortable reality is that we find ourselves faced with the imminent end of the era of cheap oil, the prospect of steadily rising commodity prices, the degradation of air, water and soil, conflicts over land use, resource use, water use, forestry and fishing rights, and the momentous challenge of stabilizing the global climate. And we face these tasks with an economy that is fundamentally broken, in desperate need of renewal.

In these circumstances, a return to business as usual is not an option. Prosperity for the few founded on ecological destruction and persistent social injustice is no foundation for a civilized society. Economic recovery is vital. Protecting people's jobs – and creating new ones – is absolutely essential. But we also stand in urgent need of a renewed sense of shared prosperity. A deeper commitment to justice in a finite world.

Delivering these goals may seem an unfamiliar or even incongruous task to policy in the modern age. The role of government has been framed so narrowly by material aims and hollowed out by a misguided vision of unbounded consumer freedoms. The concept of governance itself stands in urgent need of renewal.

But the economic crisis presents us with a unique opportunity to invest in change. To sweep away the short-term thinking that has plagued society for decades. To replace it with considered policy capable of addressing the enormous challenge of delivering a lasting prosperity.

For at the end of the day prosperity goes beyond material pleasures. It transcends material concerns. It resides in the quality of our lives and in the health and happiness of our families. It is present in the strength of our relationships and our trust in the community. It is evidenced by our satisfaction at work and our sense of shared meaning and purpose. It hangs on our potential to participate fully in the life of society.

Prosperity consists in our ability to flourish as human beings – within the ecological limits of a finite planet. The challenge for our society is to create the conditions under which this is possible. It is the most urgent task of our times.

2
The Age of Irresponsibility

This has been an age of global prosperity. It has also been an era of global turbulence. And where there has been irresponsibility, we must now clearly say: the age of irresponsibility must be ended.

Gordon Brown, September 2008[1]

The conventional formula for achieving prosperity relies on the pursuit of economic growth. Higher incomes will increase well-being and lead to prosperity for all, in this view.

This book challenges that formula. It questions whether economic growth is still a legitimate goal for rich countries, when huge disparities in income and well-being persist across the globe and when the global economy is constrained by finite ecological limits. It explores whether the benefits of continued economic growth still outweigh the costs and scrutinizes the assumption that growth is essential for prosperity. In short, it asks: is it possible to have prosperity *without* growth?

This question was thrown into sharp relief during the course of writing the book. The banking crisis of 2008 led the world to the brink of financial disaster and shook the dominant economic model to its foundations. It redefined the boundaries between market and state and forced us to confront our inability to manage the financial – let alone social or environmental – sustainability of the global economy.

Consumer confidence was shattered. Investment stalled completely and unemployment rose sharply. Advanced economies (and some developing countries) were faced with the prospect of a deep and long-lasting recession. Trust in financial markets is likely to suffer for some considerable time to come. Public sector finances will be stretched for a decade or more.

Raising deep, structural questions about the nature of prosperity in this climate might seem inopportune if not insensitive. 'That is not what people are interested in when financial markets are in turmoil,' admits billionaire George Soros of his own attempt to dig deeper into the global credit crisis.[2]

But it's clear that some serious reflection is in order. Not to stand back and question what has happened would be to compound failure with failure: failure of vision with failure of responsibility. If nothing else, the economic crisis presents a unique opportunity to address financial and ecological sustainability together. And, as this chapter argues, the two things are intimately related.

In search of villains

The causes of the crisis are disputed. The most prominent villain was taken to be subprime lending in the US housing market. Some highlighted the unmanageability of the 'credit default swaps' used to parcel up 'toxic debts' and hide them from the balance sheet. Others pointed the finger of blame at greedy speculators and unscrupulous investors intent on making a killing at the expense of vulnerable institutions.

A dramatic rise in basic commodity prices during 2007 and early 2008 (Figure 1.2) certainly contributed to economic slowdown by squeezing company margins and reducing discretionary spending. At one point in mid-2008, advanced economies were facing the prospect of 'stagflation' – a simultaneous slowdown in growth with a rise in inflation – for the first time in 30 years. Oil prices doubled in the year to July 2008, while food prices rose by 66 per cent, sparking civil unrest in some poorer nations.[3]

All of these can be counted as contributory factors. None on its own offers an adequate explanation for how financial markets managed to destabilize entire economies. Why loans were offered to people who couldn't afford to pay them off. Why regulators failed to curb individual financial practices that could bring down monolithic institutions. Why unsecured debt had become so dominant a force in the economy. And why governments had consistently turned a blind eye or actively encouraged this 'age of irresponsibility'.

Political response to the crisis provides us with some clues. By the end of October 2008, governments across the world had committed a staggering $7 trillion of public money – more than the GDP of any country in the world except the US – to secure risky assets, underwrite threatened savings and recapitalize failing banks.[4]

No-one pretended that this was anything other than a short-term and deeply regressive solution, a temporary fix that rewarded those responsible for the crisis at the expense of the taxpayer. It was excused on the grounds that the alternative was simply unthinkable.

Collapse of the financial markets would have led to a massive and completely unpredictable global recession. Entire nations would have been bankrupted. Commerce would have failed *en masse*. Livelihoods would have been destroyed. Homes would have been lost. The humanitarian cost of failing to save the banking system would have been enormous. Those who resisted the US's Troubled Assets Relief Program (TARP) on its first reading through Congress appeared oblivious to these consequences, inflamed as they were with commendable indignation over the unjustness of the solution.

But the harsh reality was that politicians had no choice but to intervene in the protection of the banking sector. In the language of the media, Wall Street is the lifeblood of Main Street. The health of the modern economy hangs on the health of the financial sector. Anything less than total commitment to its survival would have been unthinkable. The appropriate goal of policy at that point in time was incontestably to stabilize the system: to reassure savers, to encourage investors, to assist debtors, to restore confidence in the market: very much as governments around the world tried to do.

They were only partially successful – halting an immediate slide into chaos but failing to avert the prospect of a deep recession across the world. This prompted a further round of economic recovery packages early in 2009 which aimed to 'kick-start' consumer spending, protect jobs and stimulate economic growth again. In Chapter 7 we explore some of these 'stimulus packages' in more detail.

It was abundantly clear, by the time the G20 nations convened in London in April 2009, that a little reflection was in order. Political leaders, economists and even financiers accept the point. The suspension of practices like short-selling; increased regulation of financial derivatives; better scrutiny of the conditions of lending: all of these had become widely accepted as inevitable and necessary responses to the crisis. There was even a grudging acceptance of the need to cap executive remuneration in the financial sector.[5]

Admittedly, this last concession was born more of political necessity in the face of huge public outcry over the bonus culture than through recognition of a point of principle. In fact, huge executive bonuses were still being paid. Goldman Sachs paid out $2.6 billion in end of year (2008) bonuses in spite of its $6 billion dollar bailout by the US government, justifying these on the basis that they helped to 'attract and motivate' the best people.[6]

But many of these responses were seen as short-term interventions, designed to facilitate the restoration of business as usual. Short-selling was suspended for six months, rather than banned.

The part-nationalization of financial institutions was justified on the basis that shares would be sold back to the private sector as soon as reasonably possible. The capping of executive remuneration was 'performance related'.

Extraordinary though some of these interventions were, they were largely regarded as temporary measures, necessary evils in the restoration of a free-market economy. The declared aim was clear. By pumping equity into the banks and restoring confidence to lenders, the world's leaders hope to restore liquidity, re-invigorate demand and halt the recession.

Their ultimate goal was to protect the pursuit of economic growth. Throughout the crisis, that was the one non-negotiable: that growth must continue at all costs. Renewed growth was the end that justified interventions unthought of only a few months previously. No politician seriously questioned it.

And yet allegiance to growth was the single most dominant feature of an economic and political system that led the world to the brink of disaster. The growth imperative has shaped the architecture of the modern economy. It motivated the freedoms granted to the financial sector. It stood at least partly responsible for the loosening of regulations, the over-extension of credit and the proliferation of unmanageable (and unstable) financial derivatives. It is generally agreed that the unprecedented consumption growth between 1990 and 2007 was fuelled by a massive expansion of credit and increasing levels of debt.

The labyrinth of debt

The capitalist economy runs on debt. For such a central feature of the society in which we live it's remarkably poorly understood by many of us. But that's partly because it's become so complex. Even the basic terminology isn't straightforward. Consumer debt is different from public debt is different from external debt. Gross debt is different from net debt. Media coverage during the crisis consistently confused these terms. And to make matters worse, the different kinds of debt have very different implications for households, for the government and for the nation as a whole (Box 2.1).

One clearly identifiable feature of advanced economies in the period preceding the crisis was the rise and rise of consumer indebtedness. Over the course of more than a decade consumer debt served as a deliberate mechanism for freeing personal spending from wage income and allowing consumption to drive the dynamics of growth.

Not all economies were equally susceptible to this dynamic. Indeed it's a feature of the system of debt that for one part of the global economy to be highly indebted, another part must be saving hard. During the first decade of the 21st century, the savers were largely in the emerging economies. The savings rate in China during 2008 was around 25 per cent of disposable income, while in India it was even higher at 37 per cent.

Even within the advanced economies, there were clear distinctions between nations. One of the most interesting of these is between the different 'varieties' of capitalism identified by Harvard historian Peter Hall and Oxford economist David Soskice.

In an extensive study of differences across market economies, Hall and Soskice distinguish two main types of capitalism within advanced nations. The so-called 'liberal market economies' (specifically Australia, Canada, New Zealand, the UK and the US) led the march towards liberalization, competition and deregulation during the 1980s and 1990s. The so-called 'coordinated market economies' (including Belgium, France, Germany, Japan and the Scandinavian countries) were much slower to de-regulate and tend to depend more heavily on strategic interactions between firms – rather than competition – to coordinate economic behaviour.[7]

Both varieties of capitalism are in common agreement about the pursuit of economic growth. But they differ on the right prescription for it. One of the key differences lies in levels of consumer indebtedness. Typically the liberal market economies have encouraged higher levels of consumer debt than coordinated market economies in order to maintain consumption growth.

The UK and the US seem to have been particularly prone to this. Consumer debt in the UK more than doubled in the decade before the crisis. Even during 2008, as recession loomed, debt was growing at the rate of £1 million every 11 minutes. Though the rate of growth slowed down – as it tends to do in a recession – by the end of 2008, the cumulative consumer debt still stood at almost £1.5 trillion, higher than the GDP for the second year running.[8] Savings, on the other hand, had plummeted. During the first quarter of 2008, the household savings ratio in the UK fell below zero for the first time in four decades (Figure 2.1).

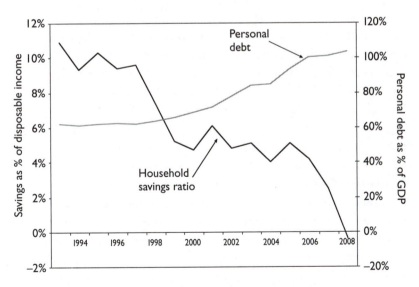

Figure 2.1 UK Consumer debt and household savings 1993–2008[9]

Source: Drawn by the author using data sources in note 9.

Box 2.1 Debt in perspective

Lending and borrowing money is (in normal times at least) a fundamental feature of the modern economy (see Chapter 6). Households, companies and governments all participate both in lending (e.g. through savings and investments) and in borrowing (e.g. through loans, credit accounts and mortgages). Financial debts (sometimes called liabilities) are the accumulated money owed at any one point in time by a person, a firm, a government or indeed the nation as a whole.

A fundamental principle of capitalism is that these accumulated liabilities attract interest charges over time. Debt rises in two ways: firstly by borrowing more money (e.g. for increased public spending) and secondly through interest accumulated on the debt. For any given interest rate, a higher level of debt places a greater demand on people's income to pay off the interest and stop the debt accumulating.

Some of this requirement could be met from revenues generated by people's own financial 'assets' or savings. By participating in the economy both as savers and as borrowers, people can try and balance their financial liabilities (money borrowed) against their financial assets (money lent). The extent to which it 'matters' how much debt we hold depends (in part) on this balance between assets and liabilities. And as the current crisis has shown, on the financial reliability of the assets.

Three aspects of debt have attracted media and policy attention over the last decade: consumer (or personal) debt, the national debt and the gross external debt. Though all are concerned with money owed, these debts are quite different and have different policy implications. The following paragraphs set out the key elements of each and their relevance for economic sustainability.

Consumer debt

Consumer (or personal) debt is the amount of money owed by private citizens. It includes home loans, credit card debt and other forms of consumer borrowing. Personal debt in the UK is currently dominated by home loans, which at the end of 2008 comprised 84 per cent of the total. For as long as the value of homes continued to rise, people's financial liabilities (home loans) are offset by the value of their physical assets (homes). Problems arise when house values collapse. Liabilities are no longer balanced by assets. When this is compounded (as in a recession) by falling incomes, debt – and the financial viability of households – becomes highly unstable. Like much of the growth economy (Chapters 4 and 6), financial stability turns out to be dependent in an unsustainable way on growth – in this case growth in the housing market.

National debt

The national (or public sector) debt is the money that government owes to the private sector.[10] When a government continually runs a deficit (spends more than it receives in revenues) the national debt rises. Just as for households, reducing the debt is only possible when the public sector runs a surplus (it spends less than it receives). Increased debt is a common feature of public finances during recession. But servicing this debt – without compromising public services – depends heavily on future government revenues increasing. This can happen in only three ways. First, by achieving the desired aim of growth. Second, by increasing the tax rate. And third, by using the debt to invest in productive assets with positive returns to the public purse. A continually rising public debt in a shrinking economy is a recipe for disaster.

External debt

The total debt held outside the country by government, business and households is called the external debt. The sustainability of this debt depends on a complex mix of factors including the extent to which it is balanced by external assets, the form of both assets and liabilities (including the currency in which they are held) and the relative strength of domestic currency on the international market. Particular pressure is placed on an economy when its economy is shrinking and its currency is losing value. In extreme circumstances, a country may find itself unable to attract investors willing to support its spending and unable to liquidate its assets to compensate for this. At this point the level of external debt relative to the GDP becomes critical. Calling in debts worth almost five times the national income, for instance, would be catastrophic.

Debt and the money supply

The amount of debt held by government, business and households is closely linked to the supply of money in the economy. Most of the 'new' money in national economies is now created by commercial banks in the form of loans to customers. Governments through their central banks attempt to control how much money is created in the form of debt through two related instruments. One is the base rate – the rate at which the central bank loans money to commercial banks. The other is the reserve requirement – the percentage of deposits that banks are required to hold in reserve and which cannot therefore be used to make loans. The higher the reserve requirement the fewer loans are made. The lower the base rate, the more likely commercial banks are to make loans. Over the last decade, the US Federal Reserve (and many other central banks) used an expansionary monetary policy to boost consumer spending. This worked to protect growth for a while but ultimately led to unsustainable levels of debt and destabilized the money markets. This is one of the reasons for calls to increase the reserve requirement (see Chapter 11).

People are encouraged into debt by a complex mix of factors, including their own desire for social status and the incentives put in place to boost high-street sales. We return to the importance of this twin dynamic in later chapters of the book. But it's also salient to note that the structural requirement for increased consumption has been facilitated over the last two decades by expanding the money supply. And this has directly affected the level of indebtedness (Box 2.1).

The important point here is that when this strategy becomes unstable – as it did during 2008 – it places large sections of the population at risk of lasting financial hardship. Inevitably, that risk falls mainly on those who are most vulnerable already – the lower income groups who profited less from the last two decades of growth.[11] Far from delivering prosperity, the culture of 'borrow and spend' ends up detracting from it.

The same vulnerability can afflict the nation as a whole. The public sector debt measures how much government owes to the private sector. Again, levels of indebtedness tend to vary widely across nations, though the pattern is less obvious than for consumer debt. France, Germany, Canada and the US all have public sector debts above 60 per cent of GDP. Italy and Japan hold public sector debts that are higher than their GDP. Norway by contrast holds no public debt at all; on the contrary it has enormous financial assets.

Typically, the public sector debt rises sharply through times of crisis. This has been particularly noticeable during wartime, when public sector borrowing can increase dramatically to fund the war effort. Between 1939 and 1944, US military spending rose from 2 per cent of national income to 54 per cent of national income. Germany's military spending reached 60 per cent of national income at its peak in 1944. This extraordinary mobilization of national resources for war is of interest in its own right as an illustration of the possibilities for mobilizing economic activity in times of crisis. But it was only achieved by increasing the national debt. The US debt rose from around 40 per cent of GDP to over 100 per cent of GDP in the space of half a decade.[12]

Similar things happen during periods of financial crisis when governments tend to borrow money in order to stimulate recovery (see Chapter 7). The enormous sums of money needed to stabilize the banking system in late 2008 and early 2009 were largely funded through increased public sector borrowing. Partly as a result of the bailouts, the UK public sector debt is expected to double from less than 40 per cent of GDP (the Treasury's self-imposed ceiling) in 2007 to at least 80 per cent of GDP by 2012. This is still lower than the public sector debt in Japan which has struggled with a faltering economy for many years.

Public sector debt is not in itself a bad thing. It simply reflects the amount of money that government owes to the private sector. This includes money saved by its own citizens. And the idea that citizens hold a financial interest in the public sector has some clear advantages. It can be thought of as part of the 'social contract' between citizen and state. But when the household savings rate collapses (Figure 2.1) and the national debt rises, further borrowing increases what is called the external debt (Box 2.1) – the money a country borrows from outside its own boundaries. This inevitably exposes the nation to the volatility of international markets.

Some countries are better placed than others to weather this volatility. External debt varied widely across nations (Figure 2.2) during 2007/8, from as little as 5 per cent of GDP (in China and India for example) to over 900 per cent of GDP (in Ireland). In the UK, the gross external debt increased seven and a half times in the space of just two decades. By the end of 2008, it was equivalent to almost five times the GDP and ranked as the second highest absolute level of external debt in the world after the US.

These external liabilities were set off – at least in part – by a higher than usual level of external assets. But in an unstable market this placed the UK in a vulnerable financial position. More to the

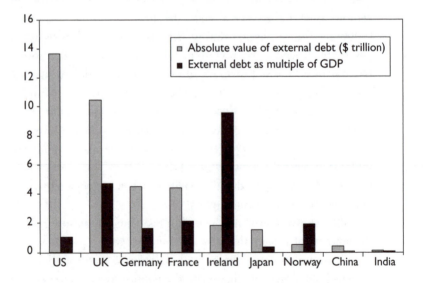

Figure 2.2 Gross external debt across nations (2007/8)[13]
Source: CIA World Factbook, see note 13.

point, as the International Monetary Fund (IMF) points out, this position was deliberately courted by the UK in its role as an international centre of finance.

The architecture of financial recovery in the wake of the 2008 crisis – and in particular the role of the public sector as an equity-holder in the banks – owed much to the UK Prime Minister, Gordon Brown. In this respect, the UK government attracted deserving praise for its response to the crisis. Part-nationalizing the banks may have been suboptimal from a free-market perspective but it was considerably more progressive than simply pumping in cash or guarantees to ensure liquidity. At least it allowed for the possibility of a financial return to the public purse.

At the same time, what became clear through the crisis was the extent to which economic policy over two decades had positioned the UK slap bang across an emerging fault line in the financial sector. High levels of consumer debt and the second highest level of external debt in the world were not just accidental features of economic life, but the result of specific policies to increase liquidity and boost spending. The one area of fiscal prudence in the UK – a relatively low level of public sector debt – became the first casualty of the collapse.

This is not to suggest that the UK is alone in facing the severity of the current crisis. On the contrary, in an increasingly globalized world, it was difficult for any country to escape the recession. Even those economies – like Germany, Japan and China – which retained strong manufacturing sectors, largely avoided consumer debt and delivered strong public sector surpluses, still suffered. During the last quarter of 2008, Germany's economy sank faster than any other European nation, contracting by 2.1 per cent.[14]

Ironically, Germany had found it hard to increase domestic consumption fast enough over the preceding decade. Unable to persuade its own consumers to spend, it had achieved growth by building a strong manufacturing sector and exporting to countries like the US where consumers were still prepared to spend rather than save. But when credit collapsed and consumer spending slowed everywhere, these export markets dried up too, hitting the German economy harder than most.

Differences in the structure of economic growth hold some interesting lessons for the challenge of devising a sustainable economy. We'll return to the implications of this in later chapters. What's clear for now is that the roots of the economic crisis are much deeper than one particular country's dalliance in the banking sector or another's reliance on export markets. In fact, they lie at least in part in the concerted effort to free up credit for economic expansion across the world.

In *The New Paradigm for Financial Markets*, George Soros traces the emergence of what he calls a 'super-bubble' in global financial markets to a series of economic policies to increase liquidity as a way of stimulating demand. Loosening restraints on the US Federal Reserve, de-regulating financial markets and promoting the securitization of debts through complex financial derivatives were also deliberate interventions. Their overriding aim was to promote economic growth.[15]

In short, what emerges from all this is that the market was not undone by isolated practices carried out by rogue individuals. Or even through the turning of a blind eye by less than vigilant regulators. The very policies put in place to stimulate growth in the economy led eventually to its downfall. The market was undone by growth itself.

The enemy within

Securitization of mortgage debts (for example) was championed at the highest level, spearheaded by Alan Greenspan, former chairman of the Federal Reserve. In *The Age of Turbulence*, Greenspan defends the practice explicitly, arguing that 'transferring risk away from ...

highly leveraged loan originators can be critical for economic stability, especially in a global environment.'[16]

In testimony to US Congress in late October 2008, Greenspan admitted to being 'shocked' that markets hadn't worked as expected.[17] But this only underlines the point that these interventions were deliberate. All along the way, decisions to increase liquidity were made with a view to expanding the economy. As an *Economist* leader article remarked: 'Amid the crisis of 2008 it is easy to forget that liberalization had good consequences as well: by making it easier for households and businesses to get credit, deregulation contributed to economic growth.'[18]

For over two decades, de-regulation of financial markets was championed under monetarism as the best way to stimulate demand. The monetarists may have been reacting against the levels of public debt incurred by Keynesian spending programmes in the 1970s.[19] But a strategy that ended up replacing public debt with private debt was always a risky one. 'When the music stops, in terms of liquidity, things will be complicated,' the CEO of Citibank reportedly remarked, just before the bubble burst. 'But as long as the music is playing, you've got to get up and dance. We're still dancing.'[20]

By the end of 2008, Citibank was no longer dancing. No bank was. The music had clearly stopped – and things were definitely complicated.[21] Just how complicated was indicated by the sheer size of the international bailout and the fact that even an estimated $7 trillion of taxpayers' money proved insufficient to guarantee stability and avoid recession.

In short, the message from this chapter is that the 'age of irresponsibility' is not about casual oversight or individual greed. The economic crisis is not a consequence of isolated malpractice in selected parts of the banking sector. If there has been irresponsibility, it has been much more systematic, sanctioned from the top, and with one clear aim in mind: the continuation and protection of economic growth.

Ecological debts

The realization that the credit crisis and the ensuing recession were part of a systemic failure in the current economic paradigm is reinforced by an understanding of the resource and environmental implications of economic growth.

The commodity price 'bubble' that developed over several years and peaked in mid-2008 had clearly burst by the end of the year (Figure 1.2). It now seems likely that the very high prices attributed to key commodities in mid-2008 were in part the result of speculation and in part the result of identifiable supply-side problems such as limited refinery capacity in the face of high demand.

But this short-term bubble sat on top of a rising trend in commodity prices that cannot entirely be explained away in these terms. Environmental factors, resource and land scarcities, also played a key part and will inevitably continue to do so as the economy recovers. As Chapter 1 has already suggested, concerns around peak oil are gathering momentum. The natural rate of decline in established oil fields is now believed to be as high as 9 per cent a year.[22]

Economic expansion in China and the emerging economies has accelerated the demand for fossil fuels, metals and non-metallic minerals (see Chapter 5) and will inevitably reduce the reserve life of finite resources. The competition for land between food and bio-fuels clearly played a part in rising food prices. And these demands in their turn are intimately linked to accelerating environmental impacts: rising carbon emissions, declining biodiversity, rampant deforestation, collapsing fish stocks, declining water supplies and degraded soils.

The material and environmental impacts of growth were paramount in prompting this inquiry. The economic crisis may appear to be unrelated; but it is not. The age of irresponsibility demonstrates a long-term blindness to the limitations of the material world. This blindness is as evident in our inability to regulate financial markets as it is in our inability to protect natural resources and curtail ecological damage. Our ecological debts are as unstable as our financial debts. Neither is properly accounted for in the relentless pursuit of consumption growth.

To protect economic growth we have been prepared to countenance – and have even courted – unwieldy financial and ecological liabilities, believing that these are necessary to deliver security and keep us from collapse. But this was never sustainable in the long-term. The financial crisis has shown us that it isn't even sustainable in the short-term.

The truth is that we have failed to get our economies working sustainably even in financial terms. For this reason, responses to the crisis which aim to restore the status quo are deeply misguided and doomed to failure. Prosperity today means nothing if it undermines the conditions on which prosperity tomorrow depends. And the single biggest message from the financial meltdown of 2008 is that tomorrow is already here.

3
Redefining Prosperity

The good life of the good person can only be fully realised in
the good society. Prosperity can only be conceived as a condition that includes obligations and responsibilities to others.

Zia Sardar, November 2007[1]

The prevailing vision of prosperity as a continually expanding
economic paradise has come unravelled. Perhaps it worked better
when economies were smaller and the world was less populated.
But if it was ever fully fit for purpose, it certainly isn't now.

Climate change, ecological degradation and the spectre of
resource scarcity compound the problems of failing financial
markets and economic recession. Short-term fixes to prop up a
bankrupt system aren't good enough. Something more is needed.
An essential starting point is to set out a coherent notion of prosperity that doesn't rely on default assumptions about consumption
growth.

Accordingly, this chapter searches for a different kind of vision
for prosperity: one in which it is possible for humans beings to
flourish, to achieve greater social cohesion, to find higher levels of
well-being and yet still to reduce their material impact on the environment.

Any cursory examination of the literature reveals that, beyond
the narrow economic framing of the question, there are some
strong competing visions of prosperity.[2] Some of these visions hail

from psychology and sociology; others from economic history. Some draw on secular or philosophical viewpoints; others from the religious or 'wisdom' traditions.[3]

There are differences between these approaches. But there are also some striking similarities. Many perspectives accept that prosperity has material dimensions. It is perverse to talk about things going well if you lack the basic material resources required to sustain yourself: food and water to be adequately nourished or materials for clothing and shelter. Security in achieving these aims is also important.

But from at least the time of Aristotle, it has been clear that something more than material security is needed for human beings to flourish. Prosperity has vital social and psychological dimensions. To do well is in part about the ability to give and receive love, to enjoy the respect of your peers, to contribute useful work and to have a sense of belonging and trust in the community. In short, an important component of prosperity is the ability to participate freely in the life of society.[4]

Some approaches suggest a 'transcendental' need in human beings. For the more religious perspectives this may entail belief in some higher power. But even secular understandings accept that the human psyche craves meaning and purpose in life.

Some perspectives – particularly from the wisdom traditions – add in an important moral or ethical component to prosperity. Islamic commentator Zia Sardar argues that 'prosperity can only be conceived as a condition that includes obligations and responsibilities to others.'[5] The same principle is enshrined in the Quaker's *Moral Economy Project*.[6] My prosperity hangs on the prosperity of those around me, these traditions suggest, as theirs does on mine.

There is an interesting overlap between components of prosperity and the factors that are known to influence subjective well-being or 'happiness' (Figure 3.1). Indeed, to the extent that we are happy when things go well and unhappy when they don't, there is an

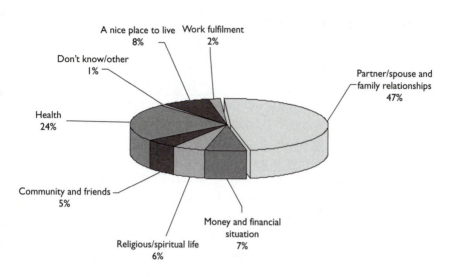

Figure 3.1 Factors influencing subjective well-being (happiness)[8]

Source: GfK NOP, October 2005. See note 8.

obvious connection between prosperity and happiness. This doesn't necessarily mean that prosperity is the same thing as happiness. But the connection between the two provides a useful link into recent policy debates about happiness and subjective well-being.[7]

In fact, there are at least three different candidates on offer here as concepts of prosperity. It's useful to distinguish carefully between them. Perhaps the easiest way to do this is to borrow from Amartya Sen, who set out the distinctions very clearly in a landmark essay on 'the living standard' first published in 1984.[9] One of Sen's concepts was characterized by the term *opulence*, another, by the term *utility* and a third through the idea of *capabilities for flourishing.*

Prosperity as opulence

Broadly speaking, Sen's first concept – opulence – corresponds to a conventional understanding that prosperity is about material satisfactions. Opulence refers to the ready availability and steady throughput of material commodities. An increase in the volume flow of commodities represents an increase in prosperity. The more we have the better off we are, in this view.

The logic of abundance as the basis for doing well dates back to Adam Smith. In those days providing material commodities to meet the necessities of life was a priority. But it is pretty straightforward to see that this simple equation of quantity with quality, of more with better, is false in general. Even economic theory recognizes this limitation. The 'diminishing marginal utility' of goods (indeed of income itself) reflects the fact that having more of something usually provides less additional satisfaction.

The sense that more can sometimes be less provides the beginnings of an understanding of the dissatisfactions of the consumer society (Chapter 9). It also offers a strong humanitarian argument for re-distribution.

When you've had no food for months and the harvest has failed again, any food at all is a blessing. When the American style fridge-freezer is already stuffed with overwhelming choice, even a little extra might be considered a burden, particularly if you're tempted to eat it. Once my appetite for strawberries, say, is sated, more of them provide no further joy at all. On the contrary, they may even make me feel ill. And if I'm tempted to ignore these bodily feedback mechanisms against excess I will find myself on the road to obesity and ill-health: outcomes which it is nonsensical to describe as desirable or satisfying.

Prosperity as utility

Quantity is not the same thing as quality. Opulence is not the same thing as satisfaction. Sen's second characterization of prosperity – as utility – recognizes this. Rather than focusing on the sheer volume of commodities available to us, this second version relates prosperity to the satisfactions which commodities provide.[10]

Though it is easy enough to articulate this difference, it is more difficult to define exactly how commodities relate to satisfaction, as many people have noted.[11] The one thing that's pretty easy to figure out is that the relationship is highly non-linear. Even something as basic as food doesn't follow a simple linear pattern in which more is always better.

There's a particularly important complexity here. Increasingly, the uses to which we put material commodities are social or psychological in nature rather than purely material.[12] In the immediate post-war years it was a challenge to provide for basic necessities, even in the most affluent nations. Today, consumer goods and services increasingly furnish us with identity, experience, a sense of belonging, perhaps even meaning and a sense of hope (Chapter 6).

Measuring utility in these circumstances is even more difficult. What is the 'psychic satisfaction' from an iPhone? A new bicycle? A holiday abroad? A birthday present for a lover? These questions are practically impossible to answer. Economics gets round the difficulty by assuming their value is equivalent to the price people are prepared to pay for them in freely functioning markets. It casts utility as the monetary value of market exchanges.

The GDP sums up all these market exchanges. Broadly speaking, it measures the total spending by households, government and investment across the nation. Spending is taken as a proxy for utility. And this, in a nutshell, is the case for believing that the GDP is a useful measure of well-being.

But the case is deeply problematic at best. There is a huge literature critiquing the value of GDP as a well-being measure.[13] Obvious limitations include its failure to account for non-market services (like household or voluntary labour) or negative utilities (externalities) like pollution. Critics point to the fact that the GDP counts both 'defensive' and 'positional' expenditures even though these don't contribute additionally to well-being.[14] And, perhaps most critically, the GDP fails to account properly for changes in the asset base which affect our future consumption possibilities.

Some have argued that the underlying concept of utility as exchange value is itself fundamentally flawed. A key finding here is the so-called happiness (or life-satisfaction) paradox. If GDP really does measure utility, it's a mystery to find that reported life satisfaction has remained more or less unchanged in most advanced economies over several decades in spite of significant economic growth. Real income per head has tripled in the US since 1950, but the percentage of people reporting themselves very happy has barely increased at all, and has declined since the mid-1970s. In Japan, there has been little change in life-satisfaction over several decades. In the UK the percentage reporting themselves 'very happy' declined from 52 per cent in 1957 to 36 per cent today, even though real incomes have more than doubled.[15]

Actually, as Figure 3.2 illustrates, the so-called life-satisfaction paradox is largely a malaise of the advanced economies. It is only after an income level of about $15,000 per capita, that the life-satisfaction score barely responds at all even to quite large increases in GDP. In fact the assumed relationship between income and life-satisfaction can be turned on its head here. Denmark, Sweden, Ireland and New Zealand all have higher levels of life-satisfaction than the USA, but significantly lower income levels.

By contrast, at very low incomes there is a huge spread in terms of life satisfaction, but the general trend is a quite steeply rising curve. A small increase in GDP leads to a big rise in life satisfaction.

These data underline one of the key messages of this book. There is no case to abandon growth universally. But there is a strong case for the developed nations to make room for growth in poorer countries. It is in these poorer countries that growth really does make a difference. In richer countries the returns on further growth appear much more limited. In the language of economics, marginal utility (measured here as subjective well-being) diminishes rapidly at higher income levels.

More importantly, it becomes clear from this analysis that a happiness-based measure of utility and an expenditure-based measure of utility behave in very different ways. And since they both claim to measure utility we can conclude that there is a problem somewhere. One or other – perhaps both – of these measures appears not to be doing its job properly.

The well-being protagonists claim it's the GDP that's failing. But the self-report measures also have their critics. One of the most worrying criticisms is that people are known to be inconsistent in assessments of their own happiness.[17]

Nobel-Prize winner Daniel Kahneman has shown that if you 'add up' people's assessments of subjective well-being over time you don't get the same answer as you would if you 'take all things together'. This may partly be because people adapt quickly to any given level of satisfaction and this changes their future valuations. Even something simple like a change in the order of events can alter our assessment of how well things have gone overall.[18]

One of the difficulties in comparing the self-report measure against the GDP is that they are simply different kinds of scales. The GDP is (in principle at least) unbounded. It can (politicians hope) go on growing indefinitely. The life-satisfaction measure on the other hand is a bounded scale. You can only score from 0 to 10, however often you go on making the assessment. It is implicit in the definition of the self-report scale that utility itself is bounded.[19]

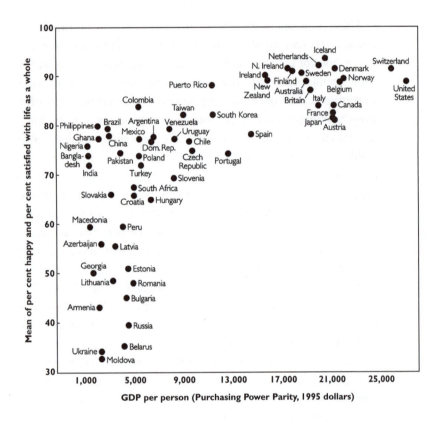

Figure 3.2 Happiness and average annual income[16]

Source: Worldwatch Institute, see note 16.

Here we come close to the crux of the matter. Obviously the two measures presume fundamentally different *concepts* of utility. In one interpretation there is no limit to the satisfaction that humans can achieve. The other is more circumspect in its view of the human psyche. Whatever else we may say about the relationship between GDP and life satisfaction, it's clear they are *not* measuring the same kind of utility.

When it comes to finding a reliable concept of prosperity, we appear to be no further forwards. Arguably, there are as many reasons for not equating prosperity with happiness as there are for not equating prosperity with exchange values. For one thing, the overriding pursuit of immediate pleasure is a very good recipe for things not going well in the future. This point has been highlighted incisively by economic historian Avner Offer: 'True prosperity is a good balance between short-term arousal and long-term security' he argues.[20]

Neither the GDP, which counts mainly present consumption, nor self-report measures, which count mainly present happiness, provide an accurate reflection of this balance. Just because humans suffer from myopic choice and find it hard to make a sacrifice now even for the sake of something better later doesn't justify taking a view of prosperity based on more or less instantaneous gratification.[21]

More fundamentally, to equate prosperity with happiness goes against our experience of what it means to live well. People can be unhappy for all sorts of reasons, some of them genetic, even when things do go well. Equally, they may be undernourished, poorly housed, with no prospect of improvement and yet declare themselves (some might say foolishly) completely content with their lot.

Prosperity as capabilities for flourishing

Sen uses these distinctions to argue (with a nod to Aristotle) for a third concept of the living standard based on the *capabilities* that people have to *flourish*. The key questions we should be asking, he insists, are to do with how well people are able to function in any given context.

'Are they well nourished? Are they free from avoidable morbidity? Do they live long?' he asks. 'Can they take part in the life of the community? Can they appear in public without shame and without feeling disgraced? Can they find worthwhile jobs? Can they keep themselves warm? Can they use their school education? Can they visit friends and relations if they choose?'[22]

There is a clear resonance between Sen's questions and the dimensions of prosperity identified at the beginning of this chapter.[23] In fact, the functionings he cites in this extract – nutritional health, life expectancy, participation in society – coincide closely with constituents of prosperity identified from time immemorial in a wide range of writings.

In his later work, Sen stresses not so much the functionings themselves – whether people actually live long, have a worthwhile job or participate in the community – as the capabilities or freedoms they have to do so.[24] His point is that in a liberal society, people should have the right to choose whether or not to participate in society, to work in paid employment and perhaps even whether to live a healthy life. It is the *capability* to flourish that is important.

Nonetheless, there are some clear reasons to retain the central importance of functionings themselves. In the first place, abstract capabilities are pretty uninformative. Any attempt to operationalize this idea of development ends up needing to specify what the important functionings are. This point is emphasized in a recent report to the Netherlands Environmental Assessment Agency on the feasibility of a capabilities approach within public policy. Even when it is the freedom to function that people value most, argues the report, this is largely because the functionings themselves are valued too.[25]

There is another reason not to take the focus on freedom too far. In a world of limits, certain kinds of freedoms are either impossible or immoral. The freedom endlessly to accumulate material goods is one of them. Freedoms to achieve social recognition at the expense of child labour in the supply chain, to find meaningful work at the expense of a collapse in biodiversity or to participate in the life of the community at the expense of future generations may be others.

Bounded capabilities

This is the most important lesson that a consideration of limits brings to any attempt to conceptualize prosperity. Capabilities for flourishing are a good starting point from which to define what it means to prosper. But this vision needs to be interpreted carefully: not as a set of disembodied freedoms, but as a range of 'bounded capabilities' to live well – within certain clearly defined limits.

These limits are established in relation to two critical factors. The first is the finite nature of the ecological resources within which life on earth is possible. These resources include the obvious material ones: fossil fuels, minerals, timber, water, land and so on. They also include the regenerative capacity of ecosystems, the diversity of species and the integrity of the atmosphere, the soils and the oceans.

None of these resources is infinite. Each stands in a complex relationship to the web of life on earth. We may not yet know exactly where all the limits lie. But we know enough to be absolutely sure that, in most cases, even the current level of economic activity is destroying ecological integrity and threatening ecosystem functioning, perhaps irreversibly. To ignore these natural bounds to flourishing is to condemn our descendents – and our fellow creatures – to an impoverished planet.

The second limiting factor on our capability to live well is the scale of the global population. This is simple arithmetic. With a finite pie and any given level of technology, there is only so much in the way of resources and environmental space to go around. The bigger the global population the faster we hit the ecological buffers, the smaller the population the lower the pressure on ecological resources. This basic tenet of systems ecology is the reality of life for every other species on the planet. And for those in the poorest nations.

The point is that a fair and lasting prosperity cannot be isolated from these material conditions. Capabilities are bounded on the one hand by the scale of the global population and on the other by the finite ecology of the planet. In the presence of these ecological limits, flourishing itself becomes contingent on available resources, on the entitlements of those who share the planet with us, on the freedoms of future generations and other species. Prosperity in this sense has both intra-generational and inter-generational dimensions. As the wisdom traditions suggest, there is an irredeemably moral dimension to the good life.

A prosperous society can only be conceived as one in which people everywhere have the capability to flourish in certain basic ways.

Deciding on those basic 'entitlements' is not a trivial task. What does it mean for humans to flourish? What are the functionings that society should value and provide for? How much flourishing is sustainable in a finite world?

Sen has tended to stop short of clear prescriptions, even though some are implicit in his writing. The philosopher Martha Nussbaum has gone furthest in this direction. Her list of 'central human capabilities' includes the following:

- life (being able to live to the end of a human life of normal length); bodily health;
- bodily integrity (to be secure against violent assault; having opportunities for sexual satisfaction and choice in matters of reproduction);
- practical reason (being able to form a conception of the good life);
- affiliation (being able to live with and toward others);
- play, and control over one's environment.[26]

Ultimately, as the Dutch report cited above recognizes, any such list needs to be negotiated in open dialogue before it can be taken as the basis of policy. But in practice, there is a striking resonance between the components in such lists and the constituents of prosperity identified in this chapter.

Physical and mental health matter. Educational and democratic entitlements count too. Trust, security and a sense of community are vital to social well-being. Relationships, meaningful employment and the ability to participate in the life of society appear to be important almost everywhere. People suffer physically and mentally when these things are absent. Society itself is threatened when they decline.

The challenge for society is to create the conditions in which these basic entitlements are possible. This is likely to require a closer attention to the social, psychological and material conditions of living – for example, to people's psychological well-being and to the resilience of communities – than is familiar in free-market societies.

Crucially though, this doesn't mean settling for a vision of prosperity based on curtailment and sacrifice. Capabilities are inevitably bounded by material and social conditions. Some ways of functioning may even be forestalled completely, particularly where they rely heavily on material throughput. But social and psychological functionings are not in any case best served by materialism, as we shall see more clearly in Chapter 9. As social psychologist Tim Kasser has pointed out (Kasser, 2007), this new vision of prosperity may serve us better than the narrow materialistic one that has ensnared us thus far.

The possibility that humans can flourish, achieve greater social cohesion, find higher levels of well-being and still reduce their material impact on the environment is an intriguing one. It would be foolish to think that it is easy to achieve – for reasons that will be discussed in more detail in the next chapter. But it should not be given up lightly. It may well offer the best prospect we have for a lasting prosperity.

4

The Dilemma of Growth

> One of the 'paradoxes of prosperity' is that people in rich
> countries don't realise how good things really are.
>
> Baumol et al, 2007[1]

Prosperity is not just about income. That much is clear. Rising prosperity is not the same thing as economic growth. But this does not in itself ensure that prosperity without growth is possible. A distinct possibility remains that growth is functional for prosperity: that continued economic growth is *a necessary condition* for a lasting prosperity. And that without growth our ability to flourish diminishes substantially.

Evidence for this would certainly need to be taken seriously. Perhaps the growth model is, after all, as good as it gets in terms of delivering prosperity. Are we guilty, as William Baumol and his colleagues claim in the quote above, of not realizing how good things really are under free-market capitalism? This chapter explores that possibility.

It examines three closely related propositions in defence of economic growth. The first is that opulence – though not synonymous with prosperity – is a necessary condition for flourishing. The second is that economic growth is closely correlated with certain basic entitlements – for health or education, perhaps – that are essential to prosperity. The third is that growth is functional in maintaining economic and social stability.

Any of these propositions, if supported, could threaten our prospects for achieving prosperity without growth and would place us instead between the horns of an extremely uncomfortable dilemma. On the one hand, continued growth looks ecologically unsustainable; on the other, it appears essential for lasting prosperity. Making progress against such an 'impossibility theorem' would be vital.

Material opulence as a condition of flourishing

At first sight it might seem odd to reopen the relationship between opulence and prosperity. Chapter 3 disposed of any simple linear relationship between material flow and flourishing. More isn't always better, even in something as basic as nutrition.

Admittedly, our ability to flourish declines rapidly if we don't have enough food to eat or adequate shelter. And this motivates a strong call for increasing incomes in poorer nations. But in the advanced economies, aside from some pernicious inequalities, we are largely beyond this. Material needs are broadly met and disposable incomes are increasingly dedicated to different ends: leisure, social interaction, experience. Clearly though, this hasn't diminished our appetite for material consumption.

Why is it that material commodities continue to be so important to us, long past the point at which material needs are met? Are we really natural-born shoppers? Have we been genetically programmed, as the psychologist William James believed, with an 'instinct for acquisition'? What is it about consumer goods that continues to entrance us even beyond the point of usefulness?

The clue to the puzzle lies in our tendency to imbue material things with social and psychological meanings. A wealth of evidence from consumer research and anthropology now supports this point. And the insight is devastating. Consumer goods provide a symbolic language in which we communicate continually with each other, not just about raw stuff, but about what really matters to us: family, friendship, sense of belonging, community, identity, social status, meaning and purpose in life.[2]

And crucially, these social conversations provide, in part, the means to participate in the life of society. Prosperity itself, in other words, depends on them. 'The reality of the social world', argues sociologist Peter Berger, 'hangs on the thin thread of conversation.'[3] And this conversation hangs in turn on the language of material goods.

There's a lovely illustration of the power of this seductive relationship in a study led by consumer researcher Russ Belk. He and his colleagues explored the role of desire in consumer behaviour across three different cultures. Commenting on what fashion meant to them, one of Belk's respondents remarked: 'No one's gonna spot you across a crowded room and say "Wow! Nice personality!"'[4]

The goal of this respondent is immediately identifiable as a basic human desire to be noticed, to be included, to be liked, to find friendship – possibly more (as the singles ads put it). All of these things are fundamental components of participating in the life of society, of flourishing.

It's tempting to think that this is a predominantly western (and relatively modern) phenomenon. Belk's study and numerous others suggest otherwise. The objective of the consumer, quite generally, according to anthropologist Mary Douglas, is 'to help create the social world and find a credible place in it'.[5] The symbolic role of material commodities has been identified, by anthropologists, in every single society for which records exist.

It is of course abundantly true in consumer society. Matter matters to us. And not just in material ways. But this is no longer unique to the west. 'One of the defining features of India's middle classes at the turn of the millennium,' argues anthropologist Emma Mawdsley, 'is their appetite for "global" culture, and their pursuit of "western" lifestyles, possessions and values.'[6] Very similar values and views are clearly discernible in China, Latin America and even in parts of Africa.

The consumer society is now, to all intents and purposes, a global society. One in which, for sure, there are still 'islands of prosperity, oceans of poverty'. But in which the 'evocative power of things'[7] increasingly creates the social world and provides the dominant arbiter of personal and societal progress.

In short, the material and the non-material dimensions of prosperity are inextricably intertwined with each other through the language of goods. Though it is essentially a social rather than a material task, our ability to participate in the life of society depends on this language. Anyone who has ever felt – or watched their kids feel – the enormous pressure of the peer group to conform to the latest fashion will understand how access to the life of society is mediated by sheer stuff.

Little wonder then that people regard income as one of the factors important to their well-being (Figure 3.1).[8] Incomes after all provide the material means for flourishing.

Prosperity depends more on opulence, it would seem, than is obvious at first glance. But there is an important subtlety in this relationship. And this subtlety provides a vital clue as to how we might confront – and get beyond – our dependency on material things.

The importance of income in well-being is largely played out (within nations) through relative effects. What matters – more than the absolute level of income – is having more or less than those around us.[9] This is particularly true in highly unequal societies where income disparities signal significant differences in social status. Income levels speak directly of status and sometimes of authority, power and class as well. But, in addition, as we now see, income provides access to the 'positional' or status goods that are so important in establishing our social standing.

And there is little doubt that at the individual level, social position counts. 'A positive social ranking produces an inner glow that is also matched with a clear advantage in life expectation and health', argues economic historian Avner Offer.[10] And this claim is backed up by persuasive evidence on the pernicious health effects of income inequality. Healthy life expectancy for English females was 16 years higher for those in the top decile in the late 1990s than it was for those in the bottom decile.[11]

The importance of social position is reinforced by Defra's recent ground-breaking study of the distribution of subjective well-being in the UK. Figure 4.1 shows reported satisfactions with different life 'domains' across different 'social grades'. Those in the higher social grades tend to report significantly higher levels of satisfaction than those in the lower social grades.[12]

Being at or near the top of the pile matters, it seems, both in terms of health and in terms of happiness or subjective well-being.

At the societal level though, there is a clear danger that this positional race doesn't contribute much to overall prosperity. 'The stock of status, measured as positive advantages, showed a sustained increase in the post-war years' acknowledges Offer. 'Much of the pay-off, however, was absorbed in positional competition.'[13]

This reasoning suggests that, at the level of society as a whole, income growth – and the associated material throughput – may be a 'zero-sum game'. The population as a whole gets richer. Some people are better off than others and positions in society may change. But overall this positional competition adds little or nothing to the levels of well-being in the nation. This is one of the arguments that has been used to explain the life-satisfaction paradox (Chapter 3).[14]

If it's right, it suggests the possibility that a different form of social organization – perhaps a more equal society – in which social positioning is either less important or signalled differently – could change things. This suggestion is borne out by the remarkable

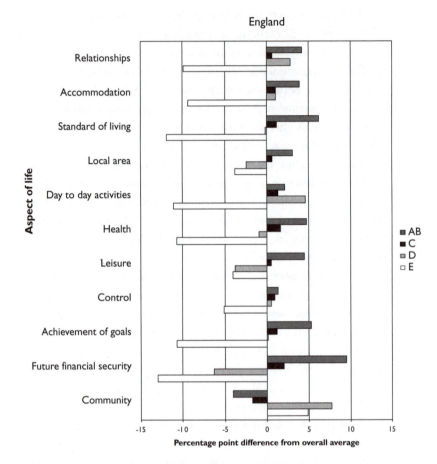

Figure 4.1 Well-being inequalities in England (2007)

Notes: Social grade is a classification based on occupation developed from the National Readership Survey. Examples of occupation in each grade include:

AB: Doctor, solicitor, accountant, teacher, nurse, police officer;

C: Junior manager, student, clerical worker, foreman, plumber, bricklayer;

D: Manual workers, shop workers, apprentices; E: Casual labourers, state pensioners, unemployed.

Separate grades A and B, and C1 and C2, have been joined (to AB and C) due to very similar distributions.

The results presented here show the difference between each group and the overall average presented on the previous graph.

Source: Defra 2007.

evidence marshalled by Richard Wilkinson and Kate Pickett in *The Spirit Level.* Looking at a range of health and social issues across OECD nations they conclude that the benefits of equality don't just accrue to the less fortunate members of society. Inequality has damaging impacts across the nation as a whole.[15]

Clearly, we would still need to confront the social logic that conspires to lock people into positional competition (Chapter 6). We would also have to identify less materialistic ways for people to participate in the life of society (Chapter 9). But in principle, these strategies could allow us to distinguish prosperity from opulence and reduce our dependency on material growth. In other words, this particular aspect of the dilemma of growth may just turn out to be avoidable.

But relative (or distributional) effects don't exhaust the relationship between income and human flourishing. There remains a distinct possibility that rising levels of income are required in and of themselves to establish and maintain absolute levels of capability for functioning.

Income and basic entitlements

This is where the second proposition comes in. The possibility that certain basic entitlements – such as life expectancy, health and educational participation – rely inherently on rising income would cast a serious doubt on our ability to flourish without growth.

The following paragraphs test this proposition using cross-country correlations between income and certain key components of human flourishing. The analysis uses data collected over several decades by the United Nations Development Programme (UNDP). These data in themselves can neither prove nor disprove a causal link between income and prosperity. But they provide a useful starting point in understanding how important GDP might be in human flourishing.

Figure 4.2, for example, maps life expectancy against average annual income levels in 177 different nations. The pattern is similar to the one in Figure 3.2 (Chapter 3), which looked at the relationship between life satisfaction and income. But now the 'dependent variable' is life expectancy rather than life-satisfaction.

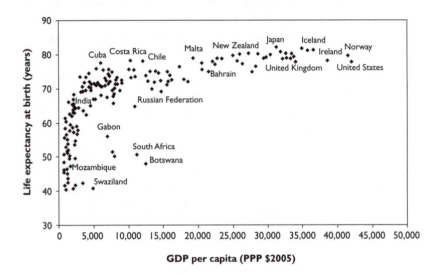

Figure 4.2 Life expectancy at birth v. average annual income

Note: PPP = purchasing power parity.

Source: Data are taken from statistics compiled for the Human Development Report, available online at the UNDP website: http://hdr.undp.org/en/statistics/

The difference between the poorest and the richest countries is striking, with life expectancies as low as 40 years in parts of Africa and almost double that in many developed nations. But the advantage of being richer as a nation shows diminishing returns. As income rises, the additional benefits in terms of increased life expectancy are reduced substantially.

Some low income countries have life expectancies that are on a par with developed nations. Chile (with an average annual income of $12,000) has a life expectancy of 78.3 years, greater than that of Denmark (whose average income is almost three times higher at $34,000). But it is also possible to find countries with incomes in the same range as Chile (South Africa and Botswana, for instance) where life expectancy is 30 years lower.

A similar story emerges from the data on infant mortality (Figure 4.3). In sub-Saharan Africa, 18 per cent of children die before their fifth birthday, whereas in OECD countries the proportion is 0.6 per cent. But as incomes increase, the gains from growth again diminish quite rapidly. Infant mortality in Cuba is 6 deaths per 1000 live births, as low as it is in the US – even though Cubans, with an average per capita income of $6000 enjoy less than 15 per cent of the income enjoyed by Americans.

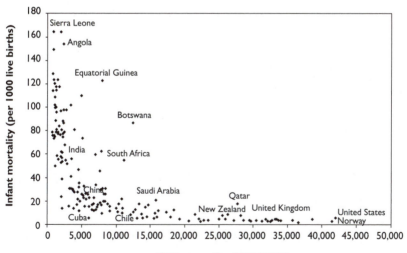

Figure 4.3 Infant mortality v. per capita income[16]

Source: See note 16.

At the same time, it is possible to find countries with an average income somewhat higher than $6000 per capita, whose infant mortality rates are much worse than those in Cuba. Equatorial Guinea is a striking example, with a per capita income of $8000 and infant mortality of 123 deaths per 1000 live births.

The ambivalent relationship between income and health indicators is echoed in the relationship between income and education. The Human Development Report's Education Index – based on a composite of educational participation rates – illustrates the same disparity between the very poor and the very rich. It also shows the familiar pattern of diminishing returns with respect to income growth (Figure 4.4).

Once again, it is possible to find low income countries providing educational participation rates that are as high as the most

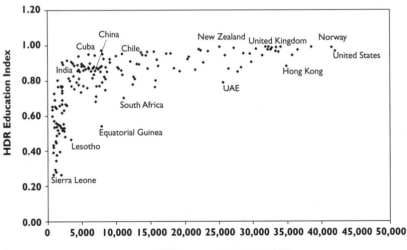

Figure 4.4 Participation in education v. income per capita

Source: see note 16.

developed nations. Kazakhstan, with in average income of less than $8000, scores higher on the index than Japan, Switzerland or the US, countries with income levels four and five times higher. Equally though, it isn't hard to find countries with income levels of $8000 whose educational participation rates are only two-thirds of those in most developed nations.

Interestingly, there is no hard and fast rule here on the relationship between income growth and improved flourishing. The poorest countries certainly suffer extraordinary deprivations in life expectancy, infant mortality and educational participation. But as incomes grow beyond about $15,000 per capita the returns to growth diminish substantially. Some countries achieve remarkable levels of flourishing with only a fraction of the income available to richer nations.

More exploration of these relationships is warranted. Understanding the structural dependencies between income and

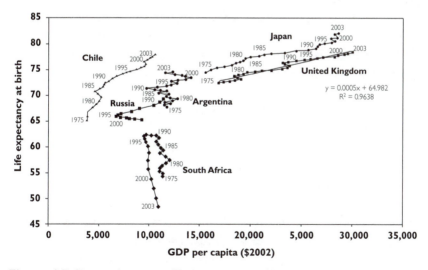

Figure 4.5 Changes in average life-expectancy and income over time

Source: See note 16.

human flourishing is a vital subject for study.[17] One of the questions that needs answering is how things change over time, within countries. Figure 4.5 illustrates the importance of this question for changes in life expectancy.

Again there is no single pattern. Three or four different modes of development emerge. One belongs to the developed nations – exemplified in Figure 4.5 by the UK and Japan. In these countries, there is a very strong but quite 'shallow' correlation between income growth and increased life expectancy. In the UK, for example, life expectancy has increased quite gradually but very consistently over the last few decades in spite of short periods of recession.[18]

Japan offers an even more interesting example. The country was hit quite severely during the Asian crisis in the late 1990s and suffered a prolonged period of economic turbulence. And yet life expectancy subsequently increased faster than at any time in the preceding two decades.

The ability to improve life expectancy despite a faltering economy is also evident in another group of countries, exemplified by Chile and Argentina in the graph. Here, rises in life expectancy appear much less dependent on income growth. In Argentina, in particular, economic output has been highly erratic over the last three decades, but the gains in life expectancy have been substantial and consistent.

Finally though, there are some countries (exemplified in Figure 4.5 by Russia and South Africa) which show significant declines in life expectancy when the economy falters. In fact, almost all the former Soviet bloc countries experienced reduced life expectancy in the post-Soviet era. In Russia itself, life expectancy remained more or less constant between 1970 and 1989 but fell by 6 per cent following the collapse of the Soviet Union. Perhaps most strikingly, this decline continued, even after the economy started to recover.

The same phenomenon – decline in spite of economic recovery – is visible in the case of South Africa. Here, the context and the contributing factors are rather different. A striking feature of human development across Africa since 1990 is the collapse in life expectancy irrespective of growth rates. This is largely due to the devastating impact of Aids.

Clearly growth doesn't guarantee improved prosperity, even in such basic components of flourishing as life expectancy. Incremental improvements have been possible in most developed nations, alongside more or less continuous economic growth. But there are also examples where life expectancy has increased much faster than income and one or two where it has increased even in the face of prolonged or severe recession.

In Cuba (not shown in Figure 4.5), the formal economy (GDP) more or less collapsed after the breakup of the Soviet Union in 1989, partly because of the sudden removal of subsidized Soviet oil. But one recent study suggests that there were significant health improvements in the aftermath. Calorific intake was reduced by over a third. Obesity was halved and the percentage of physically active adults more than doubled. Between 1997 and 2002, 'there were declines in deaths attributed to diabetes (51%), coronary heart disease (35%) [and] stroke (20%)'.[19]

Income growth and economic stability

This brings us on to the third proposition identified above: that growth is functional in maintaining economic and social stability. It is clear from the evidence here that collapsing economies do present a risk of humanitarian loss. Economic stability or, at the very least, some form of social resilience, is important for prosperity.

Even so there are interesting differences between countries faced with economic hardship. Some countries – notably Cuba, Japan and Argentina – have been able to ride out quite severe economic turbulence and yet maintain or even enhance national health. Others have watched life expectancy tumble in the face of economic recession.

Some of the explanation for these differences must lie in social structure. The transition of ex-Soviet states to a market economy was characterized by very profound changes in social structure, not the least of which was a collapse in state provision of health and social care. Little surprise, in these circumstances, that life expectancy faltered. In Cuba, by contrast, continuing state-led social provision was almost certainly a contributing factor in the health improvements that followed the economic collapse.

Humanitarian loss in the face of economic turbulence, in other words, may be more dependent on social structure than on the degree of economic instability that is encountered. There are some interesting policy lessons here (Chapter 11) for the prospect of prosperity without growth.

But the risk of humanitarian collapse is enough to place something of a question mark over the possibility that we can simply halt economic growth. If halting growth leads to economic and social collapse, then times look hard indeed. If it can be achieved without collapse, prospects for maintaining prosperity are considerably better.

Critical here is the question of whether a growing economy is essential for economic stability. Is growth functional for stability? Do we need economic growth after all simply to keep the economy stable?

The conventional answer is certainly that we do. To see why, we need to explore a little further how economies work. A detailed discussion of this is deferred to Chapter 6. But the broad idea is simple enough to convey.

Capitalist economies place a high emphasis on the efficiency with which inputs to production (labour, capital, resources) are utilized. Continuous improvements in technology mean that more output can be produced for any given input.[20] Efficiency improvement stimulates demand by driving down costs and contributes to a positive cycle of expansion. But crucially it also means that fewer people are needed to produce the same goods from one year to the next.

As long as the economy grows fast enough to offset this increase in 'labour productivity' there isn't a problem. But if it doesn't, then increased labour productivity means that someone somewhere loses their job.[21]

If the economy slows for any reason – whether through a decline in consumer confidence, through commodity price shocks or through a managed attempt to reduce consumption – then the systemic trend towards improved labour productivity leads to unemployment. This in its turn leads to diminished spending power, a loss of consumer confidence and further reduces demand for consumer goods.

From an environmental point of view this may be desirable because it leads to lower resource use and fewer polluting emissions. But it also means that retail falters and business revenues suffer. Incomes fall. Investment is cut back. Unemployment rises further and the economy begins to fall into a spiral of recession.

Recession has a critical impact on the public finances. Social costs rise with higher unemployment. But tax revenues decline as incomes fall and fewer goods are sold. Lowering spending risks real cuts to public services. Cutting spending affects people's capabilities for flourishing – a direct hit on prosperity.

Governments must borrow more not just to maintain public spending but to try and re-stimulate demand. But in doing so, they inevitably increase the national debt. Servicing this debt in a declining economy – as we noted in Chapter 2 – is problematic at best. Just maintaining interest payments takes up a larger proportion of the national income.

The best that can be hoped for here is that demand does recover and it's possible to begin paying off the debt. This could take decades. It took Britain almost half a century to pay off public debts accumulated through World War II. The Institute for Fiscal Studies has estimated that the 'debt overhang' from the current recession could last into the 2030s.[22] Alternatively, if the debt accumulates and the economy fails to recover, the country is doomed to bankruptcy.

Crucially, there is little resilience within this system. Once the economy starts to falter, feedback mechanisms that had once contributed to expansion begin to work in the opposite direction, pushing the economy further into recession.[23] With a growing (and aging) population these dangers are exacerbated. Higher levels of growth are required to protect the same level of average income and to provide sufficient revenues for (increased) health and social costs.

In short, modern economies are driven towards economic growth. For as long as the economy is growing, positive feedback mechanisms tend to push this system towards further growth. When consumption growth falters the system is driven towards a potentially damaging collapse with a knock on impact on human flourishing. People's jobs and livelihoods suffer.

There is, of course, something of an irony here. Because at the end of the day the answer to the question of whether growth is functional for stability is this: in a growth-based economy, growth is functional for stability. The capitalist model has no easy route to a steady state position. Its natural dynamics push it towards one of two states: expansion or collapse.

Later (Chapter 8) we explore the possibilities for amending this conclusion. In the meantime, we appear to have returned to the dilemma with which this chapter started, or at least to a more precise incarnation of it. Put in its simplest form the 'dilemma of growth' can now be stated in terms of two propositions:

- Growth is unsustainable – at least in its current form. Burgeoning resource consumption and rising environmental costs are compounding profound disparities in social well-being.
- 'De-growth'[24] is unstable – at least under present conditions. Declining consumer demand leads to rising unemployment, falling competitiveness and a spiral of recession.

This dilemma looks at first like an impossibility theorem for a lasting prosperity. But it cannot be avoided and has to be taken seriously. The failure to do so is the single biggest threat to sustainability that we face.

5

The Myth of Decoupling

> From a world of seemingly unlimited resources, mankind is
> gradually accustoming itself to the Earth as a limited, crowded
> and finite space, with limited resources for extraction and a
> narrowing capacity for waste disposal of pollution.
>
> Jean-Claude Trichet, June 2008[1]

The conventional response to the dilemma of growth is to appeal to the concept of 'decoupling'. Production processes are reconfigured. Goods and services are redesigned. Economic output becomes progressively less dependent on material throughput. In this way, it is hoped, the economy can continue to grow without breaching ecological limits – or running out of resources.

It's vital here to distinguish between 'relative' and 'absolute' decoupling. Relative decoupling refers to a decline in the ecological intensity per unit of economic output. In this situation, resource impacts decline relative to the GDP. But they don't necessarily decline in absolute terms. Impacts may still increase, but at a slower pace than growth in the GDP.

The situation in which resource impacts decline in absolute terms is called 'absolute decoupling'. Needless to say, this latter situation is essential if economic activity is to remain within ecological limits. In the case of climate change, for instance, absolute reductions in global carbon emissions of 50–85 per cent are required by 2050 in order to meet the Intergovernmental

Panel on Climate Change's (IPCC's) 450 ppm stabilization target.[2]

The aim of this chapter is to explore the evidence for both relative and absolute decoupling. It concentrates in particular on trends in the consumption of finite resources and the emission of greenhouse gases. These examples don't exhaust the concerns associated with a continually growing economy. But they are already of immediate concern and illustrate clearly the scale of the problem.

How much decoupling has been achieved in these examples? How much needs to be achieved? Is it really possible for a strategy of 'growth with decoupling' to deliver ever-increasing incomes for a world of 9 billion people and yet remain within ecological limits? These questions are central to the inquiry here.

As the title of this chapter suggests, the evidence that decoupling offers a coherent escape from the dilemma of growth is far from convincing. The 'myth' of decoupling is the claim that decoupling will necessarily achieve ecological targets. This is not to say that decoupling itself is unnecessary. On the contrary it's vital – with or without growth.

Relative decoupling

Put very simply, relative decoupling is about doing more with less: more economic activity with less environmental damage; more goods and services with fewer resource inputs and fewer emissions. Decoupling is about doing things more efficiently. And since efficiency is one of the things that modern economies are good at, decoupling has a familiar logic and a clear appeal as a solution to the dilemma of growth.

Resource inputs represent a cost to producers. So the profit motive should stimulate a continuing search for efficiency improvement in industry to reduce input costs. Some evidence supports this hypothesis. For example, the amount of primary energy needed to produce each unit of the world's economic output has fallen more or less continuously over most of the last half century. The global 'energy intensity' is now 33 per cent lower than it was in 1970.[3]

These gains have been most evident in the advanced economies. Energy intensities have declined three times faster in the OECD countries over the last 25 years than they have in non-OECD countries.[4] Energy intensity in both the US and the UK is some 40 per cent lower today than it was in 1980.[5]

Outside the most advanced nations, the pattern has been much less clear. Even in some southern European countries (for example Greece, Turkey and Portugal) energy intensity has increased in the last 25 years. And in emerging economies and developing nations achievements have been very mixed. Across the Middle East, energy intensity more than doubled between 1980 and 2006; in India it increased at first but has declined slowly since the peak in 1993. In China, energy intensity fell by over 70 per cent to the turn of the 21st century but has now begun to climb again.[6]

Overall, however, energy intensities declined significantly during the last three decades, across the OECD countries in particular. The same is true of material intensities more generally. Figure 5.1 shows a measure of material intensity for five advanced nations, including the UK, over the final quarter of the 20th century. The figure shows clear evidence of 'relative decoupling'.

Not surprisingly, improved resource efficiency is also leading to declining emission intensities. Figure 5.2 shows the changing carbon dioxide intensity of GDP over the last 25 years. The global carbon intensity declined by almost a quarter from just over 1 kilogram of carbon dioxide per US dollar ($kgCO_2/\$$) in 1980 to 770 grams of carbon dioxide per US dollar ($gCO_2/\$$) in 2006.

Again, steady improvements across the OECD countries were accompanied by a slightly more uneven pattern across non-OECD countries. Significant growth in carbon intensity occurred across

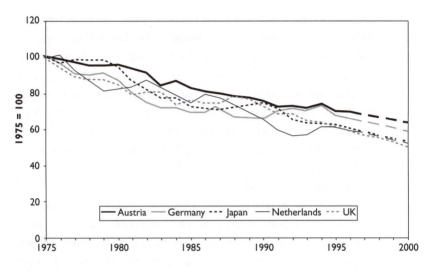

Figure 5.1 Relative decoupling in OECD countries 1975–2000[7]

Source: See note 7.

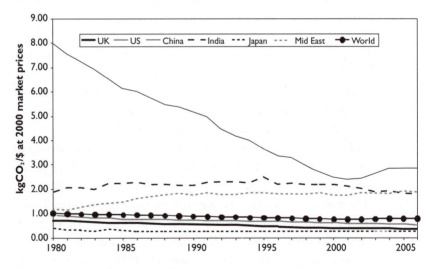

Figure 5.2 CO_2 intensity of GDP across nations: 1980–2006[8]

Source: see note 8.

the Middle East and during the earlier stages of development in India. China witnessed some striking improvements early on. But these have been partly offset by increasing carbon intensity in recent years. Worryingly, the declining global trend in carbon intensity has also faltered in recent years, even increasing slightly since its low point in 2000.

Clearly, there is little room for complacency here. The efficiency with which the global economy uses fossil resources and generates carbon dioxide emissions is improving in some places. But overall we are making faltering progress at best.

To make matters worse, relative decoupling is barely half the story. It measures only the resource use (or emissions) per unit of economic output. For decoupling to offer a way out of the dilemma of growth, resource efficiencies must increase at least as fast as economic output does. And they must continue to improve as the economy grows, if overall burdens aren't to increase. To achieve this more difficult task, we need to demonstrate absolute decoupling. Evidence of this is much harder to find.

Absolute decoupling

Despite declining energy and carbon intensities, carbon dioxide emissions from fossil fuels have increased by 80 per cent since 1970. Emissions today are almost 40 per cent higher than they were in 1990 – the Kyoto base year – and since the year 2000 they have been growing at over 3 per cent per year (see Figure 5.3).

Figure 5.3 does illustrate some relative decoupling: the world GDP has risen faster than carbon dioxide emissions over the last 18 years. But there is no absolute decoupling here. And a surge in world consumption of coal has increased the rate of growth in carbon dioxide emissions since the year 2000.

What's true for fossil resources and carbon emissions is true for material throughputs more generally. Figure 5.4 illustrates direct

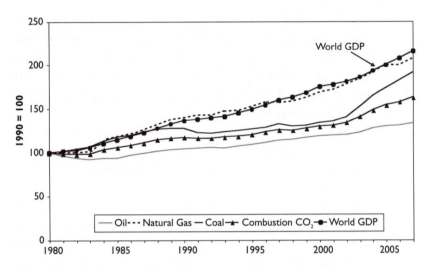

Figure 5.3 Trends in fossil fuel consumption and related CO_2: 1980–2007[9]

Source: see note 9.

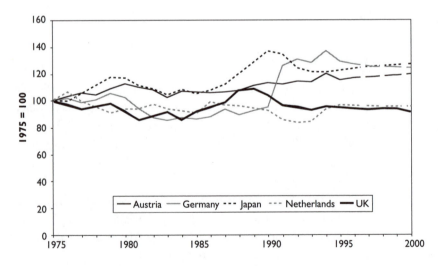

Figure 5.4 Direct material consumption in OECD countries: 1975–2000[10]

Source: see note 10.

material consumption for the same five OECD countries shown in Figure 5.1. Despite very clear evidence of relative decoupling in the earlier figure, there is far less evidence here of an absolute decline in material consumption.

The best that can be observed – in only a couple of countries – is something of a stabilization in resource requirements, particularly since the late 1980s. But even this finding is not entirely to be trusted. The problem is that it's difficult to pick up all the resources embedded in traded goods. The measure shown here – direct material consumption – does its best to identify traded flows of specific resources. But it misses out on the resources (and emissions) used to manufacture finished and semi-finished products abroad.

This question is important precisely because of the structure of modern developed economies, which have typically tended to move progressively away from domestic manufacturing. Unless the demand for consumer goods also declines, more and more finished and semi-finished goods need to be imported from abroad. And since concepts like direct material consumption omit such accounts, Figure 5.4 underestimates the resource requirements of developed economies.

Correcting this failing calls for more sophisticated resource and economic models than are currently available. In the case of carbon dioxide, however, several recent studies for the UK have confirmed that national accounts systematically fail to account for the 'carbon trade balance'. In other words, there are more (hidden) carbon emissions associated with UK consumption patterns than appear from the numbers we report to the United Nations (UN) under the Framework Convention on Climate Change (FCCC).

In fact, this difference is enough to undermine the progress made towards the UK's Kyoto targets. An apparent reduction in emissions of 6 per cent between 1990 and 2004, as reported under UN FCCC guidelines is turned into an 11 per cent increase in emissions, once emissions embedded in trade are taken into account.[11]

Without more detailed work, it's difficult to know whether this pattern is true more generally for material resources. But given the trend away from manufacturing in advanced economies, it's clearly wise to view Figure 5.4 with some caution. There is an outside chance that some stabilization of resource consumption has occurred. But Figure 5.4 doesn't provide a lot of confidence in absolute decoupling, even within the richer nations.

Ultimately, in any case, what count most in terms of global limits are worldwide statistics. Both climate change and resource scarcity are essentially global issues. So the final arbiter on the feasibility of absolute decoupling – and the possibilities for escaping the dilemma of growth – are worldwide trends. Figure 5.3 confirmed a rising global trend in fossil fuels and carbon emissions. Figure 5.5 shows the global trend in the extraction of another vital set of finite resources – metal ores.

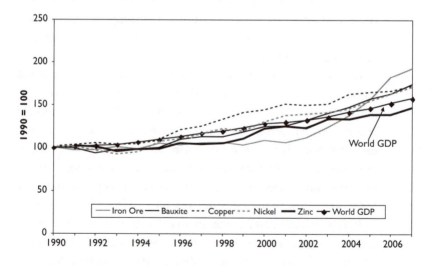

Figure 5.5 Global trends in primary metal extraction: 1990–2007[12]

Source: see note 12.

What's striking from Figure 5.5 is not just the absence of absolute decoupling. There is little evidence of relative decoupling either. Some improved resource efficiency is evident in the earlier years, but this appears to have been eroded more recently. Particularly notable is the increased consumption of structural metals. Extraction of iron ore, bauxite, copper and nickel is now rising faster than world GDP.

Reasons for this are not particularly hard to find. China's hunger for iron ore is well-documented.[13] As the emerging economies build up their infrastructures, the rising demand for structural materials is one of the factors that put an upward pressure on commodity prices during 2007 and the first half of 2008 (see Chapter 2, Figure 2.2). The impact on certain non-metallic minerals is just as striking. Worldwide cement production has more than doubled since 1990, surpassing growth in world GDP by some 70 percentage points. Global resource intensities (the ratios of resource use to GDP), far from declining, have increased significantly across a range of non-fuel minerals. Resource efficiency is going in the wrong direction. Even relative decoupling just isn't happening.

It's clear from this that history provides little support for the plausibility of decoupling as a sufficient solution to the dilemma of growth. But neither does it rule out the possibility entirely. A massive technological shift; a significant policy effort; wholesale changes in patterns of consumer demand; a huge international drive for technology transfer to bring about substantial reductions in resource intensity right across the world: these changes are the least that will be needed to have a chance of remaining within environmental limits and avoiding an inevitable collapse in the resource base at some point in the (not too distant) future.

The message here is not that decoupling is unnecessary. On the contrary, absolute reductions in throughput are essential. The question is, how much is achievable? How much decoupling is technologically and economically viable? With the right political will, could relative decoupling really proceed fast enough to achieve real reductions in emissions and throughput, and allow for continued economic growth? These critical questions remain unanswered by those who propose decoupling as the solution to the dilemma of growth. More often than not, the crucial distinction between relative and absolute decoupling isn't even elucidated.

It's far too easy to get lost in general declarations of principle: growing economies tend to become more resource efficient; efficiency allows us to decouple emissions from growth, so the best way to achieve targets is to keep growing the economy. This argument is not at all uncommon in the tangled debates about environmental quality and economic growth.

It contains some partial truths – for example, that some efficiency improvements occur in some advanced economies.[14] It draws some support from some limited evidence on air pollutants such as sulphur dioxide and particulates. These emissions sometimes show an inverted-U shaped relationship with economic growth: emissions grow in the early stage of growth but then peak and decline.[15]

But this relationship only holds, according to ecological economist Douglas Booth, for local, visible environmental effects like smoke, river water quality and acid pollutants. It isn't uniformly true even for these pollutants. And it simply doesn't exist at all for key indicators of environmental quality such as carbon emissions, resource extraction, municipal waste generation and species loss.[16]

As an escape from the dilemma of growth it is fundamentally flawed. Ever greater consumption of resources is itself a driver of growth. As industrial ecologist Robert Ayres has pointed out: 'consumption (leading to investment and technological progress) drives growth, just as growth and technological progress drives consumption'.[17] Protagonists of growth seldom compute the consequences of this relationship.

The arithmetic of growth

Arithmetic is key here. A very simple mathematical identity governs the relationship between relative and absolute decoupling. It was put forward almost 40 years ago by Paul Ehrlich and John Holdren. The Ehrlich equation tells us quite simply that the impact (I) of human activity is the product of three factors: the size of the population (P), its level of affluence (A) expressed as income per person and a technology factor (T), which measures the impact associated with each dollar we spend (Box 5.1).

For as long as the T factor is going down, then we are safe in the knowledge that we have relative decoupling. But for absolute decoupling we need I to go down as well. And that can only happen if T goes down fast enough to outrun the pace at which population (P) and income per capita (A) go up.

Over the last five decades this has been a tough ask. Both affluence and population have gone up substantially, each being about equally responsible for the overall five-fold growth in the economy. In recent years, the affluence factor has exceeded the population factor in driving growth. But both are clearly important, as Ehrlich himself recognized.[18] And neither has proved particularly tractable to policy. Increasing affluence has been seen as synonymous with improved well-being. Advocating limits to population growth has been seen as contravening basic human liberties.

Ironically, both these pre-conceptions are wrong. Increasing incomes don't always guarantee well-being and sometimes detract from it. And the fastest population growth has occurred in the developing world – driven not by liberty but by a lack of education and inadequate access to contraception.[19]

Nonetheless, the intractability of addressing both population and income has tended to reinforce the idea that only technology can save us. Knowing that efficiency is key to economic progress, it is tempting to place our faith in the possibility that we can push relative decoupling fast enough that it leads in the end to absolute decoupling. But just how feasible is this?

Box 5.1 Unravelling the arithmetic of growth

The Ehrlich equation states that environmental (I) is a product of population (P) times affluence or income level (A) times the technological intensity (T) of economic output.

$$I = P \times A \times T$$

For carbon dioxide emissions from fuel combustion, for example, the total emissions are given by the product of population (P) times income (measured as dollars of GDP/person) times the carbon intensity of economic activity (measured as $gCO_2/\$$):

$$C = P \times \$/person \times gCO_2/\$$$

Using this arithmetic for the year 2007, when the global population was about 6.6 billion, the average income level in constant 2000 dollars (at market prices) was $5900, and the carbon intensity was $760gCO_2/\$$, we find that the total carbon dioxide emissions C were:

$$6.6 \times 5.9 \times 0.77 = 30 \text{ billion tonnes of } CO_2.$$

In 1990, when the population was only 5.3 billion and the average income was $4700 but carbon intensity was $860gCO_2/\$$, total carbon dioxide emissions C were given by:

$$5.3 \times 4.7 \times 0.87 = 21.7 \text{ billion tonnes of } CO_2.$$

These numbers are confirmed against those reported in the Energy Information Administration's *International Energy Annual*. The cumulative growth in emissions between 1990 (the Kyoto base year) and 2007 was 39 per cent (30/21.7 = 1.39) with an average growth rate in emissions (r_i) of almost 2 per cent ($r_i = (1.39)^{1/17} - 1 = 1.96$ per cent).

There is a convenient 'rule of thumb' to figure out when relative decoupling will lead to absolute decoupling. In a growing population with an increasing average income, absolute decoupling will occur when the rate of relative decoupling is greater than the rates of increase in population and income combined.[20]

With this rule of thumb in mind, it's instructive to explore what's happened historically (and why) to global carbon dioxide emissions.

Carbon intensities have declined on average by 0.7 per cent per year since 1990. That's good, but not good enough. Population has increased at a rate of 1.3 per cent and average per capita income has increased by 1.4 per cent each year (in real terms) over the same period. Efficiency hasn't even compensated for the growth in population, let alone the growth in incomes. Instead, carbon dioxide emissions have grown on average by 1.3 + 1.4 − 0.7 = 2 per cent per year, leading over 17 years to an almost 40 per cent increase in emissions (Box 5.1).[21]

The same rule of thumb allows us a quick check on the feasibility of decoupling carbon dioxide emissions from growth in the future. The IPCC's Fourth Assessment Report suggests that achieving a 450 ppm stabilization target means getting global carbon dioxide emissions down to below 4 billion tonnes per annum by 2050 or soon after. This would be equivalent to reducing annual emissions at an average rate of 4.9 per cent per year between now and 2050.[22]

But income and global population are going in the opposite direction. According to the UN's mid-range estimate, the world's population is expected to reach 9 billion people by 2050 – an average growth of 0.7 per cent each year. Under business as usual conditions, the decline in carbon intensity just about balances the growth in population and carbon dioxide emissions will end up growing at about the same rate as the average income – 1.4 per cent a year. It might not sound much, but by 2050, under these assumptions, carbon dioxide emissions are 80 per cent *higher* than they are today. Not quite what the IPCC had in mind.

To achieve an average year-on-year reduction in emissions of 4.9 per cent with 0.7 per cent population growth and 1.4 per cent income growth, T has to improve by approximately 4.9 + 0.7 + 1.4 = 7 per cent each year – almost ten times faster than it is doing right now. By 2050 the average carbon content of economic output would need to be less than $40gCO_2/\$$, a 21-fold improvement on the current global average (Figure 5.6, Scenario 1).

In fact, things could get even worse than this. At the higher end of the UN's population estimates – in a world of almost 11 billion people – business as usual would more than double global carbon dioxide emissions over today's level. Achieving the 2050 target in these circumstances would put even more pressure on technological improvements, to drive the carbon intensity of output down to less than $30gCO_2/\$$ (Figure 5.6, Scenario 2).[23]

Notably, this would still be a deeply unequal world. Business as usual income growth is usually taken to mean a steady 2 per cent growth rate in the most developed countries while the rest of the world does its best to catch up – China and India leaping ahead at 5–10 per cent per annum at least for a while, with Africa, South America and parts of Asia languishing in the doldrums for decades to come. In most of these scenarios, both the incomes and the carbon footprints of the developed nations would be more than an order of magnitude higher by 2050 than those in the poorest nations.

If we're really serious about fairness and want the world's 9 billion people all to enjoy an income comparable with EU citizens today, the economy would need to grow 6 times between now and 2050, with incomes growing at an average rate of 3.6 per cent a year. Achieving the IPCC's emission target in this world means pushing down the carbon intensity of output by 9 per cent every single year for the next 40 or so years.[24] By 2050, the average carbon intensity would need to be 55 times lower than it is today at only $14gCO_2/\$$ (Figure 5.6, Scenario 3).

And this scenario still hasn't factored in income growth in the developed nations. Imagine a scenario in which incomes everywhere are commensurate with a 2 per cent increase per annum in the current EU average income. The global economy grows almost 15 times in this scenario and carbon intensity must fall by over 11 per cent every single year. By 2050 the carbon content of each dollar has to be no more than $6gCO_2/\$$. That's almost 130 times lower than the average carbon intensity today (Figure 5.6, Scenario 4).

Beyond 2050, of course, if growth is to continue, so must efficiency improvements. With growth at 2 per cent a year from 2050 to the end of the century, the economy in 2100 is 40 times the size of today's economy. And to all intents and purposes, nothing less than a complete decarbonization of every single dollar will do to achieve carbon targets. Under some more stringent stabilization scenarios,

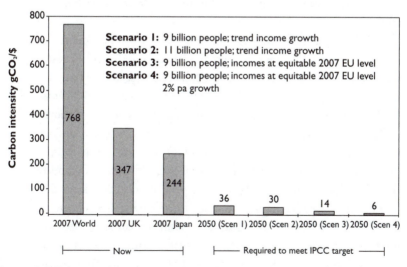

Figure 5.6 Carbon intensities now and required to meet 450 ppm target[25]

Source: see note 25.

by 2100 we will need to be taking carbon out of the atmosphere. The carbon intensity of each dollar of economic output will have to be less than zero!

What kind of economy is that? What are its consumption activities? What are its investment activities? What does it run on? What keeps it going? How is economic value created by removing carbon from the atmosphere? One thing is clear. It's a completely different kind of economy from the one we have at the moment which drives itself forward by emitting more and more carbon.

Stark choices

Playing with numbers may seem like dancing angels on the head of a pin. But simple arithmetic hides stark choices. Are we really committed to eradicating poverty? Are we serious about reducing carbon emissions? Do we genuinely care about resource scarcity, deforestation, biodiversity loss?[26] Or are we so blinded by conventional wisdom that we daren't do the sums for fear of revealing the truth?

One thing is clear. Business as usual is grossly inadequate, as even the International Energy Agency (IEA) – the world's energy watchdog – now accepts. Their 'Reference' scenario has the demand for primary energy growing by 45 per cent by 2030, on-track for the 80 per cent hike in carbon emissions alluded to above.

The IEA's 'Stabilization' scenario reveals the scale of the challenge. 'Our analysis shows that OECD countries alone cannot put the world onto a 450 ppm trajectory, even if they were to reduce their emissions to zero', the World Energy Outlook 2008 admits.[27]

The report also highlights the scale of investment that is likely to be needed over the coming decades. Stabilizing carbon emissions (and addressing problems of energy security) requires a whole-scale transition in global energy systems. Technological change is essential, with or without growth. Even a smaller economy would face this challenge: declining fossil energy requirements and substantially reduced carbon emissions are vital.

We can never entirely discount the possibility that some massive technological breakthrough is just round the corner. But it's clear that early progress towards carbon reduction will have to rely on options that are already on the table: enhanced energy efficiency, renewable energy and perhaps carbon capture and storage.[28]

Just how much decoupling could be achieved in this way is an open question. The truth is, we haven't yet tried that hard to achieve it. As environmental economist Paul Ekins has pointed out, current policies barely scratch the surface of what could be done to deliver decoupling.[29] Substantial early investment in low carbon technologies is obviously essential.

In fact, it is this need for what we might call 'ecological investment', particularly by the advanced economies, which begins to transform the economics of the 21st century. As we'll see in more detail in Chapter 7, carbon reduction is only one of many competing targets for ecological investment. Others include resource efficiency, resource substitution, infrastructure changes, ecosystem protection and ecological enhancement.

The impact on global growth from a substantial up-scaling of ecological investment is far from certain. The Stern Review famously argued that 'the annual costs of achieving stabilization … are around 1 per cent of global GDP.'[30] But the stabilization target was a less punishing one (550 ppm) than is now believed to be necessary.

In the original report, Nicholas Stern dismissed the possibility of achieving a more stringent stabilization target, precisely because it would 'be very difficult and costly to aim to stabilise at 450 ppm'. He later revised this opinion slightly, suggesting that a 500 ppm target was now needed, because climate change was proceeding faster than previously anticipated. His estimate of the cost to GDP of achieving the higher target was revised upwards to 2 per cent.

Accountancy firm PriceWaterhouse Coopers estimated the costs of achieving a 50 per cent reduction in global carbon emissions at 3 per cent of global GDP.[31]

Though all these numbers look rather small, there's something very confusing about cost estimates like this: they are already about the same order of magnitude as the difference between a growing economy and a non-growing economy. So if these costs really represented an annual hit of around 2–3 per cent of GDP they would essentially already wipe out growth.

It's therefore very important to the Stern argument – although often not explicitly pointed out – that the annual costs rise from quite low levels to reach 1 per cent of GDP by 2050. In 2015, for instance, they are still low enough (0.3 per cent of GDP in the Stern central case) to suppose that we could squeeze them out of the variability in productivity and still achieve annual 2 per cent GDP growth in the background. At twice or three times that level in the early years, the assumption becomes a lot more problematic.[32]

So the speed and rate at which carbon emissions have to be reduced becomes crucially important to the argument about its impacts on GDP. And the emerging scientific evidence (see Chapter 1) suggests that we need to act sooner and faster rather than later. But there's yet another reason for questioning whether the assumption of an easy hit on GDP growth is robust.

The Stern Review costs represent a cost to global GDP based on global emission reductions. For all sorts of reasons, the costs to advanced nations could and indeed should be considerably higher. In the first place, current emission levels are higher in richer nations, so there is further to go in terms of reductions. In addition, the historical responsibility for climate change rests firmly with the developed nations. Richer countries have a moral duty to be doing much more than poorer countries in achieving stabilization. This will have to include abating not just their own emissions, but those of developing nations too.

This point is made forcefully by energy economist Dieter Helm. In a lecture given in Oxford in February 2009 he concludes that the task we're faced with 'is to apply (much) more expensive low carbon technologies in countries like China quickly. That will, in turn, require developed countries to transfer considerable sums (considerably more than 1% of GDP) to countries like China so that they can increase their competitiveness and be low carbon. The corollary is that Americans and Europeans will have to correspondingly lower their own consumption considerably – and quickly.'[33] In short, there are significant limitations to the original Stern analysis and as yet no reliable indication of the impacts of substantial ecological investment on GDP growth in the advanced nations. 'The easy compatibility between economic growth and climate change, which lies at the heart of the Stern Report, is an illusion,' claims Helm. He suggests that Stern's micro-economic appraisals suffer from serious 'appraisal optimism' by assuming that wholesale transformation of energy systems can be achieved by scaling up marginal cost estimates.[34]

Helm also attacks the macro-economics of current stabilization scenarios. Not only could carbon abatement policies interfere more seriously with productivity than many macro-economic assessments suggest, but early climate change impacts could themselves reduce potential growth. Assuming that economic growth simply rolls onwards in the background despite high mitigation and adaptation costs is untenable, claims Helm.[35]

Besides all this, the Stern stabilization scenario could not deliver global income parity without extensive redistribution from richer to poorer nations. As with most such scenarios, income growth in the developed nations is taken as read in the Stern analysis. Parts of the developing world are assumed to catch up a little with the richer nations. But this is not a scenario in which incomes are distributed equally across nations. Unless growth in the richer nations is curtailed, or some kind of completely unforeseen technological breakthrough happens, the carbon implications of a shared prosperity are truly daunting to contemplate.

The truth is that there is as yet no credible, socially just, ecologically sustainable scenario of continually growing incomes for a world of 9 billion people.

In this context, simplistic assumptions that capitalism's propensity for efficiency will allow us to stabilize the climate or protect against resource scarcity are nothing short of delusional. Those who promote decoupling as an escape route from the dilemma of growth need to take a closer look at the historical evidence – and at the basic arithmetic of growth.

Resource efficiency, renewable energy and reductions in material throughput all have a vital role to play in ensuring the sustainability of economic activity. But the analysis in this chapter suggests that it is entirely fanciful to suppose that 'deep' emission and resource cuts can be achieved without confronting the structure of market economies.

6

The 'Iron Cage' of Consumerism

As every hunted animal knows, it is not how fast you run that counts, but whether you are slower than everyone else.

The Economist, November 2008[1]

A sense of anxiety pervades modern society. At times it tips over into visceral fear. The economic crisis of 2008 was such a time. Financial institutions became almost paralysed by fear. Banks refused to lend even to each other; consumers stopped spending because of it. Governments displayed signs of being totally bewildered, both by the speed of change and by the implications of failure.

Fear may not be all bad. The threat of imminent collapse may have been the only force strong enough to bring so many countries together in late 2008, with a pledge to 'achieve needed reforms in the world's financial systems'. Decisiveness in the face of fear is what the G20 leaders called for during the early phase of financial recovery.

And yet the sense of a more fundamental, a more pervasive anxiety underlying the modern economy is an enduring one.[2] Could it really be the case, as *The Economist* suggests, that we are still behaving like hunted animals, even in the 21st century, driven by the fine distinction between predator and prey? If we are, it would be good to recognize it. And to understand why. For without that understanding, solutions to the dilemmas we face will inevitably prove elusive.

Admittedly, the dilemma of growth isn't helping much, looking as it does like an impossibility theorem for lasting prosperity. Perhaps at some instinctive level, we have always understood this. Maybe we're haunted by the subconscious fear that the 'good life' we aspire to is already deeply unfair and can't last forever. That realization – even repressed – might easily be enough to taint casual joy with existential concern.

And of course the analysis in Chapter 5 doesn't allay those fears. It more or less closes down the most obvious escape from the dilemma of growth. Efficiency is a grand idea. And capitalism sometimes delivers it. But even as the engine of growth delivers productivity improvement, so it also drives forward the scale of throughput. Nowhere is there any evidence that efficiency can outrun – and continue to outrun – scale in the way it must do if growth is to be compatible with sustainability.

There is still a possibility that we just haven't tried hard enough. With a massive policy effort and huge technological advances, perhaps we could reduce resource intensities the two or three orders of magnitude necessary to allow growth to continue – at least for a while. And yet, the idea of running faster and faster to escape the damage we're already causing is itself a strategy that smacks of panic. So before we settle for it, a little reflection may be in order.

Accordingly, this chapter confronts the structure of modern capitalist economies head on. In particular, it explores two inter-related features of economic life that are central to the growth dynamic. On the one hand, the profit motive stimulates newer, better or cheaper products and services through a continual process of innovation and 'creative destruction'. At the same time, the expanding consumer demand for these goods is driven forwards by a complex social logic.

These two factors combine to drive 'the engine of growth' on which modern economies depend and lock us in to an 'iron cage' of consumerism.[3] It's essential to get a better handle on this twin dynamic, not least so that we can identify the potential to escape from it. The starting point is to unravel some of the workings of modern capitalism.

Structures of capitalism

Capitalism isn't a single homogenous entity. We've seen already (Chapter 2) that it exists in different varieties. Peter Hall and David Soskice distinguished between liberal market economies and coordinated market economies. The former place more faith in the power of liberalized, deregulated markets. The latter argue for stronger social institutions and more strategic relationships (rather than competition) between firms. An argument rages over which variety achieves more growth.[4]

In *Good Capitalism, Bad Capitalism*, William Baumol and his colleagues classify the economies of capitalist countries in four different categories: state-guided capitalism, oligarchic capitalism, big-firm capitalism and entrepreneurial capitalism.[5] 'About the only thing these systems have in common is that they recognize the right of private ownership of property', the authors write. 'Beyond that they are very different.'[6]

Private ownership of the means of production is, broadly speaking, Baumol's definition of capitalism. An economy is 'capitalistic' when 'most or at least a substantial proportion of its means of production [is] in private hands, rather than being owned and operated by the government'. But he also recognizes that this definition is fluid, with even the most capitalistic states prepared to take ownership in some sectors. The financial crisis has blurred this boundary even more, of course, with national governments taking substantial equity stakes in financial institutions.

The main thesis of Baumol and his colleagues is that not all types of capitalism are equally good. Some of them lead to growth; others lead to 'stagnation'. Specifically, the 'good' ones lead to growth and the 'bad' ones lead to stagnation! This moral judgement is fascinating in its own right. It's also interesting in suggesting that a capitalist economy doesn't after all inevitably have to be growth-based. We'll come back to this question later in the book (Chapters 8 and 12).

For now, the most useful part of Baumol's thesis is his claim that 'good' capitalism (that is, growth-based capitalism) is entrepreneurial capitalism with a dose of big-firm capitalism thrown in. It won't escape anyone's attention of course that this is pretty much the version of capitalism that characterizes the consumer economies of the west. In fact, much of Baumol's book is focused on how to nurture and protect this rare and beautiful creature and persuade others to adopt it, so that we can all get as much growth as possible from it.

Though it could clearly do with a dose of ecological realism, the book is nonetheless a useful resource for those interested in understanding how long-run economic growth is supposed to work in this kind of economy, at least in principle. In practice as we've seen, things can go badly wrong. At its heart, however, consumer capitalism is strikingly simple (Figure 6.1).

In broad terms, firms employ labour (people) and capital (buildings and machinery) to produce the goods and services that households want and need. Households (people) offer up their labour and capital[7] (savings) to firms in exchange for incomes. Revenue from the sale of goods and services is what allows firms to provide people with incomes. People spend some of this income on more consumer goods. But some of it they save. These savings are invested (directly or indirectly) back into firms. This, in a nutshell, is the 'circular flow' of the economy.[8]

Missing from this oversimplified picture of the economy (and from Figure 6.1) are what's called the public sector (government), the foreign sector (overseas firms, households and governments), and the financial sector – which mediates the financial flows of the circular economy.

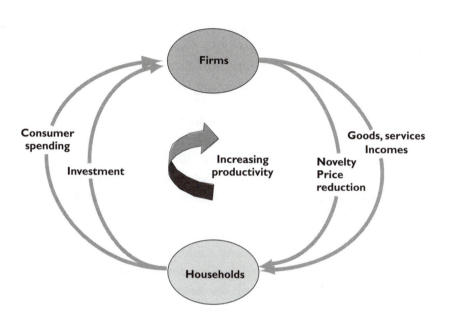

Figure 6.1 The 'Engine of Growth' in market economies

Source: Drawn by the author based on standard economic texts (see note 8).

All of these are crucial. Partly because they introduce a whole new set of actors and a whole new set of possibilities: different ways of spending and producing, saving and investing. These offer some potential (as we shall see in Chapter 8) for reconfiguring the economy. But they also complicate the basic simplicity of Figure 6.1 enormously.

In one sense, the financial crisis emerged precisely out of the complexity generated by the evolution of a global financial sector. And as we saw in Chapter 2, that complexity was in part the result of trying to keep the system going. Global credit markets facilitate one of the most fundamental features of capitalism: the dual role of saving and investment.

The basic functioning of this feature is simple enough. Households give over part of their income to savings. These savings are invested – either directly or through an intermediary (for example a bank, building society or investment house) in businesses to generate profits.

Profit is key to this system. Why would households give their savings to firms rather than simply hanging on to them or spending the money on consumer goods? Only because they expect to receive a healthy 'return' on their capital at some point in the future. This return is created out of the stream of profits from the firms they invest in.

Firms themselves seek profit for several reasons. In the first place, it provides them with working capital (cash) to invest in maintenance and improvements themselves. Secondly, it's needed to pay off the company's creditors – people who've lent the firm money in expectation of a return. Thirdly, it's used to pay dividends to shareholders – people who've bought a share in the company.

A company that shows good returns attracts more investment. The value of the company will rise because people are prepared to pay more for shares in it. When share values are rising, more people will be keen to buy them. Creditors know they will get their money back with interest. Shareholders know that the value of their shares will rise. The company knows that it has sufficient resources to maintain its capital stock and invest in new processes and technologies.

This ability to re-invest is vital. At a basic level, it's needed to maintain quality. Without it, buildings and equipment inevitably get run down.[9] Product quality is lost. Sales decline. The company loses its competitive position and risks going out of business.

Investment is also needed continually to improve efficiency, in particular labour productivity. The role of efficiency in capitalism has already been noted (Chapter 5). The driver for efficiency is essentially the profit motive: the need to increase the difference between revenues from sales and the costs associated with the so-called factor inputs: capital, labour and material resources.

Cost minimization becomes a core task for any firm. But it involves some inherent trade-offs. Amongst these is that capital investment is needed, in addition to its role in maintenance, to achieve cost reduction in the other two factors: labour and materials.[10] Switching to more energy efficient appliances or less labour intensive processes requires capital. This continuing capital need both motivates the search for low-cost credit and highlights the dangers of credit drying up. It also explains why reducing capital costs indefinitely isn't an option.[11]

When it comes to choosing which of the other two factors to target, a lot depends on the relative price of labour and materials. In a growing economy, wages rise in real terms. Until very recently at least, material costs have been falling in real terms. So in practice, companies have invested preferentially in technologies that reduce labour costs even if this increases material costs: an obvious counter to the trend of resource productivity discussed in Chapter 5.[12]

For a company then, higher labour productivity lowers the cost of its products and services. Forgoing that possibility runs the risk that the company finds itself at a disadvantage compared with national and international competitors. In this case, it would sell fewer goods, report lower profits to its shareholders and risk capital flight from the company. At the national level, this dynamic plays out as the ability to compete in international markets.

This dynamic explains some of the concern over labour productivity in Europe over the last decade or so. Labour productivity growth in the EU has slowed considerably in recent years. Though it grew on average by 2.7 per cent per year between 1980 and 1995, the growth rate fell to 1.7 per cent for the period 1995–2005. The GDP growth rate remained fairly constant at 2.2 per cent over the period, but this is largely because people are working longer hours now than they were before. A 3 per cent decline in the hours worked during the first period turned into an 8 per cent increase in hours worked over the second period.[13]

One of the concerns for the EU is how well it's doing against its competitors. The contrast between the EU and the US over the two periods is striking. Growth in GDP in the EU already lagged behind the US during the first period (Figure 6.2). This difference was entirely due to the decline in working hours in the EU compared to an increase in working hours in the US.

During the second period, the gap between the EU GDP growth and the US GDP growth increased in spite of a faster increase in working hours in the EU than in the US. The difference was almost entirely due to changes in the labour productivity growth rate. As we noted, this fell dramatically in the EU during the second period. But in the US, it doubled from 1.2 per cent per year in the earlier period to 2.4 per cent per year in the later period.[14]

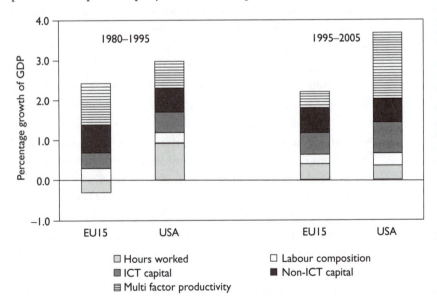

Figure 6.2 Contributions to market economy GDP growth: EU 15 v. US[15]

Source: Timmer et al 2007, Figure 3.

Understanding the dynamic between labour productivity, working hours and economic growth is important for all sorts of reasons. Not least is the insight it provides into the minds of economists. For instance, the conventional view on labour productivity allows the authors of the EU study cited here to describe the US as 'forging ahead' because of its higher labour productivity and to condemn the performance of certain EU countries as 'dismal' because of their low labour productivity.

We'll have occasion later (Chapter 8) to question these normative judgements. But for now the key point is that the general trend in capitalist economies is quite clearly towards increasing labour productivity. Since this means producing the same quantity of goods and services with fewer people, the cycle creates a downward pressure on employment that's only relieved if output increases.

Efficiency quite literally drives growth forwards. By reducing labour (and resource) inputs, efficiency brings down the cost of goods over time. This has the effect of stimulating demand and promoting growth. Far from acting to reduce the throughput of goods, technological progress serves to increase production output by reducing factor costs.[16]

The phenomenon of 'rebound' attests to this.[17] Money saved through energy efficiency, for example, gets spent on other goods and services. These goods themselves have energy costs that offset the savings made through efficiency, and sometimes wipe them out entirely (a situation described as 'backfire'). Spending the savings from energy efficient lighting (say) on a cheap short-haul flight is one sure-fire recipe for achieving this.

This somewhat counter-intuitive dynamic helps explain why simplistic appeals to efficiency will never be sufficient to achieve the levels of decoupling required for sustainability. In short, *relative* decoupling sometimes has the perverse potential to *decrease* the chances of *absolute* decoupling.

But efficiency alone doesn't guarantee success in business. Making the same thing more and more efficiently doesn't work for a couple of reasons. The first is that there are physical limits to efficiency improvement in specific processes. At the basic level, these constraints are laid down by the laws of thermodynamics.[18] The second is that failing to diversify and innovate risks losing out to competitors producing newer and more exciting products.

The economist Joseph Schumpeter was the first to suggest that it is in fact novelty, the process of innovation, that is vital in driving economic growth.[19] Capitalism proceeds, he said, through a process of 'creative destruction'. New technologies and products continually emerge and overthrow existing technologies and products. Ultimately, this means that even successful companies cannot survive simply through cost-minimization.[20]

The ability to adapt and to innovate – to design, produce and market not just cheaper products but newer and more exciting ones – is vital. Firms who fail in this process risk their own survival. The economy as a whole doesn't care if individual companies go to the wall. It does care if the process of creative destruction stops because without it economic growth eventually stops as well.[21]

The role of the entrepreneur – as visionary – is critical here. But so is the role of the investor. It is only through the continuing cycle of investment that creative destruction is possible. When credit dries up, so does innovation. And when innovation stalls, according to Schumpeter, so does the long-term potential for growth itself.

At this point, it's tempting to wonder what the connection is between this self-perpetuating but somewhat abstract vision of creative capitalism, and the needs and desires of ordinary human beings. The circular flow of production and consumption may once have been a useful way of organizing human society to ensure that people's material needs are catered for. But what does this continual cycle of creative destruction have to do with human flourishing?

Does this self-perpetuating system really contribute to prosperity in any meaningful sense? Isn't there a point at which enough is enough and we should simply stop producing and consuming so much?

One of the things that prevents this happening, clearly, is the structural reliance of the system itself on continued growth. The imperative to sell more goods, to innovate continually, to stimulate higher and higher levels of consumer demand is driven forwards by the pursuit of growth. But this imperative is now so strong that it seems to undermine the interests of those it's supposed to serve.

The cycles of creative destruction become ever more frequent. Product lifetimes plummet as durability is designed out of consumer goods and obsolescence is designed in. Quality is sacrificed relentlessly to volume throughput. The throw-away society is not so much a consequence of consumer greed as a structural prerequisite for survival. Novelty has become a conscript to the drive for economic expansion.

This doesn't mean that innovation is always destructive. Or that creativity is intrinsically bad. On the contrary, the creative spirit can and does enrich our lives. Its potential to do so has already been demonstrated. Proponents point quite rightly to the human benefits that creative entrepreneurship can bring: advances in medical science, for example, which have contributed to increased longevity; or the sheer variety of experience which now contributes to the quality of modern life.[22]

But neither can we see novelty as entirely neutral in the structural dynamic played out through capitalism. In fact, there is something even more deep-rooted at play here, conspiring to lock us firmly into the cycle of growth. The continual production of novelty would be of little value to firms if there were no market for the consumption of novelty in households. Recognizing the existence, and understanding the nature, of this demand is essential.

Social logic

It is perhaps not surprising to discover that the desire for novelty is linked intimately to the symbolic role that consumer goods play in our lives. It has already been noted (Chapter 4) that material artefacts constitute a powerful 'language of goods' that we use to communicate with each other, not just about status, but also about identity, social affiliation, and even – through giving and receiving gifts for example – about our feelings for each other, our hopes for our family, and our dreams of the good life.[23]

This is not to deny that material goods are essential for our basic material needs: food, shelter, protection. On the contrary, this role is critical to our physiological flourishing: health, life expectancy, vitality.

But stuff is not just stuff. Consumer artefacts play a role in our lives that goes way beyond their material functionality. Material processes and social needs are intimately linked together through commodities. Material things offer the ability to facilitate our participation in the life of society. And in so far as they achieve this, they contribute to our prosperity (Chapter 3).

One of the vital psychological processes here is what consumer researcher Russ Belk called *cathexis*: a process of attachment that leads us to think of (and even feel) material possessions as part of the 'extended self'.[24] This process is evident everywhere. Our relationships to our homes, our cars, our bicycles, our favourite clothes, our books, our CD or DVD collection, our photographs and so on all have this character.

Our attachments to material things can sometimes be so strong that we even feel a sense of bereavement and loss when they are taken from us. 'Hollow hands clasp ludicrous possessions because they are links in the chain of life. Without them, we are truly lost' claimed the marketing guru Ernest Dichter in *The Science of Desire*.[25]

Some of these attachments are fleeting. They burn with novelty momentarily and are extinguished as suddenly when something else attracts our attention. Others last a lifetime. Possessions sometimes offer a sanctuary for our most treasured memories and feelings. They allow us to identify what is sacred in our lives and distinguish it from the mundane.

This kind of materialism, flawed though it may be, even offers some kind of substitute for religious consolation. In a secular world, having something to hope for is particularly important when things are going badly. Retail therapy works for a reason.[26]

Novelty plays an absolutely central role in all this. In the first place, of course, novelty has always carried information about social status. As Thorstein Veblen pointed out over a century ago, 'conspicuous consumption' proceeds through novelty. Many of the latest consumer appliances and fashions are accessible at first only to the rich. New products are inherently expensive, because they are produced on a small scale. They may even be launched at premium prices deliberately to attract those who can afford to pay for social distinction.[27]

After distinction comes emulation. Social comparison – keeping up with the Joneses – rapidly expands the demand for successful products and facilitates mass production, making once luxury goods accessible to the many. And the sheer wealth and enormous variety of material goods has a democratizing element to it. It allows more and more people to go about inventing and reinventing their social identities in the search for a credible place in society.

Arguably it is precisely this cornucopia of material goods and its role in the continual reinvention of the self that distinguishes a consumer society from its predecessors. Material artefacts were always capable of carrying symbolic meaning. They were often used to establish social position. Only in modernity has this wealth of material artefacts been so deeply implicated in so many social and psychological processes.

According to some commentators, the symbolic role of goods is even appropriated in modern society to explore deep existential questions about who we are and what our lives are about. Novelty is seductive in its own right here. It offers variety and excitement; it allows us to dream and hope. It helps us explore our dreams and aspirations for the ideal life and escape the sometimes harsh reality of our lives.[28]

And it is precisely because material goods are flawed, but somehow plausible, proxies for our dreams and aspirations, that consumer culture seems on the surface to work so well. Consumer goods, suggests anthropologist Grant McCracken, provide us with a tangible bridge to our highest ideals. They fail, of course, to provide a genuine access to those ideals, but in failing they leave open the need for future bridges and so stimulate our appetite for more goods. Consumer culture perpetuates itself here precisely because it succeeds so well at failure![29]

Again, it is important to remember that this dynamic doesn't by any means exhaust our relationship to material goods. Consumption is also vital to us in simple material ways. It is as much about ordinary everyday survival as it is about the social and psychological processes of identity, affiliation, aspiration and self-expression. But it is this social dynamic, rather than physiological flourishing, which serves to explain why our desire for material goods appears so insatiable. And why novelty matters to us.

Novelty and anxiety

It is tempting to dismiss such a system as pathological. And in some senses it clearly is. Psychologist Philip Cushman has argued that the extended self is ultimately an 'empty self' which stands in continual need of 'being "filled up" with food, consumer products, and celebrities'.[30]

But it is also vital to recognize that this pathology is not simply the result of some terminal quality in the human psyche. We are not by nature helpless dupes, too lazy or weak to resist the power of manipulative advertisers. On the contrary, human creativity, emotional intelligence and resilience in the face of adversity are visible everywhere, even in the face of an apparently pathological consumerism.

Rather, what emerges from this analysis is that the empty self is itself a product of powerful social forces and the specific institutions of modern society. Individuals are at the mercy of social comparison. Institutions are given over to the pursuit of consumerism. The economy is dependent on consumption for its very survival.

Perhaps the most telling point of all is the rather too perfect fit between the continual consumption of novelty by households and the continuous production of novelty in firms. The restless desire of the 'empty self' is the perfect complement for the restless innovation of the entrepreneur. The production of novelty through creative destruction drives (and is driven by) the appetite for novelty in consumers.

Taken together these two self-reinforcing processes are exactly what is needed to drive growth forwards. As the ecological economist Douglas Booth remarks: 'The novelty and status seeking consumer and the monopoly-seeking entrepreneur blend together to form the underpinning of long-run economic growth.'[31]

It's perhaps not surprising that this restlessness doesn't necessarily deliver genuine social progress. Sometimes (see Chapter 4) it even undermines well-being and contributes to social recession. And there are some pretty clear reasons for that. Amongst them is that this is a system driven by anxiety.

The extended self is motivated by the angst of the empty self. Social comparison is driven by the anxiety to be situated favourably in society. Creative destruction is haunted by the fear of being left behind in the competition for consumer markets. Thrive or die is the maxim of the jungle. It's equally true in the consumer society. Nature and structure combine together here to lock us firmly into the iron cage of consumerism.

It's an anxious, and ultimately a pathological, system. But at one level it works. The relentless pursuit of novelty may undermine well-being. But the system remains economically viable as long as liquidity is preserved and consumption rises. It collapses when either of these stalls.

These understandings provide us with our clearest insight yet into the enormity of the challenge implied in delivering a truly sustainable form of prosperity. Perhaps first and foremost, that challenge compels us to develop a different kind of economic structure (see Chapters 7 and 8).

But it's clear that this task isn't sufficient. We also have to find a way through the institutional and social constraints that lock us into a failing system. In particular, we need to identify opportunities for change within society – changes in values, changes in lifestyles, changes in social structure – that will free us from the damaging social logic of consumerism (see Chapters 9 and 10).

Only through such changes will it be possible to get ourselves 'unhooked' from growth, free ourselves from the relentless flow of novelty that drives material throughput and find instead a lasting prosperity – the potential to flourish, within ecological and social limits.

7

Keynesianism and the 'Green New Deal'

The new, green economy would provide a new engine of growth, putting the world on the road to prosperity again. This is about growing the world economy in a more intelligent, sustainable way.

Achim Steiner, October 2008[1]

One of the most striking features of the global financial crisis of 2008 was the consensus on the need to re-invigorate economic growth. From the International Monetary Fund (IMF) to the United Nations Environment Programme (UNEP), from political parties across the political spectrum and from within both liberal and coordinated market economies, the call was for mechanisms that would 'kick-start' consumer spending and get the economy growing again.

The reason is obvious enough. When spending slows down, unemployment looms large. Firms find themselves out of business. People find themselves out of a job. And a government that fails to respond appropriately will soon find itself out of office. In the short-term, the moral imperative to protect jobs and prevent any further collapse is incontrovertible.

The clarion call from every side was to get the economy 'back on the growth path'. And this call was not just to increase the GDP. It was quite specifically to stimulate consumption growth: to restore consumer confidence and stimulate high-street spending. It was, in effect, a more or less united call to re-inspire the dynamics described in Chapter 6, the dynamics that will continue to drive unsustainable throughput.

Those inclined to question the consensus wisdom were swiftly denounced as cynical revolutionaries or modern day luddites. 'We do not agree with the anti-capitalists who see the economic crisis as a chance to impose their utopia, whether of a socialist or eco-fundamentalist kind', roared the *Independent on Sunday* late in 2008. 'Most of us in this country enjoy long and fulfilling lives thanks to liberal capitalism: we have no desire to live in a yurt under a workers' soviet.'[2]

With that confusingly attired bogey-man looming over us, kick-starting consumer confidence to boost high-street spending looks like a no-brainer. And internecine warfare is all saved for arguing over how this is to be achieved.

This chapter outlines some of those arguments. It highlights, in particular, the international consensus that emerged around a very simple idea. Economic recovery demands investment. The transition to a low-carbon society also requires investment. Let's put the two things together and create an investment package with multiple benefits. Specifically, a 'green stimulus' has the potential to secure jobs and economic recovery in the short-term, to provide energy security and technological innovation in the medium-term and to ensure a sustainable future for our children in the long-term.

Although this idea makes a great deal of sense, the default assumption of even the 'greenest' stimulus package is to return the economy to a condition of continuing consumption growth. Since this condition is unsustainable, it is difficult to escape the conclusion that in the longer term something more is needed. That's something we take up in the next chapter.

Options for kick-starting growth

There are four main contenders for the boot that will kick-start growth. But none of them is risk free. The first is hardly a boot at all; it's a 'do nothing' option. The argument here is that, given time and left to its own devices, the economy will recover by itself. Unemployment will rise, but that will push down wages, reduce the cost of goods and so stimulate both more consumption and a higher demand for labour.

The difficulty with this option, aside from its political unacceptability, is that while things are recovering, life could get very tough indeed, particularly for those without jobs. Worse, if there are long-term trends at play in labour or capital markets, recovery could be a long time coming, as Japan found out to its cost during the 1990s.

A second option is to stimulate demand through monetary expansion. This was the way the consumer boom was protected for so long throughout the 1990s and early 2000s. And there is a sort of logic to it. Stimulating credit increases the availability of investment capital to firms and at the same time reduces the cost of debt to consumers. We've seen already how crucial both of these things are in keeping consumption going.[3]

But making credit easier and cheaper also played a critical role (Chapter 2) in creating the global financial crisis. The danger is that many advanced economies are already at the limits of consumer indebtedness and face a sharply rising public sector debt as well. Pushing these any further stretches the boundaries of financial prudence.

Reducing the interest rate also reduces the incentive to save. At a point when savings rates have collapsed, this route appears to be an encouragement away from economic prudence by firms and households. Although, perversely, as we see below, this may work in favour of recovery.

The third option is to put more money in people's pockets by cutting taxes or increasing benefits. The risk here is that government doesn't have much control over where this extra money gets spent. Some of it may get spent on imported goods and contribute nothing to domestic recovery. Some of it may get saved. People are more inclined to save during a recession anyway. If your financial security looks threatened, it's not a bad idea to have something put away for the future. Ironically, more saving is the last thing that governments want in these circumstances, in spite of widespread concern over levels of consumer indebtedness.

This is what economist John Maynard Keynes called the 'paradox of thrift'. The normal rules of prudence are turned on their head. It's entirely rational for each individual (or firm) to save a bit more in a crisis. But it turns out to be bad for the economy – at least with the system designed the way it is right now. Increased saving reduces high-street spending still further, deepening and lengthening the recession.[4]

A further challenge lies in funding these tax cuts. At a time when the tax base is already declining and social costs (for instance to meet unemployment benefits) are rising, this can only be done by increasing public sector borrowing. If we're going to put ourselves deeper in debt, many argue, then perhaps we should be doing it through some form of meaningful investment in the future.

This is the basis for option four, a classic Keynesian public spending programme. The most well-known example of this was Franklin D. Roosevelt's New Deal in the 1930s, implemented as the world struggled to escape the great Depression. The New Deal entailed a massive investment in public sector works. It may not have had the short-term effect some claim for it. It didn't in fact achieve a full economic recovery within Roosevelt's first two terms in office. But its long-term impact was enormous.[5]

As Paul Krugman, winner of the 2008 Nobel Prize for economics, has pointed out: 'The New Deal famously placed millions of

Americans on the public payroll via the Works Progress Administration [WPA]... To this day we drive on WPA-built roads and send our children to WPA-built schools.'[6] Not surprisingly, there was a lot of talk about the New Deal during the financial crisis. Krugman called for a Keynesian-type stimulus equivalent to 4 per cent of the US GDP.[7]

Green New Deal

The most interesting variation on this theme during 2008 was the call for a (global) Green New Deal. If the public sector is going to spend money to re-invigorate the economy, argued its advocates, wouldn't it be as well to spend it investing in the new technologies that we know we are going to need to address the environmental and resource challenges of the 21st century?

'Investments will soon be pouring back into the economy' suggested Pavan Sukdhev, the Deutsche Bank economist leading research on UNEP's Green Economy Initiative. 'The question is whether they go into the old extractive short-term economy of yesterday, or a new green economy that will deal with multiple challenges while generating multiple economic opportunities for the poor and the well-off alike.'[8]

By early 2009, a strong international consensus had emerged in support of the idea of a 'green' stimulus. Targeting public sector investment carefully towards energy security, low-carbon infrastructures and ecological protection could offer numerous benefits, including:

- freeing up resources for household spending and productive investment by reducing energy and material costs;
- reducing reliance on imports and exposure to the fragile geo-politics of energy supply;
- providing a boost to jobs in the expanding 'environmental industries' sector;[9]

- making progress towards the demanding carbon emission reduction targets needed to stabilize the global atmosphere;
- protecting valuable ecological assets and improving the quality of our living environment for generations to come.

Consensus had also formed around the appropriate targets for a green stimulus. During 2008, the Green New Deal group (a UK-based group with representatives from business, the media and non-government organizations (NGOs) suggested that stimulus spending should be focused on the twin challenges of climate change and energy security. The group put forward proposals for a low-carbon energy system that would make 'every building a power station' and the creation and training of 'a "carbon army" of workers to provide the human resources for a vast environmental reconstruction programme.'[10]

Later in the year, UNEP's global Green New Deal widened the remit of spending to include investment in natural infrastructure: sustainable agriculture and ecosystem protection. Ecosystems already provide tens of trillions of dollars worth of services to the world economy.[11] So protecting and enhancing ecosystems is vital to economic productivity in the future, UNEP pointed out. They also called for substantial investments in clean technologies, sustainable agriculture and sustainable cities.

The case for a stimulus focused on energy and carbon is clearly strong. Re-capitalising the world's energy systems for a low-carbon world will be a major investment challenge over the next 50 years. The International Energy Agency (IEA) has estimated that energy investment needs between 2010 and 2030 will be in excess of $35 trillion.[12] Bringing forward some of this investment and targeting it specifically at renewable energy, low-carbon technologies and energy efficiency could pay massive dividends later.[13]

In a report published towards the end of 2008, the Deutsche Bank identified a 'green sweet spot' for stimulus spending, consisting of investment in energy efficient buildings, the electricity grid, renewable energy and public transportation. 'One of the reasons that the "green sweet spot" is an attractive focus for an economic stimulus is the labor-intensity of many of its sectors' claimed the Bank.[14]

A study by the University of Massachusetts Political Economy Research Institute supported that view. It identified six priority areas for investment: retrofitting buildings, mass transit/freight rail, smart grid, wind power, solar power and next generation bio-fuels. The authors calculated that spending $100 billion on these interventions over a two-year period would create 2 million new jobs. By contrast, the same money directed at household spending would generate only 1.7 million jobs and directed at the oil industry fewer than 600,000 jobs.[15]

Strategies for job creation

If replicable elsewhere, these findings provide vital insights into the appropriate way to approach economic recovery. Job creation is one of the key aims of an economic stimulus programme. Not only are jobs essential for economic recovery. Meaningful employment is itself a key constituent in prosperity (Chapter 3).

Understanding how best to protect employment is vital. Several strategies are possible, including the direct creation of public sector jobs, financial support to boost employment in specific sectors or indirect support for jobs through measures to stimulate demand.

Public sector employment was the route favoured in Roosevelt's New Deal. Apart from the obvious social benefit in providing jobs, public sector employment seeks its return in several ways. Firstly, there are the benefits to the economy from investment in productive infrastructure (road building, for example, in the New Deal). In addition, public sector jobs generate a part of what has been called the 'social wage' – a return to households from government spending in the form of wages, health and education benefits and social services.[16]

The stimulus packages to emerge from the 2008 crisis favoured a mixture of strategies. Specific sectors received (or sought) direct support from government in a number of different countries. Most obviously of course, enormous sums of money were committed to the direct support of the financial sector. By the end of 2008, an estimated $7 trillion had been spent globally in underwriting toxic assets, recapitalizing banks and attempting to restore confidence in the financial sector and stimulate lending (Chapter 2).

Direct recovery packages were also sought (and sometimes offered) in other sectors. Most notably, the car industry received direct support in both the UK and the US. The US government committed over $23 billion to bail out the ailing giants GM and Chrysler at the end of 2008.[17] Early in 2009, the UK government promised to underwrite loans to the car industry totalling £2.3 billion.

Perhaps most bizarrely, representatives from the US porn industry approached US Congress for support early in 2009, following the car industry bailout. 'Americans can do without cars and such, but they cannot do without sex' argued Larry Flynt, the founder of *Hustler* magazine.[18] Surely more of a publicity stunt than a serious claim, the call nonetheless highlights the profound mess created by the financial crisis, with the vulnerable and not-so-vulnerable alike lobbying for direct support in the matter of their livelihoods.

Beyond direct support to specific sectors, a number of wider fiscal recovery packages were established across the world during 2008 and 2009. One of the first acts of the Obama administration was to bring in a fiscal stimulus package equivalent to 5 per cent of US GDP (spread over a decade) through the American Recovery and Reinvestment Act 2009 (ARRA). The $787 billion package comprised around $290 billion in tax cuts and almost $500 billion in 'thoughtful and carefully targeted priority investments'; its aim 'to create and save 3 to 4 million jobs, jumpstart our economy, and begin the process of transforming it for the 21st century'.[19]

The potential for 'green' recovery

In principle, each of these different approaches to economic recovery could have contained a 'green stimulus' component. Public sector employment could be directed explicitly at 'green jobs'. Direct support for the financial sector could be allied with requirements that lending be preferentially targeted at sustainable investments. Sectoral bailouts like those afforded to the car industry could be made conditional on shifting towards greener manufacturing and low-carbon vehicles.[20]

In practice not much of this happened. All the same, by early 2009, the idea of linking fiscal stimulus with green investment was taking hold. As an HSBC Global Research report remarked at the time, the 'colour of stimulus' was going green. Out of a total commitment of almost $2.8 trillion to economic recovery plans to date, $436 billion (15.6 per cent of the total) could be characterized as green stimulus, according to the HSBC analysis.[21]

As Table 7.1 illustrates, the extent of green stimulus varied considerably across countries. Some plans had no green component at all while others (notably China, the EU package and South Korea) incorporated green investment that represented a very substantial proportion of the recovery funding.

The 'greenest' recovery package was in South Korea where over 80 per cent of the stimulus was targeted towards environmental goals. The funding was allocated to four main areas:

- conservation (low-carbon vehicles, clean energy and recycling);
- quality of life (green neighbourhoods and housing);
- environmental protection (including flood defence); and
- infrastructure (IT and green transport networks).

Table 7.1 Green elements of economic stimulus plans – February 2009

Country/Region	Fund $b	Period	Green Fund $b	% Green
Asia Pacific				
Australia	26.7	2009–12	2.5	9.3
China	586.1	2009–10	221.3	37.8
India	13.7	2009		0
Japan	485.9	2009–	12.4	2.6
South Korea	38.1	2009–12	30.7	80.5
Thailand	3.3	2009		0
Subtotal	**1,153.8**		**266.9**	**23.1**
Europe				
EU	38.8	2009–10	22.8	58.7
Germany	104.8	2009–10	13.8	13.2
France	33.7	2009–10	7.1	21.2
Italy	103.5	2009–	1.3	1.3
Spain	14.2	2009	0.8	5.8
UK	30.4	2009–12	2.1	6.9
Other EU States	308.7	2009	6.2	2.0
Subtotal	**634.2**		**54.2**	**16.7**
Americas				
Canada	31.8	2009–13	2.6	8.3
Chile	4.0	2009		0
US EESA	185.0	10 years	18.2	9.8
US ARRA	787.0	10 years	94.1	12.0
Subtotal	**1,007.8**		**114.9**	**11.4**
TOTAL	**2,796**		**436**	**15.6**

Note: EESA, Emergency Economic Stabilization Act of 2008.

Source: HSBC 2009

Employment benefits were estimated to include the creation of 960,000 new jobs over the next four years. Interestingly, the government seems to view its Green New Deal as a way of placing South Korea at the forefront of 21st century economies. Launching the package on 6 January, South Korea's Prime Minister Han Seung-soo said: 'We are in an unprecedented global economic crisis. We must respond to the situation in an urgent manner... The Green New Deal will provide these. The 21st century global environment is here and we will find new growth engines for this era.'[22]

The largest absolute level of commitment to a green stimulus came through the US ARRA. Around $94 billion (12 per cent) of the total stimulus of $787 billion could be characterized as green stimulus according to HSBC Global Research. This included $26 billion for low-carbon power (mainly renewables), $27.5 billion for energy efficiency in buildings, $4 billion for low-carbon vehicles, around $10 billion for rail and $11 billion to upgrade the electricity grid.[23]

Even these commitments may have been too low. The total stimulus commitment of $2.8 trillion identified in the HSBC report amounted to a little over 5 per cent of global GDP ($55 trillion) at the time. Spread over the three years or so of the commitment programmes, this implies a stimulus commitment at a level of approximately 1.5 per cent of GDP. But the green component of this commitment represented less than a quarter of a per cent of global GDP.[24]

By comparison with Krugman's suggestion of a 4 per cent stimulus or indeed the 2–3 per cent resource costs that might be required to achieve a transition to a low-carbon society, this could simply be too little too late. A report from the Grantham Institute early in 2009 suggested that green spending should comprise at least 20 per cent of a 4 per cent stimulus package. The UK Sustainable Development Commission (SDC) went even further arguing that green spending should be at least 50 per cent of a 4 per cent stimulus package.[25]

In the event, nothing anywhere near as substantial as this emerged from the stimulus spending commitments in advanced economies. Nonetheless, the argument for a substantial green stimulus remains strong. A much higher level of investment is clearly essential if we are to have a chance of meeting climate change targets and protecting against energy scarcities.

Equally, there is a nasty possibility that generic recovery spending – with no green focus – will jeopardize sustainability. Investing in road building, for example, may be a decent-ish way of protecting jobs and boosting economic activity. But it won't lead to green growth. On the contrary, it's quite possible for stimulus investments in high-carbon infrastructures to make it all but impossible to achieve environmental targets later. The US stimulus package included $27 billion to be spent on new roads – dwarfing the much smaller sums set aside for low-carbon electric and hydrogen vehicles.

Perhaps most strikingly of all, a fiscal stimulus dedicated towards a generic increase in high-street spending could have entirely perverse consequences. Even if it is successful in boosting consumption – evidence suggests that households are just as likely either to save the additional income or spend it on non-domestic goods and services – there is no way of targeting this spending towards low-carbon outcomes.[26]

In short, there is a clear case to suggest that green investment and green jobs should be seen not as a marginal addition to conventional packages, but as the single biggest element in economic recovery. The returns on such spending appear to be at least as good as those on more conventional stimulus spending. And green investment is absolutely essential to achieve sustainability targets.

Funding recovery

Any recovery package – and certainly something of the size proposed above – raises the question of how it is to be paid for. One of the advantages of a green stimulus is that it offers the potential for direct financial returns to the economy. These returns take a variety of forms. Most obviously they arise in the form of fuel and resource savings. For instance, some simple measures to improve the energy efficiency of the domestic housing stock have payback times of less than two years.

Some – but not all – of these returns accrue directly to government and can therefore offset the fiscal costs of stimulus spending. Direct returns include fuel cost savings to government, as well as savings in public expenditure resulting from reduced health costs, lower congestion and lower levels of pollution. Internalizing some of these costs – for instance through a carbon price – would increase the visibility of these direct returns to the government purse (Chapter 11).

Some of the returns accrue to businesses and households rather than to government. In a recession, this is clearly in the national interest, because it boosts household income and reduces the pressure on firms. But it also raises the question of where government is to find the funding.

The broad assumption in Keynesianism is that fiscal stimulus is funded by increasing the national debt (deficit spending). This is justified because such spending stimulates growth through a 'multiplier' effect.[27] By growing consumption (and incomes) now, governments can pay off the debt through higher tax revenues in the future.

Nonetheless there are reasons to be wary of this rationale. One of them is that existing levels of public sector debt are already high. And increasing this exposure, particularly if it's achieved through greater external debt, could be costly later.[28] At the very least, it could take decades to recover from a rapid rise in national debt.

Besides, there are also questions of 'saturation' in conventional debt markets, with a real prospect of failure in some governments' ability to fund conventional debt.[29]

So there's a strong case for serious consideration of other funding options.

Green bonds are one such option. These are bond issues linked directly to low-carbon (or green) investments. The idea is interesting for a variety of reasons. In the first place, it is clear that many of these investments offer considerable returns, at a time when the returns on conventional household savings mechanisms are disappearing.

The absence of suitable savings vehicles is particularly frustrating when the propensity for households to save is finally emerging from the doldrums – even in the liberal market economies. Keynes's 'paradox of thrift' is frustrating for government policies aimed at encouraging people to spend. But instead of going against the grain of people's natural prudence at such times, there is a good case for providing robust and credible vehicles to save in a form which could provide the basis for stimulus funding. And the evidence from consumer research suggests that people are desperate for options not just to change their lifestyles to be 'greener', but also to shift their investment decisions.[30]

In summary, green bonds provide a differentiated savings product when the propensity to save is high and conventional bond markets are saturating; and in doing so they inject investment funds directly into green recovery. Nonetheless, bond issues of any kind increase the public sector debt at a time when it is already high. So other mechanisms for recovering the rewards from public sector investment are going to be needed. Broadly speaking, there are two options here.

One of them is fiscal tightening – using existing or new local or national taxes to recover investment spending. A pure Keynesian would reject this measure, at least in the short-term, precisely because it could suppress or even wipe out the multiplier effect. But with rising national debt, there will clearly be a need to re-assess the long-term sustainability of the tax base in advanced economies. The idea of an ecological tax reform – a shift towards environmental taxes – should be a part of that discussion. We'll return to this in Chapter 11.

Secondly, there are arguments to suggest that government itself could take an equity stake in energy-related assets. The argument here is not dissimilar to the one used to justify public ownership in the banks. There is a legitimate public claim on the return from public investment, wherever those funds are directed. The case for public equity funding in the energy sector is at least as strong as it is in the financial sector.

One thing is clear: achieving long-term social goals in the energy sector already requires innovative thinking and creative approaches to asset ownership and investment architecture. The case for a green recovery package simply pulls these issues to the fore. Before consigning the nation to additional years of public sector debt, it's clearly crucial to explore the full range of funding options in much greater depth.

Beyond recovery

In summary, the idea of a green stimulus has many strengths. Investment in the transition to a sustainable economy is vital. Targeting stimulus spending towards that investment makes perfect sense.

Stimulus measures which support the least well-off are particularly to be welcomed. The poorest will inevitably be hardest hit through the recession and are already struggling with rising costs for food and fuel. Income inequality is higher in the OCED nations than it was in the mid-1980s.[31]

An unequal society is an anxious society, one given too readily to 'positional consumption' that adds little to overall happiness but contributes significantly to unsustainable resource throughput. A Green New Deal worthy of the name would signal clearly to the post-crisis world that we are serious about fighting climate change, preventing resource scarcity and creating a fairer society.

At the same time, the broad assumption behind all the recovery packages put forward through the crisis was that they would help to stimulate consumption growth. Credit would flow, consumers would spend, business would invest and innovate, productivity would return and the wheels of the machine would start turning again. This is the logic of Keynesianism.[32]

Recovery means a return to business as usual. Let's kick-start the circular flow of the economy and watch it grow again. The outcome (assuming it works) will be thoroughly predictable. Business innovation (creative destruction) and consumer demand (novelty seeking) will drive consumption forwards again. And with employment depending on it, there's no chance of anyone getting off the treadmill. We are right back at the structural impasse identified in Chapter 6.

Clearly, the Green New Deal advocates weren't proposing a return to the status quo. UNEP called for 'transformational thinking'. The call was for a different kind of growth – what Achim Steiner, Executive Director of UNEP, called a 'green engine of growth'. But growth nonetheless. 'Any public spending should be targeted so that domestic companies benefit, and then the wages generated create further spending on consumer goods and services', argued the UK group.[33]

And yet, it is difficult to escape the conclusion that in the longer term, we're going to need something more than this. Returning the economy to a condition of consumption growth is the default assumption of Keynesianism. But for all the reasons highlighted in preceding chapters this condition remains as unsustainable as ever.

There is still no consistent vision of an economy founded on continual consumption growth that delivers absolute decoupling. And the systemic drivers of growth push us relentlessly towards ever more unsustainable resource throughput. A different way of ensuring stability and maintaining employment is essential. A different kind of economic structure is needed for an ecologically constrained world. It is to this possibility that we now turn.

8

Ecological Macro-economics

Under existing macro-economic arrangements, growth is the only real answer to unemployment – society is hooked on growth.

Douglas Booth, 2004[1]

Put bluntly, the dilemma of growth has us caught between the desire to maintain economic stability and the need to remain within ecological limits. This dilemma arises because stability seems to require growth, but environmental impacts 'scale with' economic output: the more the economy grows, the greater the environmental impact – all other things being equal.

Of course, other things aren't equal. And the dominant attempt to escape the dilemma relies precisely on this fact. Things change as economies grow. One of the things that changes is technological efficiency. It's now widely accepted that technological efficiency is both an outcome from and a fundamental driver of economic growth.

Proponents use this feature of capitalism to suggest that growth is not only compatible with ecological goals but necessary to achieve them. Growth induces technological efficiency as well as increases in scale. All that's needed to remain within ecological limits is for efficiency to outrun (and continue to outrun) scale.

But historical evidence for the success of this strategy is deeply unconvincing. Global emissions and resource use are still rising.

Apparent declines in carbon emissions in advanced economies turn out on closer inspection to be due to accounting errors and cross-boundary trades. Much of the growth that is desperately needed in developing countries is inherently material in nature. And rebound effects from technological change push consumption even higher. In short, efficiency hasn't outrun scale and shows no signs of doing so.

That doesn't mean such a transition is impossible. On the contrary, we've already seen how little effort has truly been dedicated towards achieving it. But it's also abundantly clear that we won't make much progress without confronting both the economic structure and the social logic that lock us into the 'iron cage' of consumerism.

In the next chapter, we'll address the social logic. Here we focus on economic structure. In particular, we explore the need for a different kind of macro-economics.[2] One in which stability no longer relies on ever-increasing consumption growth. One in which economic activity remains within ecological scale. One in which our capabilities to flourish – within ecological limits – becomes the guiding principle for design and the key criterion for success.

In a sense, it's surprising that such a macro-economics doesn't already exist. There's something distinctly odd about our persistent refusal to countenance the possibility of anything other than growth-based economics. After all, John Stuart Mill, one of the founding fathers of economics, recognized both the necessity and the desirability of moving eventually towards a 'stationary state of capital and wealth', suggesting that it 'implies no stationary state of human improvement'.

Though John Maynard Keynes's macro-economics was largely concerned with the conditions of prudent growth, he also foresaw a time when the 'economic problem' would be solved and we would 'prefer to devote our further energies to non-economic purposes'.[3]

And it's now more than three decades since Herman Daly made

such a cogent case for a 'steady state economy'. He defined the ecological conditions for this economy in terms of a constant stock of physical capital, capable of being maintained by a low rate of material throughput that lies within the regenerative and assimilative capacities of the ecosystem. Anything other than this, he argued, ultimately erodes the basis for economic activity in the future.[4]

Admittedly, this terminology doesn't roll off the tongue easily for economists, who are schooled in a language that rarely even refers to natural resources or ecological limits. And that is clearly one of the points. Economics – and macro-economics in particular – is ecologically illiterate.

Daly's pioneering work provides a solid foundation from which to rectify this. But what we still miss is the ability to establish economic stability under these conditions. We have no model for how common macro-economic 'aggregates' (production, consumption, investment, trade, capital stock, public spending, labour, money supply and so on) behave when capital doesn't accumulate. We have no models to account systematically for our economic dependency on ecological variables such as resource use and ecological services.

Though these are unfamiliar goals for economists, the aim of this chapter is to show that they are not only meaningful, but achievable. In fact, this call for a robust, ecologically-literate macro-economics is probably the single most important recommendation to emerge from this book.

Macro-economic basics

Macro-economics is scary terrain for the uninitiated. But the main parameters can be set out easily enough. The principal macro-economic variable – the one all the fuss is about, so to speak – is the GDP. Whether it deserves pride of place in a new ecological macro-economics is an open question. But it's a key element in the macro-economic vocabulary. So it's useful to set out some of its basic characteristics.

Broadly speaking, the GDP is a measure of the 'busy-ness' of the economy. All it does really is count up – in three different ways – the economic activities going on within a particular geographical boundary, usually a nation.

The first of these three accounts is the one we identified in Chapter 1. It's the sum of all the 'final' expenditures (E) on goods and services in the economy. Formally speaking, these include consumer expenditure (C), government expenditure (G), gross investment in fixed capital (I) and net exports ($\overline{X}$).[5] In mathematical terms:

$$E \equiv C + G + I + \overline{X} \tag{1}$$

In order to spend, we need to have generated an income. The second GDP account measures this income. It does so by adding up all the wages and dividends (including profits and rents) paid out within the economy. These incomes are secured – either directly or indirectly[6] – from the output generated by all the productive activities in the economy. The third GDP account measures this output as the 'value added' by productive enterprises.

So the first type of GDP account (E) tells us what people and government spend (or invest). This is sometimes referred to as aggregate demand. The second (income) tells us what people earn and the third (output) tells us how much value firms produce. The second and third are sometimes referred to as aggregate supply (Y). The economy is said to be in equilibrium when aggregate demand equals aggregate supply. That is, when expenditure equals income, or in mathematical terms when:[7]

$$Y = C + G + I + \overline{X} \tag{2}$$

Notice straightaway that there's something very formulaic about the GDP. It is literally a measure of different kinds of activity. It makes no explicit normative judgement about the nature of those activities. On the other hand, it has implicitly already made some normative judgements. Firstly, by counting only the monetary value of things exchanged in the economy, and secondly by assuming that all of these monetary values are equivalent.

These implicit judgements give rise to some of the criticisms raised against the GDP. Lots of things happen outside of markets that result from or impact on economic activity. Some of these are positive things like the value of household work, caring and voluntary work. Others are negative things, such as the ecological or social damage from economic activities.[8] No attention is paid by the GDP, for example, to the health or environmental costs of pollution or the depletion of natural resources.

By contrast, all kinds of things are included in the GDP – the costs of congestion, oil spills and clearing up after car accidents, for example – which don't really contribute additionally to human well-being. These 'defensive expenditures' are incurred because of economic activities that are also counted positively in the GDP. But to count both sets of activities as contributing meaningfully to economic welfare seems perverse.

A more general criticism of the GDP is its failure to account properly for changes in the asset base, even when it comes to financial assets. Gross fixed capital investment is measured. But depreciation of capital stocks goes unaccounted for and the GDP is almost completely blind to the levels of indebtedness identified in Chapter 2. Perhaps even more importantly from our perspective, the depreciation of natural capital (finite resources and ecosystem services) is missing completely from this macro-economic account.[9]

These perversities have generated a long-standing critique of conventional macro-economic accounting. Numerous suggestions have been made for supplementing or adjusting the natural accounts to rectify the situation. For instance, there is a strong argument in favour of including some account of positive benefits from things like household work, adjusting for the depletion of capital (both human-made and natural), subtracting external environmental and social costs and taking account of defensive expenditures.[10]

We return to the policy implications of this in Chapter 11. The main aim here is to outline how the principal macro-economic variables relate to each other. A key element in that understanding is the balance between supply and demand and the importance of this balance for labour employment.

Demand depends mostly on people (and government) spending money on goods and services in the economy. How much people spend depends partly on their income. But it also depends on how much of their income they decide to spend rather than save and on how much they're prepared to borrow in order to spend. These things in their turn depend on their confidence in the economy and their expectations about the future.[11]

Supply is determined, in conventional macro-economics, by a 'production function', which tells us how much income (Y) an economy is capable of producing with any given input of the 'factors of production'. The most important factors of production (in the conventional model) are capital (K) and labour (L). Output is calculated by multiplying the factors of production by their 'productivity'. Broadly speaking, productivity captures the technological efficiency with which inputs (factors) are transformed into outputs.[12]

Again, critics argue that this form of production function is unsatisfactory because it makes no explicit reference to the material or ecological basis for the economy at all. Clearly both consumer goods and capital stocks (buildings and machinery) do embody material resources. But the flow of goods and the stock of capital are measured only in monetary terms and don't carry any explicit reference to the material flows needed to create them.[13]

It's possible to derive production functions which do include explicit reference to material or energy resources. We might even conceive of production functions which include ecological constraints – so that, for instance, production is forced to remain within a certain carbon budget. These are some of the changes likely to be needed for a robust ecological macro-economics. They're discussed further in Appendix 2.[14]

But for now, this conventional form of production function is good enough to illustrate the key relationship between supply and demand. In fact, we can take an even simpler form of production function, in which income, Y, is calculated as the product of labour L, and the productivity of labour P_L. Explicitly we have:

$$Y = P_L \times L \tag{3}$$

In this production function the dependency on capital, on technological efficiency and on resources is all rolled into the labour productivity. P_L can be thought of as the average amount of income generated by one hour (say) of labour input. The change in P_L over time is critical in determining how much growth (increase in Y) is possible. In fact, if the labour input L remains constant, then growth is determined exactly by the increase in labour productivity.

When labour productivity increases over time, as it is generally expected to do because of technological improvement, then the only way to stabilize economic output Y is by reducing the labour input L, or in other words by accepting some under-employment.

Conversely, as we've already seen (Chapter 6), when demand falls, revenues to firms are reduced, leading to job losses and reduced investment. Reduced investment leads to a lower capital stock which, together with a lower labour input, in turn reduces the productive capability of the economy. Output falls and with less money in the economy, public revenues also fall, debt increases and the system has a tendency to become unstable.

This dynamic is basically what gives rise to the economist's insistence that continued growth is essential for long-term economic stability. But of course this assumption does nothing to alleviate the concerns about ecological impact. We're right back with the dilemma of growth.

Taking a step back for a moment, there are only two ways out of this dilemma. One is to make growth sustainable; the other is to make de-growth stable. Anything else invites either economic or ecological collapse. We'll look at the option of making de-growth stable in a moment. But first let's just revisit the possibility that a different kind of growth could deliver us from the dilemma.

Changing the 'Engine of Growth'

Would or would not a different 'engine of growth' help us here, as Achim Steiner and others have suggested. Similar proposals have been voiced for some years by ecological economists. Pointing out that 'ever greater consumption of resources is [in itself] a driver of growth' in the current paradigm, Robert Ayres argues that 'in effect, a new growth engine is needed, based on non-polluting energy sources and selling non-material services, not polluting products'.[15]

Similar visions for business models based around materially-light product-service systems have been put forward by others. A recent government taskforce report highlighted the potential for such models to reduce the requirement for personal ownership, improve the utilization of capital resources and lower the material intensity of the economy.[16]

This idea is still essentially an appeal to decoupling. Growth continues, while resource intensity (and hopefully throughput) declines. But here at least is something in the way of a blueprint for what such an economy might look like. It gives us more of a sense of what people are buying and what businesses are selling in this new economy. Its founding concept is the production and sale of de-materialized 'services', rather than material 'products'.

It's vital to note that this cannot simply be the 'service-based economies' that have characterized development in certain advanced economies. For the most part that's been achieved, as we've seen, by reducing manufacturing, continuing to import consumption goods from abroad and expanding financial services to pay for them.[17]

Nor does it necessarily look anything like what passes for service sector activity in advanced economies at the present. When the impacts attributable to these are fully accounted for, many of them turn out to be at least as resource-hungry as the manufacturing sectors. Leisure is one of the fastest growing sectors in modern economies and ought to be a prime candidate for de-materialization in principle. In practice, the way we spend our leisure time can be responsible for as much as 25 per cent of our carbon 'footprint'.[18]

So what exactly constitutes productive economic activity in this economy? It isn't immediately clear. Selling 'energy services', certainly, rather than energy supplies.[19] Selling mobility rather than cars. Recycling, re-using, leasing, maybe.[20] Yoga lessons, perhaps, hairdressing, gardening: so long as these aren't carried out using buildings, don't involve the latest fashion and you don't need a car to get to them. The humble broom would need to be preferred to the diabolical 'leaf-blower', for instance.

The fundamental question is this: can you really make enough money from these activities to keep an economy growing?[21] And the truth is we just don't know. We have never at any point in history lived in such an economy. That doesn't mean we couldn't. Again, having a convincing macro-economics for such an economy would be a good starting point. But it sounds at the moment suspiciously like something the *Independent on Sunday* would instantly dismiss as a yurt-based economy – with increasingly expensive yurts.

The dynamics described in Chapter 6 just don't seem easily amenable to moderation of the kind envisaged. Social logic, questions of scale and the laws of thermodynamics are all a significant stumbling block to the changes hoped for by those with well-meaning intentions for continued growth with drastic reductions in material intensity. However much material efficiency you squeeze out of the economy, eventually you'll reach a limit, at which point continued growth will push material throughput up again.

Daly is explicit on this point. 'The idea of economic growth overcoming physical limits by angelizing GDP is equivalent to overcoming physical limits to population growth by reducing the throughput intensity or metabolism of human beings', he wrote, over 30 years ago. 'First pygmies, then Tom Thumbs, then big molecules, then pure spirits. Indeed, it would be necessary for us to become angels in order to subsist on angelized GDP.'[22]

But this doesn't mean we should throw away the underlying vision completely. We are almost certainly still some way from absolute thermodynamic limits. And whatever the new economy looks like, low-carbon economic activities that employ people in ways that contribute meaningfully to human flourishing have to be the basis for it. That much is clear.

In fact, the seeds for such an economy may already exist in local or community-based social enterprises: community energy projects, local farmers' markets, slow food cooperatives, sports clubs, libraries, community health and fitness centres, local repair and maintenance services, craft workshops, writing centres, water sports, community music and drama, local training and skills. And yes, maybe even yoga (or martial arts or meditation), hairdressing and gardening.

People often achieve a greater sense of well-being and fulfilment, both as producers and as consumers of these activities, than they ever do from the time-poor, materialistic, supermarket economy in which most of our lives are spent.[23] But in formal terms these activities – let's call them ecological enterprises – barely count.

They represent a kind of Cinderella economy that sits neglected at the margins of consumer society.[24]

Some of them scarcely even register as economic activities in a formal sense at all. They often employ people on a part-time or even voluntary basis. These activities are usually labour intensive. So if they contribute anything at all to GDP, their labour productivity is of course 'dismal' – in the language of the dismal science.

To come back to macro-economics, their problematic status is confirmed by data on labour productivity in Europe. Where these activities exist in the formal economy, many of them are classified as 'personal and social services'. Figure 8.1 confirms just how fantastically unproductive this sector has been over the last decade!

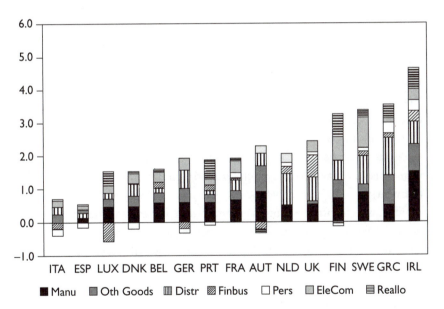

Figure 8.1 Sector contributions to EU labour productivity growth 1995–2005

Source: Timmer et al 2007, Figure 3. See note 25.

Between 1995 and 2005, labour productivity in the personal and social services sector declined by 3 per cent across the EU 15 nations; the only sector ('Pers' in Figure 8.1) to show negative productivity growth. Only in a couple of nations was there any improvement at all in labour productivity. Across Europe, output grew much more slowly in this sector than in the economy as a whole. In fact it only grew at all because more people were employed there.[26]

In short, this sector – the one where our hopes might lie for a 'different engine of growth' – just doesn't perform well by conventional standards. On the contrary, it's already 'dragging Europe down' in the productivity stakes. If we start shifting wholesale to patterns of de-materialized services, we wouldn't immediately bring the economy to a standstill, but we'd certainly slow down growth considerably.

We're getting perilously close here to the lunacy at the heart of the growth-obsessed, resource-intensive, consumer economy. Here is a sector which could provide meaningful work, offer people capabilities for flourishing, contribute positively to community and have a decent chance of being materially light.[27] And yet it's denigrated as worthless because it's actually employing people.

This finding is instructive in various ways. In the first place, it shows up the fetish with macro-economic labour productivity for what it is: a recipe for undermining work, community and environment.

This is categorically not to suggest that increases in labour productivity are always bad. There are clearly places where it makes sense to substitute away from human labour, especially where the working experience itself is poor. But the idea that labour input is always and necessarily something to be minimized goes against two well-supported understandings.

Firstly, there's a very good reason why de-materialized services don't lead to productivity growth. It's because, in most cases, human input is what constitutes the value in them. The pursuit of labour productivity in activities whose integrity depends on human interaction systematically undermines the quality of the output.[28]

Secondly, work itself is one of the ways in which humans participate meaningfully in society. Reducing our ability to do that – or reducing the quality of our experience in doing so[29] – is a direct hit on flourishing. Relentless pursuit of labour productivity in these circumstances makes absolutely no sense.

In summary, it seems that those calling for a new engine of growth based around de-materialized services are really on to something. But they may have missed a vital point. The Cinderella economy is an incredibly useful starting point from which to build a resource-light society. But the idea that it can (or should) provide for ever-increasing economic output doesn't quite stack up.

Sharing the work

Coming back to macro-economics, we have made some progress though. Looking again at equation (3) above, it's clear that the Cinderella economy offers us at least a way of questioning the downward pressure on employment in a non-growing economy. Specifically, the suggestion is that we don't after all necessarily have to accept a continually increasing labour productivity P_L.

This insight already suggests more room for re-configuring the conventional macro-economic model than is usually assumed by economists. Simply shifting the focus of economic activities from one sector to another has the potential to maintain or even increase employment, even without growth in economic output.

All the same, there are reasons not to accept declining labour productivities across the economy as a whole. Conventionally, the reason for this is that the higher the labour content of a good or service the higher its cost. In fact, in a growing economy, as we saw in Chapter 6, average wage costs rise continually. So even maintaining stable prices relies on increasing labour productivity.

In a low or no-growth economy this pressure is reduced because average incomes no longer rise continually – or rise by less. Nonetheless, to remain competitive in international markets we would still need to ensure that labour productivity doesn't fall too far, at least in our key export (and import) sectors. In this case, we have to look at equation (3) in a different way.

If labour productivity increases overall, then the only way to stabilize output is for the total hours worked by the labour force to fall. In a recession this typically leads to unemployment. But there is another possibility here. We could also systematically set about sharing out the available work more evenly across the population. Essentially, this means reduced working hours, a shorter working week and increased leisure time.

Interestingly, some of the increased labour productivity in Europe during the period between 1980 and 1995 was taken up in exactly this way, as increased leisure. This trend was reversed during the last decade, with working hours increasing and labour productivity growing more slowly. But as a route to prevent large-scale unemployment, sharing the available work has much to recommend it.

This is the option taken, for example, by Canadian ecological economist, Peter Victor, in a study designed to test a low or no-growth scenario for the Canadian economy. Astonishingly, Victor's work stands out as an almost unique attempt to develop any kind of model of a non-growing economy. It is, in short, a worthy pioneer of the idea of an ecological macro-economics.[30]

The model is calibrated against real historical data from Canada on the principal macro-economic variables: consumption, public spending, investment, productivity growth, savings rates and so on. Making specific assumptions about the future, the model then estimates the national income, computes the fiscal balance and tracks the national debt over a 30-year period to 2035. It also keeps an account of unemployment, greenhouse gas emissions and poverty levels.[31]

Figure 8.2 illustrates one of the stabilization scenarios generated by the model. By manipulating the 'drivers' of growth in the model, income growth is gradually reduced from 1.8 per cent a year to less than 0.1 per cent a year, effectively stabilizing per capita GDP. Notably though, this is achieved without compromising economic and social stability.

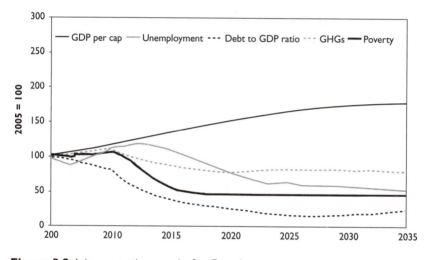

Figure 8.2 A low growth scenario for Canada
Source: Victor, 2008b.

In fact, unemployment and poverty are both halved in this scenario as a result of active social and working time policies. Even more striking is that the debt to GDP ratio has been slashed by 75 per cent. And though it falls some way short of achieving a 450 ppm stabilization target, Canada has achieved (25 years too late!) its 'Toronto target' of a 20 per cent cut in greenhouse gas emissions.[32]

The key policy intervention used to prevent wide-scale unemployment is a reduction in working hours. Labour productivity is assumed to increase in the model, pretty much in line with histor-ical increases in labour productivity in Canada. And this would normally lead through the logic discussed already to a reduction in employment. But unemployment is averted here by sharing the available work more equally across the workforce.[33]

Reducing the working week is the simplest and most often cited solution to the challenge of maintaining full employment with non-increasing output. And there is clear precedent for it, for example, from labour policies in certain European nations.[34] But it's worth noting that there are some other more radical suggestions for reorganizing work to ensure equity and to encourage continuing participation in society. These include quite radical changes to the wage structure, such as the introduction of a basic (or citizen's) income.[35]

This is not to suggest that any of these changes is easy to imple-ment. Reducing working hours, for example, only tends to succeed under certain conditions. 'One of the fundamental pre-conditions for the working time policy pursued in Germany and Denmark' writes sociologist Gerhard Bosch, 'was a stable and relatively equal earning distribution.'[36] A shift to a completely different income basis would be even more complicated.

But the point here is that – even within a relatively conventional macro-economic framework – different configurations of the key variables are possible. And these configurations deliver different outcomes. The goal of achieving economic stability while remain-ing within ecological limits begins to look more achievable.

Ecological investment

We've focused so far on the question of labour (and labour produc-tivity) in the transition to a sustainable economy. But there's another key area to address in a coherent ecological macro-economics, namely the question of capital and capital productivity.

As we've seen already, capital investment is a vital input to production. Investment maintains and improves production facilities. It provides for radical innovation which can revolutionize the productive capacity of the economy. And in particular it stimulates continual increases in labour productivity.

The starting point in an ecological macro-economics has to be slightly different. The transition to a sustainable, low-carbon economy represents an enormous challenge. Above all, this challenge is about investment. It's about allocating sufficient resources to transform our economies fast enough that they don't completely undermine the prospects for prosperity in the future.

A study by Italian ecological economists Simone d'Alessandro, Tommaso Luzzati and Mario Morroni underlines this point. Using an experimental simulation model, they explore the challenge associated with making a successful transition from a fossil fuel economy to one based on renewable energy.[37]

As we saw in Chapter 7 this is one of several key targets for substantial new investment. But there's a balance to be struck. If we invest too slowly, we run out of resources before alternatives are in place. Fuel prices soar and economies crash. If we invest too fast, there's a risk of slowing down the economy to the extent that the resources required for further investment aren't available.

The upshot, according to d'Alessandro and his colleagues, is that there is a narrow 'sustainability window' through which the economy must pass if it is to make the transition to a non-fossil world successfully. Crucially though, this 'sustainability window' is widened if the balance between consumption and investment in the economy can be changed. Specifically, if the savings ratio is increased and more of the national income is allocated to investment, the flexibility to achieve the transition is higher, according to this analysis.[38]

In other words, the balance between consumption and investment has to change in a new ecological macro-economics. From the perspective of the demand side, that needn't matter too much. A shift between C and I in equation (1) needn't necessarily lead to a reduction in aggregate demand E. It would simply reduce the importance of consumption as a driver of growth and replace it with an enhanced role for investment.

Clearly the target of investment would also need to change. The traditional function of investment, framed around increasing labour productivity, is likely to diminish in importance. Innovation will still be vital, but it will need to be targeted more carefully towards sustainability goals. Specifically, investments will need to focus on resource productivity, renewable energy, clean technology, green business, climate adaptation and ecosystem enhancement. These are precisely the kind of targets that emerge from the consensus around a global Green New Deal (Chapter 7).

Foregoing consumption growth seems inevitable if we are to sustain this enhanced need for ecological investment. What we don't yet know is whether ultimately the scale and nature of this kind of investment can maintain the growth potential of the economy as a whole.

The conventional Keynesian response suggests that increasing investment in the economy has a multiplier effect and stimulates growth. But we can't use that reasoning here for a couple of reasons. In the first place, Keynes assumed that the increase in investment is funded through increased borrowing, not by substituting savings for consumption. Secondly, the Keynesian multiplier can't be trusted here is that the calculation assumes that the marginal propensity to consumer remains constant. But the whole point about a shift from consumption to savings is that it alters that assumption. In fact, Keynes's paradox of thrift suggests that this shifting from consumption to savings will simply slow down recovery.

What we need in order to address this question properly is a fuller exploration not just of the targets for ecological investments but also of the nature of these investments. How productive are they in conventional terms? Do they have higher or lower rates of return than conventional investments? Do they have shorter or longer periods of return? Do they increase the productive capacity in the economy more than or less than conventional capital investments? Do they increase or decrease labour productivities?

Answering these questions fully again requires a macro-economic model. But it's a very different kind of macro-economic model than is currently employed to understand the growth-based economy. Essentially it requires us to explore more deeply the 'ecology' of ecological investment: the set of conditions (rate of return, nature of return, period of return and so on) that determines how the investment interacts both on the supply side and the demand side of the economy. Such a task is beyond the scope of this book. But we can already hazard some guesses about the outcome of a greatly enhanced role for ecological investment.

In the first place, the answers will depend on the composition of investment needed for the transition. Specifically, this is determined by three main types of investment:

- investments that enhance resource efficiency and lead to resource cost savings (for example energy efficiency, waste reduction, recycling);
- investments that substitute conventional technologies with clean or low-carbon technologies (for example renewables);
- investments in ecosystem enhancement (climate adaptation, afforestation, wetland renewal and so on).

The impact on the productive capacity of the economy will differ markedly across these investment types. Investments in resource productivity are likely to have a positive impact on overall productivity. But they won't necessarily bring preferential returns over conventional investments unless the relative prices of labour and materials change substantially.

Some investments in renewable energy will bring competitive returns in some market conditions. Others will only bring returns over much longer timeframes than traditional financial markets expect. Investments in ecosystem enhancement and climate adaptation might not bring conventional financial returns at all, even though they are protecting vital ecosystem services for the future and may also be contributing to employment.[39]

In other words, simplistic prescriptions in which investment contributes to future productivity won't work here. The ecology of investment will itself have to change. Investment in long-term infrastructures and public goods will have to be judged against different criteria. And this may mean rethinking the ownership of assets and the distribution of surpluses from them.

Specifically, there is likely to be a substantially enhanced role for public sector investment and asset ownership. The public sector is often best placed to identify and protect long-term social assets. Public sector rates of return are typically lower than commercial ones, allowing longer investment horizons and less punishing requirements in terms of productivity.

Appendix 2 sketches the outline for a new macro-economic investment framework that builds on these points. Particular attention is drawn there to the challenge of matching supply with demand under these new conditions. Investments in ecosystem maintenance (for example) contribute to aggregate demand, but make no direct contribution to aggregate supply – at least under the assumptions of a conventional production function. They may be vital in protecting environmental integrity. And this, is in its turn, is vital for sustaining production at all over the long-term. But in the short-term, they appear to 'soak up' income without increasing economic output.[40]

In a conventional growth-based economy this is problematic because it reduces the growth potential in the economy. In a sustainable economy this kind of investment needs to be seen as an essential component of macro-economic structure. Whether it leads to growth or not is, once again, somewhat beside the point.

Foundations for an ecological macro-economics

In summary, the aim of this chapter has been to show that a new ecological macro-economics is not only essential, but possible. The starting point must be to relax the presumption of perpetual consumption growth as the only possible basis for stability and to identify clearly the conditions that define a sustainable economy.

These conditions will still include a strong requirement for economic stability. Or perhaps 'resilience' would be a better word for what is required here. A sustainable economy must be capable of resisting the exogenous shocks and avoiding the internal contradictions which cause chaos during periods of recession.

But the requirement for resilience will need to be augmented by conditions that provide security for people's livelihoods, ensure distributional equity, impose sustainable levels of resource through-put and protect critical natural capital.

The fundamental macro-economic variables will still pertain. People will still spend and they will still save. Enterprise will still produce goods and services. Government will still raise revenues and spend them in the public interest. Both private and public sector will invest in physical, human and social assets.

But new macro-economic variables will need to be brought explicitly into play. These will almost certainly include variables to reflect the energy and resource dependency of the economy and the limits on carbon. They may also include variables to reflect the value of ecosystem services or stocks of natural capital.[41]

And there are likely to be key differences even in the way that conventional variables play out. The balance between consumption and investment, the balance between public and private sector, the role of different sectors, the nature of productivity improvement, the conditions of profitability: all of these are likely to be up for re-negotiation.

Ecological investment must play an absolutely vital role. If debt is to be kept under control this suggests that a different savings ratio will be needed. And that a different balance between consumption and investment in the aggregate demand function is likely. In addition, the level and nature of this investment almost certainly calls for a different balance between public and private sector investment.

An ecological macro-economics will require a new ecology of investment. This will mean revisiting the concepts of profitability and productivity and putting them to better service in pursuit of long-term social goals. We will almost certainly need to abandon the mindless infatuation with labour productivity and think systematically about the conditions for high employment in low-carbon sectors.

Above all, the new macro-economics will need to be ecologically and socially literate, ending the folly of separating economy from society and environment.

9
Flourishing – Within Limits

We must bring back into society a deeper sense of the
purpose of living. The unhappiness in so many lives ought to
tell us that success alone is not enough. Material success has
brought us to a strange spiritual and moral bankruptcy.

Ben Okri, October 2008[1]

Fixing the economy is only part of the problem. Addressing the
social logic of consumerism is also vital. This task is far from simple
– mainly because of the way in which material goods are so deeply
implicated in the fabric of our lives.

Prosperity is not synonymous with material wealth. And the
requirements of prosperity go beyond material sustenance. Rather,
prosperity has to do with our ability to flourish: physically, psychologically and socially. Beyond mere subsistence, prosperity hangs
crucially on our ability to participate meaningfully in the life of
society.

This task is as much social and psychological as it is material.
But the appealing idea that (once our material needs are satisfied)
we could do away with material things flounders on a simple but
powerful fact: material goods provide a vital language through
which we communicate with each other about the things that really
matter: family, identity, friendship, community, purpose in life.

There is clearly a puzzle here. If participation is really what
matters, and material goods provide a language to facilitate that,

then richer societies ought to show more evidence of it. In fact, the opposite appears to be the case. Robert Putnam's groundbreaking book *Bowling Alone* provided extensive evidence of the collapse of community across the USA.[2]

More generally, western society appears to be in the grip of a 'social recession'. There is a surprising agreement on this from across the political spectrum. For example, Jonathan Rutherford, a commentator from the political left, points to rising rates of anxiety and clinical depression, increased alcoholism and binge drinking, and a decline in morale at work. Jesse Norman, from the political right, highlights the breakdown of community, a loss of trust across society and rising political apathy.[3]

The two authors disagree on the causes of social recession. For Rutherford, the main culprit is the increasing commoditization of public goods and the rising social inequalities that are engendered by capitalism itself. For Norman it is the over-bearing influence of 'big' government in people's lives. Their prescriptions for solving the problem differ accordingly. But on the existence of a social recession there is much less disagreement.

The extent of this phenomenon clearly differs across different nations. Data from a recent module in the European Social Survey designed to measure social well-being illustrate this point. Figure 9.1 shows the different levels of trust and belonging experienced by respondents across 22 European nations. Those with the highest scores (for example Norway) experience far greater levels of trust and belonging than those with lower scores (for example the UK).

It's commonly agreed that at least some of the reasons for a breakdown in trust lie in the erosion of geographical community. A study by Sheffield University for the BBC confirms this trend in the UK. Using an index to measure geographical community in different BBC regions, the study revealed a remarkable change in British society since the early 1970s. Incomes doubled on average over the 30-year period. But the Sheffield 'loneliness index'[4]

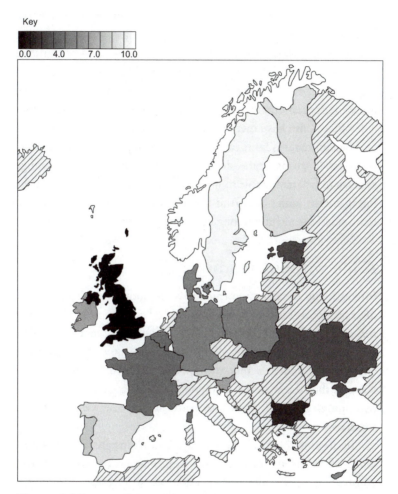

Figure 9.1 Trust and belonging in 22 European nations[5]

Note: Countries with diagonal stripes are not included in the study.

Source: nef, 2009.

increased in every single region measured. In fact, according to one of the report's authors 'even the weakest communities in 1971 were stronger than any community now'.[6]

The increasing number of people living on their own has a number of different causes, including a substantial rise in the divorce rate between 1971 and 2001.[7] The study's authors link the changes over time largely to mobility. 'Increased wealth and improved access to transport has made it easier for people to move for work, for retirement, for schools, for a new life' reports the BBC. They might also have mentioned that the mobility of labour is one of the requirements for higher productivity in the growth economy.[8]

In other words, some degree of responsibility for the change appears to be attributable to growth itself. As evidence for flourishing it doesn't look good. And it becomes even more puzzling why rich societies continue to pursue material growth.

A life without shame

Interestingly, Amartya Sen came close to addressing this puzzle in his early work on the 'living standard'. There he argued that the material requirements for physiological flourishing tend to be fairly similar in all societies. After all, the basic human metabolism doesn't change that much across the species. Crucially, however, Sen claimed that the material requirements associated with social and psychological capabilities can vary widely between different societies.

His argument harks back to Adam Smith's insight on the importance of shame in social life. As Smith wrote in *The Wealth of Nations*: 'A linen shirt, for example, is, strictly speaking, not a necessary of life... But in the present times, through the greater part of Europe, a creditable day labourer would be ashamed to appear in public without a linen shirt, the want of which would be supposed to denote that disgraceful degree of poverty which, it is presumed, nobody can well fall into without extreme bad conduct.'[9]

Sen broadens this argument to a wider range of goods, and a deeper sense of flourishing. As he claimed in 'The living standard', to lead a 'life without shame… to be able to visit and entertain one's friends, to keep track of what is going on and what others are talking about, and so on, requires a more expensive bundle of goods and services in a society that is generally richer and in which most people already have, say, means of transport, affluent clothing, radios or television sets, and so on.' In short, he suggested, 'the same absolute level of capabilities may thus have a greater relative need for incomes (and commodities)'.[10]

Putting aside for a moment the fact that higher incomes have been partly responsible for diminished flourishing, there is an even more striking point to be noted here. If we take for granted the importance of material commodities for social functioning, *there is never any point at which we will be able to claim that enough is enough.* This is the logic of Sen's argument. The baseline for social functioning is always the current level of commodities. And the avoidance of shame – a key feature of social flourishing – will drive material demand forward relentlessly.

This is in effect a different reframing of the social logic explored in Chapter 6. But the social trap is now even clearer. At the individual level it makes perfect sense to avoid shame. It is essential to social (and psychological) flourishing. But the mechanism for doing so in the consumer society is inherently flawed. At the societal level it can only lead to fragmentation and anomie. And in doing so it undermines the best intentions of the individual as well. It looks suspiciously like the language of goods just isn't doing its job properly. All that's left is an undignified scrap to try and ensure that we're somewhere near the top of the pile.

Most worrying of all is that there is no escape from this social trap within the existing paradigm. While social progress depends on the self-reinforcing cycle of novelty and anxiety, the problem can only get worse. Material throughput will inevitably grow. And the prospects for flourishing within ecological limits evaporate. Prosperity itself – in any meaningful sense of the word – is under threat. Not from the current economic recession, but from the continuing surge of materialism and from the economic model that perpetuates it.

Alternative hedonism

Change is essential. And some mandate for this change already exists. There is cross-party concern over the social recession. And alarm at evidence like the Sheffield study. Politicians struggle for solutions. Small-scale initiatives aimed at addressing the pernicious impacts of social recession are springing up at grass roots level, led by community groups or local authorities.[11]

The philosopher Kate Soper points to a growing appetite for 'alternative hedonism', sources of satisfaction that lie outside the conventional market. She describes a widespread disenchantment with modern life – what she refers to as a 'structure of feeling' – that consumer society has passed some kind of critical point, where materialism is now actively detracting from human well-being.[12]

Anxious to escape the work and spend cycle, we are suffering from a 'fatigue with the clutter and waste of modern life' and yearn for certain forms of human interaction that have been eroded. We would welcome interventions to correct the balance, according to Soper. A shift towards alternative hedonism would lead to a more ecologically sustainable life that is also more satisfying and would leave us happier.[13]

Some statistical evidence supports this view. Psychologist Tim Kasser has highlighted what he calls the high price of materialism. Materialistic values such as popularity, image and financial success are psychologically opposed to 'intrinsic' values like self-acceptance, affiliation, a sense of belonging in the community. Yet these latter are the things that contribute to our well-being. They are the constituents of prosperity.[14]

Kasser's evidence is striking here. People with higher intrinsic values are both happier and have higher levels of environmental responsibility than those with materialistic values. This finding is extraordinary because it suggests there really is a kind of double or triple dividend in a less materialistic life: people are both happier and live more sustainably when they favour intrinsic goals that embed them in family and community. Flourishing within limits is a real possibility, according to this evidence.

It's a possibility that has already been explored to some extent from within modern society. Against the surge of consumerism, there are already those who have resisted the exhortation to 'go out shopping', preferring instead to devote time to less materialistic pursuits (gardening, walking, enjoying music or reading, for example) or to the care of others. Some people (up to a quarter of the sample in a recent study) have even accepted a lower income so that they could achieve these goals.[15]

Beyond this 'quiet revolution', there have also been a series of more radical initiatives aimed at living a simpler and more sustainable life.[16] 'Voluntary simplicity' is at one level an entire philosophy for life. It draws extensively on the teachings of the Indian cultural leader Mahatma Gandhi who encouraged people to 'live simply, that others might simply live'. In 1936, a student of Gandhi's described voluntary simplicity in terms of an 'avoidance of exterior clutter' and the 'deliberate organisation of life for a purpose'.[17]

Former Stanford scientist Duane Elgin picked up this theme of a way of life that is 'outwardly simple, yet inwardly rich' as the basis for revisioning human progress.[18] More recently, psychologist Mihalyi Csikszentmihalyi has offered a scientific basis for the hypothesis that our lives can be more satisfying when engaged in activities which are both purposive and materially light. These conditions are more likely, says Csikszentmihalyi, to provide a good balance between skill and the challenge associated with the task and lead to a state of 'flow'.[19]

Individual efforts to live more simply are more likely to succeed in a supportive community. This realization has led to the emergence of so-called 'intentional communities' where people come together under the declared aim of living simpler, more sustainable lives. Some of these initiatives began, interestingly, as spiritual communities, attempting to create a space where people could reclaim the contemplative dimension of their lives that used to be captured by religious institutions.

The Findhorn community in northern Scotland is an example of this. Findhorn's roots lie in the desire for spiritual transformation. Its character as an eco-village developed more recently, building on principles of justice and respect for nature.[20] Another modern example is Plum Village, the 'mindfulness' community established by the exiled Vietnamese monk Thich Nhat Hahn in the Dordogne area of France, which now provides a retreat for over 2000 people.[21]

These initiatives are modern equivalents of more traditional religious communities like those of the Amish in North America; or the network of Buddhist monasteries in Thailand where every young male is expected to spend some time before going out into professional life.

Not all networks have this explicit spiritual character. The Simplicity Forum, for example, launched in North America in 2001, is a loose secular network of 'simplicity leaders' who are committed to 'achieving and honoring simple, just and sustainable ways of life'. Downshifting Downunder is an even more recent initiative, launched off the back of an international conference on downshifting held in Sydney during 2005; its aim is to 'catalyze and co-ordinate a downshifting movement in Australia that will significantly impact sustainability and social capital'.[22]

The downshifting movement now has a surprising allegiance across a number of developed economies. A recent survey on downshifting in Australia found that 23 per cent of respondents had engaged in some form of downshifting in the five years prior to the study. A staggering 83 per cent felt that Australians are too materialistic. An earlier study in the US found that 28 per cent had taken some steps to simplify and 62 per cent expressed a willingness to do so. Very similar results have been found in Europe.[23]

Research on the success of these initiatives is quite limited. But the findings from studies that do exist are interesting. In the first place, the evidence confirms that 'simplifiers' appear to be happier. Consuming less, voluntarily, can improve subjective well-being – completely contrary to the conventional model.[24]

At the same time, intentional communities remain marginal. The spiritual basis for them doesn't appeal to everyone, and the secular versions seem less resistant to the incursions of consumerism. Some of these initiatives depend heavily on having sufficient personal assets to provide the economic security needed to pursue a simpler lifestyle.

More importantly, even those in the vanguard of social change turn out to be haunted by conflict – internal and external.[25] These conflicts arise because people find themselves at odds with their own social world. Participation in the life of society becomes a challenge in its own right. People are trying to live, quite literally, in opposition to the structures and values that dominate society. In the normal course of events, these structures and values shape and constrain how people behave. They have a profound influence on how easy or hard it is to behave sustainably.[26]

The role of structural change

Examples of the perverse effect of dominant structures are legion: private transport is incentivized over public transport; motorists are prioritized over pedestrians; energy supply is subsidized and protected, while demand management is often chaotic and expensive; waste disposal is cheap, economically and behaviourally;

recycling demands time and effort: 'bring centres' are few and far between and often overflowing with waste.

Equally important are the subtle but damaging signals sent by government, regulatory frameworks, financial institutions, the media and our education systems: business salaries are higher than those in the public sector, particularly at the top; nurses and those in the caring professions are consistently less well paid; private investment is written down at high discount rates making long-term costs invisible; success is counted in terms of material status (salary, house size and so on); children are brought up as a 'shopping generation' – hooked on brand, celebrity and status.[27]

Policy and media messages about the recession underline this point. Opening a huge new shopping centre at the height of the financial crisis in October 2008, Mayor of London Boris Johnson spoke of persuading people to come out and spend their money, despite the credit crunch. Londoners had made a 'prudent decision to give Thursday morning a miss and come shopping', he said of the huge crowds who attended the opening.[28] George W. Bush's infamous call for people to 'go out shopping' in the wake of the 9/11 disaster is one of the most staggering examples of the same phenomenon.

Little wonder that people trying to live more sustainably find themselves in conflict with the social world around them. These kinds of asymmetry represent a culture of consumption that sends all the wrong signals, penalizing pro-environmental behaviour, and making it all but impossible even for highly motivated people to act sustainably without personal sacrifice.

It's important to take this evidence seriously. As laboratories for social change, intentional households and communities are vital in pointing to the possibilities for flourishing within ecological limits. But they are also critical in highlighting the limits of voluntarism.

Simplistic exhortations for people to resist consumerism are destined to failure. Particularly when the messages flowing from government are so painfully inconsistent. People readily identify this inconsistency and perceive it as hypocrisy. Or something worse. Under current conditions, it's tantamount to asking people to give up key capabilities and freedoms as social beings. Far from being irrational to resist these demands, it would be irrational not to, in our society.

Several lessons flow from this. The first is the obvious need for government to get its message straight. Urging people to *Act on CO_2*, to insulate their homes, turn down their thermostat, put on a jumper, drive a little less, walk a little more, holiday at home, buy locally produced goods (and so on) will either go unheard or be rejected as manipulation for as long as all the messages about high-street consumption point in the opposite direction.[29]

Equally, it's clear that changing the social logic of consumption cannot simply be relegated to the realm of individual choice. In spite of a growing desire for change, it's almost impossible for people to simply *choose* sustainable lifestyles, however much they'd like to. Even highly-motivated individuals experience conflict as they attempt to escape consumerism. And the chances of extending this behaviour across society are negligible without changes in the social structure.

Conversely, of course, social structures can and do shift people's values and behaviours. Structural changes of two kinds must lie at the heart of any strategy to address the social logic of consumerism. The first will be to dismantle or correct the perverse incentives for unsustainable (and unproductive) status competition. The second must be to establish new structures that provide capabilities for people to flourish, and particularly to participate fully in the life of society, in less materialistic ways.

What this second avenue means in practice is something that requires a more detailed exploration than is possible here. It will certainly require a keener policy attention to what flourishing means, particularly when it comes to questions of community, social participation and psychological flourishing. But these outcomes cannot be delivered in instrumental, *ad hoc* ways. Policy must pay closer attention to the structural causes of social alienation and anomie. It must have the goal of providing capabilities for flourishing at its heart.

This idea clearly has resonances with the concept of the Cinderella economy discussed in the preceding chapter. Specifically, the strategy suggested here rejects the centrality of material commodities as the basis for profitability. It replaces them with the idea of an economy designed explicitly around delivering the capabilities for human flourishing.

More than this, of course, these capabilities will have to be delivered with considerably less material input. We will need to call on the creativity of the entrepreneur in a different way from in the past. Social innovation is going to be vital in achieving change. But so too is a closer attention to the question of limits. Creating continuity and cohesion must be balanced against stimulating change.

A core element in this strategy must be the reduction of social inequality. Unproductive status competition increases material throughput and creates distress. In his book *Affluenza*, clinical psychologist Oliver James presents evidence that more unequal societies systematically report higher levels of distress than more equal societies.[30]

Richard Wilkinson and Kate Pickett have gone even further in documenting the damage caused by unequal societies. *The Spirit Level* draws together astonishing evidence of the benefits of equality across OECD nations in a range of health and social impacts (Figure 9.2). Life expectancy, child well-being, literacy, social mobility and trust are all better in more equal societies. Infant mortality, obesity, teenage pregnancy, homicide rates and incidence of mental illness are all worse in less equal ones. Tackling systemic inequality is vital, argue Wilkinson and Pickett, and not just for the least well-off. Society as a whole suffers in the face of inequality.

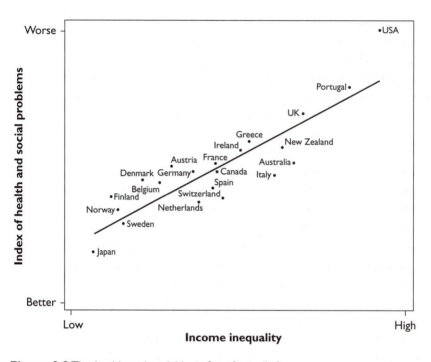

Figure 9.2 The health and social benefits of equality[31]
Source: Wilkinson and Pickett 2009.

A key point of influence here will lie in the structure of wages. The prevailing structure has consistently rewarded competitive and materialistic outcomes even when these are socially detrimental – as the lessons from the financial crisis made clear. Reducing the huge income disparities that result from this would send a powerful signal about what is valued in society. Better recognition for those engaged in child-care, care for the elderly or disabled and volunteer work would shift the balance of incentives away from status competition and towards a more cooperative, and more altruistic society.

Increased investment in public goods and social infrastructure is another vital point of influence. This has already been identified as an essential component in the macro-economics of sustainability (Chapter 8). In addition to its role in ensuring economic resilience, public investment sends a powerful signal about the balance between private interests and the public good.

In summary, we are faced with a formidable challenge. A limited form of flourishing through material success has kept our economies going for half a century or more. But it is completely unsustainable in ecological and social terms and is now undermining the conditions for a shared prosperity. This materialistic vision of prosperity has to be dismantled.

The idea of an economy whose task is to provide capabilities for flourishing within ecological limits offers the most credible vision to put in its place. But this can only happen through changes that support social behaviours and reduce the structural incentives to unproductive status competition.

The rewards from these changes are likely to be significant. A less materialistic society will be a happier one. A more equal society will be a less anxious one. Greater attention to community and to participation in the life of society will reduce the loneliness and anomie that has undermined well-being in the modern economy. Enhanced investment in public goods will provide lasting returns to the nation's prosperity.

10 | Governance for Prosperity

The current financial crisis has also become a political crisis that is reconfiguring the role of government in the economy and conventional wisdom about the appropriate relationship between the public and the private sector.

Peter Hall, October 2008[1]

Achieving a lasting prosperity relies on providing capabilities for people to flourish – within certain limits. Those limits are established not by us, but by the ecology and resources of a finite planet. Unbounded freedom to expand our material appetites just isn't sustainable. Change is essential.

Two specific components of change have been identified. The first is the need to fix the economics: to develop a new ecologically literate macro-economics (Chapter 8). This new economic framework will have to place economic activity within ecological limits. It will need to reduce the structural reliance on relentless consumption growth and find a different mechanism to achieve underlying stability.

The existing mechanism, in any case, has failed us. A resilient economy – capable of resisting external shocks, maintaining people's livelihoods and living within our ecological means – is the goal we should be aiming for here.

The second component of change lies in shifting the social logic of consumerism (Chapter 9). This change has to proceed through the provision of real, credible alternatives through which people can flourish. And these alternatives must go beyond making basic systems of provision (in food, housing and transport, for example) more sustainable. They must also provide capabilities for people to participate fully in the life of society, without recourse to unsustainable material accumulation and unproductive status competition.

Making these changes may well be the biggest challenge ever faced by human society. Inevitably it raises the question of governance – in the broadest sense of the word. How is a shared prosperity to be achieved in a pluralistic society? How is the interest of the individual to be balanced against the common good? What are the mechanisms for achieving this balance? These are some of the questions raised by this challenge. Specifically, of course, such changes raise questions about the nature and role of government itself.

The role of government

Debates over the role of the state, and in particular the question of whether we need 'more state' or 'less state', have been fiercely fought at times and have complex roots in history.[2] But some striking shifts in this debate occurred as a result of the current economic recession. The financial crisis of 2008 re-wrote the boundary between the public and the private sector and changed profoundly the landscape of 21st century politics.

Part-nationalization of financial sector institutions was an almost shocking turn of events, particularly from a free-market perspective in which government is broadly seen as a distortion of the market. And yet there was little disagreement anywhere about the role of the state in the circumstances. On the contrary, the only possible response when the economy stood on the brink of failure was for governments to intervene. Even the die-hards agreed on this. 'Finance is inherently unstable', acknowledged *The Economist* in the early days of the crisis. 'So the state has to play a big role in making it safer by lending in a crisis in return for regulation and oversight.'[3]

Extending this basic responsibility for economic stability to the task of building a credible and ecologically robust economics seems pretty straightforward. Admittedly, it's a more complex task than anything faced in conventional macro-economics; in part because it has to depart from the well-worn formula of laissez-faire consumption growth as the basis for stability; and in part because it requires a closer attention to key ecological variables. So making progress will depend on engaging a wider community of advice than conventional approaches do. But the responsibility for taking it forward lies unequivocally with government.

Beyond this quite specific responsibility, there are vital questions about the role of government – and the mechanisms for governance – in a much broader sense. Where, for example, does responsibility lie for the other key task identified here: redressing the social logic of consumerism?

Policy-makers are (perhaps rightly) uncomfortable with the idea that they have a role in influencing people's values and aspirations. But the truth is that governments intervene constantly in the social context, whether they like it or not.

A myriad of different signals is sent out by the way in which education is structured, by the importance accorded to economic indicators, by public sector performance indicators, by procurement policies, by the impact of planning guidelines on public and social spaces, by the influence of wage policy on the work-life balance, by the impact of employment policy on economic mobility (and hence on family structure and stability), by the presence or absence of product standards (on durability for example), by the degree of regulation of advertising and the media and by the support offered to community initiatives and faith groups.

In all these arenas, policy shapes and co-creates the social world. So the idea that it is legitimate for the state to intervene in changing the social logic of consumerism is far less problematic than is often portrayed. A critical task is to identify (and correct) those aspects of this complex social structure which provide perverse incentives in favour of a materialistic individualism and undermine the potential for a shared prosperity.

At one level, this task is as old as the hills. It is, in part at least, the task of balancing individual freedoms against the common good. Governance mechanisms emerged in human society for precisely this reason. The evolutionary basis for this is beginning to be understood.[4] Societies capable of protecting social behaviour have a better chance of survival.

The philosophical basis is provided by the concept of a 'social contract', an implicit arrangement between individuals and society to curb narrow individualism and support social behaviour. We hand over some of our individual freedoms. But in return we gain a certain security that our lives will be protected against the unbounded freedoms of others.[5]

Oxford economic historian Avner Offer provides a valuable extension of this idea in *The Challenge of Affluence*.[6] Left to our own devices, argues Offer, individual choices tend to be irredeemably myopic. We favour today too much over tomorrow, in ways which, to an economist, appear entirely inexplicable under any rational rate of discounting of the future. Economists call this the problem of 'hyperbolic' discounting. It's not unfamiliar in itself. Offer's unique contribution is to suggest that this fallibility has (or has in the past had) a social solution.

To prevent ourselves from trading away our long-term well-being for the sake of short-term pleasures, society has evolved a whole set of 'commitment devices': social and institutional mechanisms which moderate the balance of choice away from the present and in favour of the future.

Savings accounts, marriage, norms for social behaviour, government itself in some sense: all these can be regarded as commitment devices. Mechanisms which make it a little easier for us to curtail our appetite for immediate arousal and protect our own future interests. And indeed – although this is less obvious in Offer's exposition – the interests of affected others.

The trouble is, as Offer demonstrates, affluence itself is eroding and undermining these commitment devices. The increase in family breakdown and the decline in trust have already been noted (Chapter 9). Parenthood itself has come under attack in developed countries. The explosion of debt, the decline of savings and the financial crisis reveal the erosion of economic prudence. And the hollowing out of government has left us ill-prepared to deal with this 'crisis of commitment'.[7]

Strikingly, Offer places a key responsibility for this erosion on the relentless pursuit of novelty in modern society. This dynamic has been addressed already in structural terms (Chapter 6). Novelty keeps us buying more stuff. Buying more stuff keeps the economy going. The end result is a society 'locked in' to consumption growth by forces outside the control of individuals.

Physical infrastructure and social architecture conspire against us here. Lured by our evolutionary roots, bombarded with persuasion and seduced by novelty: we are like children in the sweet shop, knowing that sugar is bad for us but unable to resist the temptation.

These insights are damning for the prospects that laissez-faire individualism is a sufficient governance mechanism for a lasting prosperity. Left to our own individual devices, it seems, there is not much hope that people will spontaneously behave sustainably. As evolutionary biologist Richard Dawkins has concluded, sustainability just 'doesn't come naturally' to us.[8]

Selfishness and altruism

At the same time it is a mistake to assume that human motivations are all selfish. Evolution doesn't preclude moral, social and altruistic behaviours. On the contrary, social behaviours evolved in humans precisely because they offer selective advantages to the species. All of us are torn to some extent between selfishness and altruism.

The psychologist Shalom Schwartz and his colleagues have formalized this insight into a theory of underlying human values. Using a scale that has now been tested in over 50 countries, Schwartz suggests that our values are structured around two distinct tensions in our psychological make-up (Figure 10.1). One is the tension between selfishness (self-enhancement, in Schwartz's

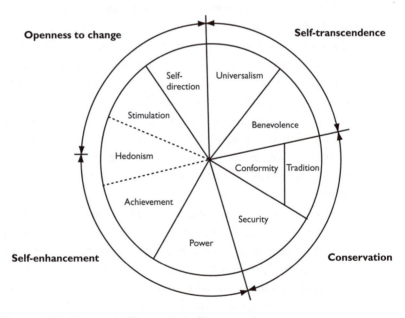

Figure 10.1 Schwartz's 'Circumplex' of human values

Source: Adapted from Schwartz 1994, p24.

scheme) and altruism (self-transcendence). The other is a tension between openness to change and conservation – or in other words between novelty and the maintenance of tradition.[9]

Schwartz provided an evolutionary explanation for these tensions. As society evolved in groups, people were caught between the needs of the individual and the needs of the group. And as they struggled for survival in sometimes hostile environments, people were caught between the need to adapt and to innovate and the need for stability. In other words, both individualism and the pursuit of novelty have played an adaptive role in our common survival. But so have altruism and conservation or tradition.

The important point here is that each society strikes the balance between altruism and selfishness (and also between novelty and tradition) in different places.[10] And where this balance is struck depends crucially on social structure. When technologies, infrastructures, institutions and social norms reward self-enhancement and novelty, then selfish sensation-seeking behaviours prevail over more considered, altruistic ones. Where social structures favour altruism and tradition, self-transcending behaviours are rewarded and selfish behaviour may even be penalized.[11]

This finding suggests that we must ask searching questions about the balance of the institutions that characterize modern society. Do they promote competition or cooperation? Do they reward self-serving behaviour or people who sacrifice their own gain to serve others? What signals do government, schools, the media, religious and community institutions send out to people? Which behaviours are supported by public investments and infrastructures and which are discouraged?

Increasingly, it seems, the institutions of consumer society are designed to favour a particularly materialistic individualism and to encourage the relentless pursuit of consumer novelty because this is exactly what's needed to keep the economy going.

The erosion of commitment is a structural requirement for growth as well as a structural consequence of affluence. Growth calls on us to be myopic, individualistic novelty seekers, because that's exactly what's needed to perpetuate the economic system. And at the same time, it supports us in this transition by undermining the commitment devices that support more altruistic and more conservative values.

And yet this doesn't just happen by itself. Government plays a crucial role here, precisely because it bears a responsibility for the stability of the macro-economy. The individualistic pursuit of novelty is a key requirement in consumption growth, and economic stability depends on consumption growth. Little surprise, then, that the drift of policy is in these directions.

Varieties of capitalism

This drift has not been uniform across all nations. As we've already seen, there are some clear distinctions between different 'varieties' of capitalism. For example, inequality tends to be higher in liberalized market economies than in coordinated market economies.[12] And it's mainly in the liberalized market economies that savings rates have fallen so dramatically in recent years and consumer debt has soared. In Germany, the government has had the opposite problem over the last decade finding it hard to persuade its citizens to save less and consume more.

Some other interesting differences emerge. Figure 10.2 shows the unemployment rates during the run-up to the economic crisis in two liberalized market economies (the UK and the US) and two coordinated market economies (Germany and Denmark). Though starting from a much higher base, unemployment in Germany fell by almost 20 per cent over the period from mid-2007 to the end of 2008.[13] In Denmark, where unemployment was already low, the fall was even greater (35 per cent) over the period. In the UK, by

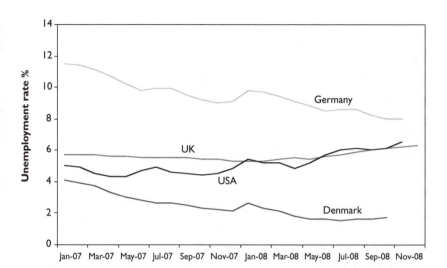

Figure 10.2 Unemployment rates in four OECD countries 2007–2008[14]

Source: see note 14.

contrast, unemployment rose by 11 per cent in the last half of 2008, while the US saw unemployment increase by over a third since July 2007.

Recent work suggests that the different varieties of capitalism also perform differently in relation to ecological impacts, opportunities for skills training and various aspects of social capital.[15] Tim Kasser and his colleagues show that people in liberalized market economies tend to have higher per capita carbon emissions, higher infant mortality, higher teenage pregnancies and a greater percentage of people reporting that they 'feel like an outsider'.[16]

Not all these findings are replicated consistently across all liberal market economies and all coordinated market economies. Indeed there is some suggestion that the distinctions between liberal and coordinated market economies are not as profound as they were through the 1980s and 1990s when Peter Hall and David Soskice carried out their original analysis.[17]

Ironically, as we saw in Chapter 2, Germany suffered more during the early months of the financial crisis from building its economy on exports, than the UK did from building its economy on domestic consumption. Both economies, ultimately, were predicated on a materialistic consumerism fuelled by debt. And it's too early to tell which one will emerge stronger in the end. In a recent article for the *Huffington Post*, Hall argues that Germany's domestic prudence and strong manufacturing base will make it more resilient in the long run.[18]

But the truth is that none of the varieties of capitalism is immune from global recession. All of them are to a greater or lesser extent bound up in the pursuit of economic growth. Differences in social and economic organization are differences in degree rather than fundamental differences in kind. And a key element in the political economy of all capitalist nations appears to be the role of government in protecting and stimulating economic growth.

The conflicted state

The principal role of government is to ensure that long-term public goods are not undermined by short-term private interests. It seems ironic then, tragic even, that governments across the world – and in particular in the liberal market economies – have been so active in championing the pursuit of unbounded consumer freedoms, often elevating consumer sovereignty above social goals and actively encouraging the expansion of the market into different areas of people's lives.

It is particularly odd to see this tendency going hand in hand with the desire to protect social and ecological goals. It's notable for example that the UK, one of the most fiercely liberal market economies, has also been a vociferous champion of sustainability, social justice and climate change policy. The UK's 2005 Sustainable Development Strategy received widespread international praise. Its 2008 Climate Change Act is a world-leading piece of legislation.

There is a real sense here of policy-makers struggling with competing goals. On the one hand government is bound to the pursuit of economic growth. On the other, it finds itself having to intervene to protect the common good from the incursions of the market. The state itself is deeply conflicted, striving on the one hand to encourage consumer freedoms that lead to growth and on the other to protect social goods and defend ecological limits.[19]

But the reason for this conflict becomes clear once we recognize the role that growth plays in macro-economic stability. With a vital responsibility to protect jobs and to ensure stability, the state is bound (under current conditions) to prioritize economic growth. And it is locked into this task, even as it seeks to promote sustainability and the common good. Government itself, in other words, is caught in the dilemma of growth.

Overcoming this dilemma is absolutely vital because the lessons from this study make it clear that without strong leadership, change will be impossible. Individuals are too exposed to social signals and status competition. Businesses operate under market conditions. A transition from narrow self-interest to social behaviours, or from relentless novelty to a considered conservation of things that matter, can only proceed through changes in underlying structure, changes that strengthen commitment and encourage social behaviour. And these changes require governments to act.

The trouble is that the thrust of policy over the last half century – particularly in the liberal market economies – has been going in almost exactly the opposite direction. Governments have systematically promoted materialistic individualism and encouraged the pursuit of consumer novelty. This trend has been perpetuated, mostly deliberately, on the assumption that this form of consumerism serves economic growth, protects jobs and maintains stability. And as a result, the state has become caught up in a belief that growth should trump all other policy goals.

But this narrow pursuit of growth represents a horrible distortion of the common good and of our underlying human values. It also undermines the legitimate role of government. A state framed narrowly as the protector of market freedom in the unbounded pursuit of consumerism bears no relation to any meaningful vision of social contract. The state is society's commitment device, *par excellence*, and the principal agent in protecting our shared prosperity. A new vision of governance that embraces this role is critical.

Knowing that family, community, friendship, health and so on are vital influences on prosperity, and that the ability of the individual to protect these factors is being eroded in modern society, there would appear to be a clear argument in favour of an increased role for government in this regard.

Equally, accepting that unemployment, injustice and inequality have impacts not just at the individual level but at the level of aggregate well-being, there would appear to be an argument in favour of government intervening to protect employment, justice and equality.

Such a role would be, in a sense, a re-invigoration of the idea of the social contract. Within such a contract, a legitimate role for government would be to strengthen and protect commitment devices which prevent myopic choice and, equally importantly, to reduce the pernicious structural impacts which increase inequality and reduce well-being.

Of course, such a vision requires a democratic mandate. 'Political change comes from leadership and popular mobilisation. And you need both of them' argued UK Climate Change Secretary Ed Miliband in December 2008.[20] Authoritarianism is damaging to human well-being in its own right.[21] And in any case it is unlikely to succeed in modern pluralistic societies. Governance for prosperity must engage actively with citizens both in establishing the mandate and delivering the change.

But this doesn't absolve government from its own vital responsibility in ensuring a shared prosperity. The role of government is to provide the capabilities for its citizens to flourish – within ecological limits. The analysis here suggests that, at this time, responsibility entails shifting the balance of existing institutions and structures away from materialistic individualism and providing instead real opportunities for people to pursue intrinsic goals of family, friendship and community.

Unfortunately, for as long as economic stability depends on growth, this isn't going to happen. There will inevitably be a tendency for governments to support social structures that reinforce materialistic, novelty-seeking individualism. Because that's what it takes to keep the economy afloat.

But it doesn't have to be like this. Freeing the macro-economy from the structural requirement for consumption growth will simultaneously free government to play its proper role in delivering social and environmental goods and protecting long-term interests. The same goal that's vital for a sustainable economy is essential to governance for prosperity. The conflicted state is itself a casualty of growth. And in rescuing the economy from that dilemma, it stands a chance, at least, of rescuing itself.

11

The Transition to a Sustainable Economy

> In the end, this economic agenda won't just require new money. It will require a new spirit of cooperation... We will be called upon to take part in a shared sacrifice and shared prosperity.
>
> Barack Obama, February 2008[1]

Consumer society seems hell-bent on disaster; but dismantling the system doesn't look easy either. Overthrowing it completely could drive us even faster along the road to ruin. But incremental changes are unlikely to be enough. Faced with this kind of intractability it's tempting to retrench. To cling more tightly to existing tenets. Or to resort to a kind of fatalism. A place where we accept the inevitability of a changing climate, an unequal world, perhaps even the collapse of society. And concentrate all our efforts on personal security.

This response is understandable. But it isn't constructive. Nor, as it happens, is it inevitable. Impossibility theorems confront us at every turn. Economies can only survive if they grow. People won't relinquish materialism. The state is powerless to intervene. But time and again axiomatic truths dissolve under a more careful scrutiny. A different kind of macro-economics is conceivable. People can flourish without more stuff. A new vision of governance does make sense. Another world is possible.

The economic crisis presents us with a unique opportunity to invest in change. To sweep away the short-term thinking that has plagued society for decades. To replace it with considered policy-making capable of addressing the enormous challenges of tackling climate change, delivering a lasting prosperity.

Of course it's one thing to have such a vision, completely another to set about achieving it. But there are basically only two possibilities for change of this order. One is revolution. The other is to engage in the painstaking work of social transformation.

There are those for whom revolution appears to be the answer. Or if not the answer, then at least the inevitable consequence of continued social and ecological dysfunction. Let's end capitalism. Let's reject globalization. Let's undermine corporate power and overthrow corrupt governments. Let's dismantle the old institutions and start afresh.

But there are risks here too. The spectre of a new barbarism lurks in the wings. A world constrained for resources, threatened with climate change, struggling for economic stability: how long could we maintain civil society in such a world if we have already torn down every institutional structure we can lay our hands on?

To reject revolution is not to accept the status quo. Or even to suggest that only incremental change is needed. It should be clear from everything that has been said that the scale of the required transformation is massive. But we also need concrete steps through which to build change. And this is still a task which calls for the engagement of governments and those able to make or influence policy.

Specifying those steps with any degree of precision relies in part on the opening out of a public and policy dialogue on the issues. Clearly it lies beyond the scope of this (or any other) volume. But it would be wrong to leave the question of policy hanging in the air completely. And it is possible already to establish some clear directions of travel.

In the following paragraphs, some specific recommendations are made. They follow directly from the analysis in the preceding chapters. Broadly speaking, they fall under three main headings:

- Establishing the limits.
- Fixing the economic model.
- Changing the social logic.

Inevitably, there are some overlaps between these categories. Undoubtedly there are things missing. Not all of the suggestions can be achieved immediately. Not all of them can be achieved unilaterally. But none of them is entirely without precedent and there are numerous points of contact with existing initiatives. Taken together they offer some policy foundations from which to initiate meaningful and lasting change.

Establishing the limits

The material profligacy of consumer society is depleting key natural resources and placing unsustainable burdens on the planet's ecosystems (Chapter 5). Establishing clear resource and environmental limits and integrating these limits into both economic functioning (Chapter 8 and Appendix 2) and social functioning (Chapter 9) is essential. The first three specific proposals relate to that task.

Resource and emission caps – and reduction targets

A much closer attention to the ecological limits of economic activity is called for. Identifying clear resource and emission caps and establishing reduction targets under those caps is vital for a sustainable economy. To the extent that they have been implemented, the stabilization targets and emission budgets established for carbon provide an exemplar here.[2]

The conditions of equity and ecological limits, taken together, suggest a key role for the model known as 'contraction and convergence' in which equal per capita allowances are established under an ecological cap that converges towards a sustainable level.[3] This approach has been applied, to some extent, for carbon. Similar caps should be established for the extraction of scarce non-renewable resources, for the emission of wastes (particularly toxic and hazardous wastes), for the drawing down of 'fossil' groundwater supplied and for the rate of harvesting of renewable resources.

Effective mechanisms for achieving targets under these caps should be set in place. Once established, these limits also need to be integrated into a convincing economic framework (see Recommendation 4 below).

Fiscal reform for sustainability

The broad principle of internalizing the external costs of economic activities has been accepted for at least two decades.[4] Taxing carbon, for example, sends a clear signal to people about the value of the climate and encourages them to shift to less carbon intensive processes, technologies and activities. A related mechanism – already established through the Kyoto Protocol's 'flexibility mechanisms' and in the EU Emissions Trading Scheme – would be to allow permits established under a cap (see Recommendation 1 above) to be traded.[5]

A useful elaboration of the argument is the principle of an ecological tax reform – a shift in the burden of taxation from economic goods (for example incomes) to ecological bads (for example pollution). Taxes on carbon (for example) could be designed to be fiscally neutral, to reduce the burden on businesses and people. New taxes on resource use or carbon would be offset through reductions in taxes on labour. This argument has been elaborated over at least a decade and has been implemented in varying degrees across Europe. But progress towards a meaningful ecological tax reform remains painfully slow.[6]

Support for ecological transition in developing countries

A key motivation for rethinking prosperity in the advanced economies is to make room for much-needed growth in poorer nations. But as these economies expand there will also be an urgent need to ensure that development is sustainable and remains within ecological limits.

Specifically, this calls for robust funding mechanisms to make resources available to developing countries. The UN Framework Convention on Climate Change has already established such a mechanism, known as the Global Environment Facility (GEF).[7] Expanding or replicating this kind of resource transfer mechanism is a priority. Investment in renewable energy, energy efficiency, resource efficiency, low-carbon infrastructures and the protection of 'carbon sinks' (forests) and biodiversity will remain vital.

There's another difficult issue for developing economies: namely, the impact of reduced consumption in advanced economies on their export markets. Interestingly, there is now some evidence to suggest that, in the longer term, this will turn out to be a less thorny issue than once thought.[8] Growth in the industrializing economies is increasingly built on domestic consumption or trade between industrializing nations. But there will remain for some time a need to provide structural support for developing countries in the transition to a sustainable economy.[9]

Funding both investment and structural needs could take several forms including a carbon levy paid by richer nations on imports from developing countries,[10] or a Tobin tax on international currency transfers (see Recommendation 6 below).

Fixing the economic model

An economy predicated on the perpetual expansion of debt-driven materialistic consumption is unsustainable ecologically, problematic socially and unstable economically (Chapters 2, 5 and 6). Changing this requires the development of a new macro-economics for sustainability (Chapters 7 and 8, Appendix 2): an economic engine that doesn't rely for its stability on relentless consumption growth and expanding material throughput. Building that new framework is an urgent priority. Policy can contribute to that task in several ways.

Developing an ecological macro-economics

A key step is to develop the technical capacity for what we might call an ecological macro-economics. Essentially this would mean being able to understand the behaviour of economies when they are subject to strict emission and resource use limits. And to explore how economies might work under different configurations of consumption, investment, labour employment and productivity growth.

A key requirement is to reframe our preconceptions about both labour and capital productivities. The continued pursuit of labour productivity drives economies towards growth simply to maintain full employment. But this trend is unlikely to continue in an economy geared towards (more labour intensive) services (Chapter 8). The impact of falling labour productivities is already an issue in the EU.[11] Rather than stimulating a continued search for high productivities, it would be better to engage in structural transition towards low-carbon, labour-intensive activities and sectors.

'Ecological investment' (see below) has also emerged as a key requirement in this analysis. The question of productivity is once again crucial. But here the question is about the productivity of capital. Ecological investments will have different rates and periods of return. In conventional terms they are likely to be 'less productive'. Ecological investment will therefore need to address the conditions as well as the targets of investment (Appendix 2).

There is also a clear case for a new macro-economics to include some account of the value of natural capital and ecosystem services.[12] Ultimately, these will need to be integrated into accounts of capital stocks and into production functions and consumption flows.

How all this might work is an enormous but exciting challenge. There are virtually no real precedents for a coherent macro-economic framework for sustainability.[13] But the new economics of sustainability is not the dismal science of Thomas Malthus. It's a place that ought to attract bright, young economists to elaborate an economic science fit for the future.

Investing in jobs, assets and infrastructures

Investment in jobs, assets and infrastructures emerges as a key component, not just of economic recovery but as one of the foundations of a new ecological macro-economics. Ecological investment has some clear targets. These include:[14]

- retrofitting buildings with energy- and carbon-saving measures;
- renewable energy technologies;
- redesigning utility networks, in particular the electricity grid;
- public transport infrastructures;
- public spaces (pedestrianization, green spaces, libraries and so on);
- ecosystem maintenance and protection.

Investment in jobs and skills will also be vital in maintaining and improving buildings and infrastructures. In fact the creation of jobs should be thought of as a legitimate focus for investment whenever employed labour is protecting or improving public assets.

But ecological investment is not just about targeting investment towards specific goals. It also demands a different 'ecology' of investment. In particular, it will need to address the conditions of investment, rates and periods of return, and the structure of capital markets. Ultimately, this will also mean raising tough questions about the ownership of assets, and control over the surpluses from those assets. The nature and role of property rights lies at the heart of these questions.

Increasing financial and fiscal prudence

Debt-driven materialistic consumption has propped up economic growth over the last two decades. But maintaining it has de-stabilized the macro-economy and contributed to the global economic crisis. There is an emerging agreement that a new era of financial and fiscal prudence needs to be ushered in. A number of important suggestions have already been discussed in the international arena.[15]

These include: reforming the regulation of national and international financial markets; outlawing unscrupulous and destabilizing market practices (such as short-selling); reducing excessive executive remuneration packages (or making them performance related); providing greater protection against consumer debt and greater incentives for domestic saving.

Some other measures also warrant consideration. One that's received attention for a number of reasons is the idea of a tax on international currency transfers. The so-called Tobin tax was originally devised (by Nobel economist James Tobin) as a mechanism to reduce the potentially destabilizing effects of currency fluctuations. It's also been supported as a mechanism to reduce the excessive mobility of capital generally, and as a way of funding development (by redistributing the revenues from the tax as development aid).[16]

Another proposal aimed at stabilizing financial markets is to increase public control over the money supply. Most of the money in circulation at any one time (in advanced economies) is now created by private banks as loans to businesses or householders. This is only possible because banks are not required to hold reserves equivalent to all deposits by savers – a so-called 'fractional' reserve system operates.

Prudence dictates that some proportion of the banks' assets are held as reserves. The higher this proportion, the higher the degree of prudence. One of the problems encountered by banks during the 2008 financial crisis was the failure to hold adequate reserves. Some have called for a 100 per cent reserve system.[17] In such a system governments would retain full control over the money supply. Liquidity would be much lower, investment and debt would be more tightly controlled.

Revising the national accounts

The GDP is really nothing more and nothing less than a measure of 'busy-ness' in the economy (Chapter 8). It measures the amount of spending and saving by consumers, or equivalently the value added from economic activities. But the shortfalls of this as a useful measure even of economic well-being are well-documented. These include the failure of the GDP to account properly for changes in the asset base; to incorporate the real welfare losses from having an unequal distribution of income; to adjust for the depletion of material resources and other forms of natural capital; to capture the external costs of pollution and long-term environmental damage; to account for the costs of crime, car accidents, industrial accidents, family breakdown and other social costs; to correct for 'defensive' expenditures and positional consumption or to account for non-market services such as domestic labour and voluntary care.

The case against the GDP has a strong economic pedigree and has attracted a lot of attention over the years. A number of attempts have been made to construct adjusted indicators that might do a better job. These include the World Bank's Adjusted Net Savings index, Nordhaus and Tobin's Measure of Economic Welfare and Daly and Cobb's Index of Sustainable Economic Welfare. The OECD's *Beyond GDP* initiative has attempted to collate these different attempts. President Sarkozy's Commission on the Measurement of Economic Performance and Social Progress is also dedicated to this question.

The time is ripe to make progress in developing national accounts that provide a more robust measure of economic performance.[18]

Changing the social logic

The social logic that locks people into materialistic consumerism as the basis for participating in the life of society is extremely powerful, but detrimental ecologically and psychologically (Chapters 4–6). An essential pre-requisite for a lasting prosperity is to free people from this damaging dynamic and provide opportunities for sustainable and fulfilling lives (Chapter 9). The final five recommendations focus on this task.

Working time policy

Working time policy is important to a sustainable economy for two reasons. Firstly, the number of hours that people work bears an important relation (via labour productivity) to output. Specifically, output is equal to the number of hours worked multiplied by the labour productivity. In an economy in which labour productivity still increases but output is capped (for instance for ecological reasons), the only way to maintain macro-economic stability and protect people's livelihoods is by sharing out the available work. This often happens already on a smaller scale during recession.

Secondly, reduced working hours have been sought for their own sake for various reasons. One of these, ironically, was in the belief that it would increase labour productivity. This was the rationale for example for the French 'experiment' with a 35-hour working week.[19] The reasoning behind this is that when people work shorter hours they are more productive during those hours because they are better rested, more alert and fitter.

These benefits of course have been called for in their own right by employee organizations and campaigners.[20] Specific policies to reduce working hours and improve the work-life balance could include: greater flexibility for employees on working time; measures to combat discrimination against part-time work as regards grading, promotion, training, security of employment and rate of pay; better incentives to employees (and flexibility for employers) for family time, parental leave and sabbatical breaks.[21]

Tackling systemic inequality

Systemic income inequalities increase anxiety, undermine social capital and expose lower income households to higher morbidity and lower life satisfaction. In fact, the evidence of negative health and social effects right across unequal populations is mounting. Systemic inequality also drives positional consumption, contributing to a material 'ratchet' that drives resources through the economy.

Tackling inequality would reduce social costs, improve quality of life and change the dynamic of status consumption. Yet too little has been done to reverse the long-term trends in income inequality, which are still increasing, particularly in the liberalized market economies, even policies and mechanisms for reducing inequality and redistributing incomes are well-established.

These include revised income tax structures, minimum and maximum income levels, improved access to good quality education, anti-discrimination legislation, anti-crime measures and improving the local environment in deprived areas. Systematic attention to these policies is now vital.

Measuring capabilities and flourishing

The suggestion that prosperity is not adequately captured by conventional measures of economic output or consumption leaves open the need to define an appropriate measurement framework for a lasting prosperity. This must certainly include a systematic assessment of people's capabilities for flourishing across the nation (and in different population segments). Such an assessment would set out specifically to measure flourishing 'outcome variables' such as healthy life expectancy, educational participation, trust, community resilience and participation in the life of society.

A number of suggestions along these lines have been made already. Perhaps the closest model to what is being suggested here is the Dutch work on developing a 'capabilities index' (see Chapter 4). But suggestions to develop national well-being accounts also draw on this logic of 'measuring what matters'. A further step would be to integrate such accounts systematically into the existing national accounting framework (see Recommendation 7 above) and perhaps even adjust economic accounts for changes in the flourishing accounts.[22]

Strengthening social capital

Understanding that prosperity consists in part in our capabilities to participate in the life of society demands that attention is paid to the underlying human and social resources required for this task. Creating resilient social communities is particularly important in the face of economic shocks. As the examples cited in Chapter 4 show, the strength of community can make the difference between disaster and triumph in the face of economic collapse.

A whole raft of policies is needed to build social capital and strengthen communities. These include: creating and protecting shared public spaces; encouraging community-based sustainability initiatives; reducing geographical labour mobility; providing training for green jobs; offering better access to lifelong learning and skills; placing more responsibility for planning in the hands of local communities, and protecting public service broadcasting, museum funding, public libraries, parks and green spaces.

There are some signs that the systematic erosion of social capital is being addressed. Third sector initiatives are beginning to focus specifically on building the resilience of communities. Examples of this include the International Resilience project in Canada, the Young Foundation's Local Well-being Project in the UK and the growing international Transition Town movement.[23] Some support is beginning to emerge from governments' own recognition of the importance of social capital.[24] But state initiatives still remain isolated and sporadic. A systematic policy framework is needed to support social cohesion and build resilient communities.

Dismantling the culture of consumerism

Consumerism has developed partly as a means of protecting consumption-driven economic growth. But it promotes unproductive status competition and has damaging psychological and social impacts on people's lives. The culture of consumerism is conveyed through institutions, the media, social norms and a host of subtle and not so subtle signals encouraging people to express themselves, seek identity and search for meaning through material goods. Dismantling these complex incentive structures requires a systematic attention to the myriad ways in which they are constructed.

Most obviously, there is a need for stronger regulation in relation to the commercial media. Particular concerns exist over the role of commercial advertising to children. Several countries (notably Sweden and Norway) have banned TV advertising to children under 12. The creation of commercial-free zones such as the one established by São Paolo's 'Clean City Law' is one way of protecting public space from commercial intrusion. Another is to provide systematic support for public media through state funding. As the Institute for Local Self-Reliance argues, 'communities should have the right to reserve spaces free of commercialism, where citizens can congregate or exchange ideas on an equal footing'.[25]

There is also a role for stronger trading standards to protect citizens both as workers and as consumers. The Fair Trade initiative is a good example of what can be achieved by companies prepared to act on a voluntary basis. But it isn't yet extensive enough to protect ecological and ethical standards along all supply chains. Or to ensure that these questions register on people's buying behaviours.

Trading standards should also systematically address the durability of consumer products. Planned and perceived obsolescence are one of the worst afflictions of the throw-away society and undermine both the rights and the legitimate interests of people as consumers and citizens.

Unravelling the culture – and changing the social logic – of consumerism will require the kind of sustained and systematic effort it took to put it in place to start with. Crucially though, this effort clearly won't succeed as a purely punitive endeavour. Offering people viable alternatives to the consumer way of life is vital. Progress depends on building up capabilities for people to flourish in less materialistic ways.

Not Utopia

The proposals outlined above flow directly from the analysis in preceding chapters of the book. But many of them sit within longer and deeper debates about sustainability, well-being and economic growth. And some of them at least connect closely with existing concerns of government – for example over resource scarcity, climate change targets, ecological taxation and social well-being.

Part of the aim of this book was to provide a coherent foundation for these policies and help strengthen the hand of government in taking them forward. At the moment, in spite of its best efforts, progress towards sustainability remains painfully slow. And it tends to stall endlessly on the overarching commitment to economic growth. A step change in political will is essential. But that too is possible – once the conflicts that haunt the state are resolved (Chapter 10).

One thing is clear. There is now a unique opportunity for governments in advanced economies – by pursuing these steps – to initiate change of a wider nature. And in the process to demonstrate economic leadership and to champion international action on sustainability. This process must start by developing financial and ecological prudence at home. It must also begin to redress the perverse incentives and damaging social logic that lock us into unproductive status competition.

Above all, there is an urgent need to develop a resilient and sustainable macro-economy that is no longer predicated on relentless consumption growth. The clearest message from the financial crisis of 2008 is that our current model of economic success is fundamentally flawed. For the advanced economies of the western world, prosperity without growth is no longer a utopian dream. It is a financial and ecological necessity.

12

A Lasting Prosperity

A new politics of the common good isn't only about finding
more scrupulous politicians. It also requires a more
demanding idea of what it means to be a citizen, and it
requires a more robust public discourse – one that engages
more directly with moral and even spiritual questions.

Michael Sandel, June 2009[1]

Society is faced with a profound dilemma. To resist growth is to risk
economic and social collapse. To pursue it relentlessly is to endan-
ger the ecosystems on which we depend for long-term survival.

For the most part, this dilemma goes unrecognized in main-
stream policy. It's only marginally more visible as a public debate.
When reality begins to impinge on the collective consciousness, the
best suggestion to hand is that we can somehow 'decouple' growth
from its material impacts. And continue to do so while the economy expands exponentially.

The sheer scale of this task is rarely acknowledged. In a world of
9 billion people all aspiring to western lifestyles, the carbon intensity
of every dollar of output must be at least 130 times lower in 2050
than it is today. By the end of the century, economic activity will
need to be taking carbon out of the atmosphere not adding to it.

Never mind that no-one knows what such an economy looks
like. Never mind that decoupling isn't happening on anything like
that scale. Never mind that all our institutions and incentive

structures continually point in the wrong direction. The dilemma, once recognized, looms so dangerously over our future that we are desperate to believe in miracles. Technology will save us. Capitalism is good at technology. So let's just keep the show on the road and hope for the best.[2]

This delusional strategy has reached its limits. Simplistic assumptions that capitalism's propensity for efficiency will stabilize the climate and solve the problem of resource scarcity are almost literally bankrupt. We now stand in urgent need of a clearer vision, braver policy-making, something more robust in the way of a strategy with which to confront the dilemma of growth.

The starting place must be to unravel the forces that keep us in damaging denial. Nature and structure conspire together here. The profit motive stimulates a continual search for newer, better or cheaper products and services. Our own relentless search for novelty and social status locks us into an iron cage of consumerism. Affluence itself has betrayed us.

Affluence breeds – and indeed relies on – the continual production and reproduction of consumer novelty. But relentless novelty reinforces anxiety and weakens our ability to protect long-term social goals. In doing so it ends up undermining our own well-being and the well-being of those around us. Somewhere along the way, we lose the shared prosperity we sought in the first place.

None of this is inevitable. We can't change ecological limits. We can't alter human nature. But we can and do create and recreate the social world. Its norms are our norms. Its visions are our visions. Its structures and institutions shape and are shaped by those norms and visions. This is where transformation is needed.

In the previous chapter we explored the potential for policy interventions that might kick-start that process. Practical steps that could be taken now to effect the transition to a sustainable economy. This final chapter returns to some of the broader questions raised by this book. It summarizes key elements of the new economy and explores some wider implications of aspiring to prosperity without growth.

Visions of prosperity

The starting point for all of this lies in a vision of prosperity as the ability to flourish as human beings – within the ecological limits of a finite planet.

This vision has undeniably material dimensions. It's perverse to talk about things going well when there's inadequate food and shelter. And that is still the case for billions in the developing world. But it's also plain to see that the simple equation of quantity with quality, of more with better, is false in general. Stuff on its own doesn't help us flourish. And sometimes it can even impede flourishing.

To do well is in part about the ability to give and receive love, to enjoy the respect of our peers, to contribute usefully to society, to have a sense of belonging and trust in the community, to help create the social world and find a credible place in it. In short, an important component of prosperity is the ability to participate meaningfully in the life of society.

These are primarily social and psychological tasks. The difficulty is that consumer society has appropriated a whole range of material goods and processes in their service. We're certainly not the first society to endow mere stuff with symbolic meaning. But we are the first to hand over so much of our social and psychological functioning to materialistic pursuits.

Our sense of identity, our expressions of love, our search for meaning and purpose; even our dreams and desires are articulated through the language of goods. The most fundamental questions we ask about the world and our place in it are played out through consumerism. Unlimited access to material goods stands in for our hopes of freedom. And sometimes even for immortality.

'The human animal is a beast that dies and if he's got money he buys and buys and buys,' says Big Daddy in Tennessee Williams' 1955 play *Cat on a Hot Tin Roof*. 'sAnd I think the reason he buys everything he can is that in the back of his mind he has the crazy hope that one of this purchases will be life ever-lasting.'

Here too delusion thrives. Of course material possessions offer novelty. Of course they comfort us and offer us hope. Of course they connect us to those we love and seek to emulate. But these connections are fickle at best. They are as likely to impede as to facilitate. They fade and distort over time. Their promise is ultimately groundless.

This is the wisdom of the sages from time immemorial. It hasn't weakened over the years. It hasn't been diluted by our material wealth. If anything it has simply become harder and harder to see where real wealth lies. To distinguish what matters from what glitters. We're trapped in a labyrinth of affluence, destined to remain there until the spell is broken. When it is, we're lost.

Two of the most fascinating responses I've received to the ideas in this book make this point in different ways. A hospice manager wrote to me after reading something I'd written on the illusory consolation of consumerism. He described how the diagnosis of terminal illness confronts people directly with this illusion. Those admitted to his care are suffering in all sorts of ways. But amongst the most difficult to negotiate is the crisis of meaning initiated by finding that the consumer dream in which they had been immersed so deeply is of no help to them whatsoever.

A community worker in the mental health sector made a similar point. He described mental breakdown as the equivalent of finding that the emotional and cognitive dimensions of your 'lifestyle package' are breaking up. 'The person in crisis can no longer hold in balance a package of habitat, relationships, work, income, debt [and so on] with the skills, aspirations, meanings and purposes that they have evolved from their childhood.' Putting yourself back together again is as much about building new supportive relationships, new purposes and new meanings as it is about drugs or therapy, he told me.

Of course we're not all confronted imminently with terminal illness or mental breakdown. But we are in the presence of a wider and perhaps more insidious crisis. Two crises, to be exact. The most immediate is the economic one. Unemployment is itself a lifestyle threat. Beyond that immediate threat lies the prospect of ecological crisis.

These days we may be encouraged to define ourselves more through our role as consumers – of goods, of time, of space – than through our role in the production of these things.[3] But work still matters. The pain of unemployment is only partly financial. The loss of a job is a kind of grief. It's still one of those situations that shakes our confidence and threatens our social world.

This risk is heightened in a more unequal world. The stigma of unemployment is played out largely through social comparison. The sharper that comparison the more debilitating the stigma. But in almost every society we've ever known, however equal, role of some kind matters.

It's interesting to find that practical responses to unemployment also point to reconstruction. And in particular to the advantages of simplicity – de-cluttering our lives and focusing on essentials. Consolidating the things that matter to us and reducing unnecessary commitments increases our resilience to external shocks and can even improve our quality of life.

This strategy also points to a powerful arena for personal responses to the dilemma in this book. The possibilities for a voluntary simplicity – sketched in Chapter 9 – are already being explored widely at individual, household and community levels. It's particularly telling that people engaged in these attempts to live more frugally seem happier than those driven by materialism.

Frugality seems alien and perhaps even harsh to our consumerist culture. But as *Financial Times* columnist Harry Eyres points out, its linguistic roots don't lie in sacrifice and hardship at all but in the Latin word for fruit.'To be more precise, the words for frugal in English and Romance languages derive from the Latin frugi, an indeclinable adjective formed from the dative of frux (fruit), and often combined with bonae – so 'to or for the good fruit'. Being 'for the good fruit' means being honest and temperate, dedicated to long-term flourishing: as vital for human beings as for the earth itself.'[4] Eyres alludes here to the second crisis. Climate change and resource scarcity may look like tomorrow's problems. Rainforests may be 'a long way from here'.[5] Extreme poverty may seem like someone else's problem. That's because we view the world myopically. We peer at the future – and at those less fortunate than ourselves – through the wrong end of a powerful telescope. Everything seems so far away.

But in doing so we undermine the prospects for a fair and lasting prosperity. Our task here, as in more immediate crises, is one of reconstruction: individual, social and institutional. Rebuilding prosperity from the bottom up is what's required. And though it may seem daunting, the reality is that we already know a lot about what's needed.

Beyond the provision of nutrition and shelter, prosperity consists in our ability to participate in the life of society, in our sense of shared meaning and purpose and in our capacity to dream. We've become accustomed to pursuing these goals through material means. Freeing ourselves from that constraint is the basis for change.

This won't happen by allowing the market free rein. Nor will it happen simply by exhortation. Individual or community-based action offers a vital avenue for change. But I've argued strongly that attempts by one group to persuade another to forego material wealth are morally suspect. It's like asking people to give up certain social and psychological freedoms.

Progress relies crucially on the construction of credible alternatives. The task is to create real capabilities for people to flourish in less materialistic ways. At a societal scale, this means re-investing in those capabilities: physically, financially and emotionally. In particular, we need to revitalize the notion of public goods. To renew our sense of public space, of public institutions, of common purpose. To invest money and time in shared goals, assets and infrastructures.

It sounds grand, but it needn't be. Green space, parks, recreation centres, sports facilities, libraries, museums, public transportation, local markets, retreats and 'quiet centres', festivals: these are some of the building blocks for a new vision of social participation. Public services have increasingly been seen as a means of looking after those who couldn't afford such services privately. But as the Harvard political philosopher Michael Sandel pointed out in his 2009 Reith Lecture, they 'are also traditionally sites for the cultivation of a common citizenship, so that people from different walks of life encounter one another and so acquire enough of a shared … sense of a shared life that we can meaningfully think of one another as citizens in a common venture.'⁶ This sense of common endeavour is one of the casualties of consumer society. Little wonder that we've lost our connection to others. Little wonder that our sense of the future is hazy and uncommitted. Little wonder that our visions of prosperity have become blind to wider and more durable social goals. We've carved up our sense of shared endeavour – sometimes (think of cars) quite literally – so that we can sell off the pieces at market price just to keep our economies growing. In the process, we leave ourselves bereft of common meaning and purpose.

The challenges here are partly economic – as we've seen – and partly social. The less we share in terms of common endeavour, the more and more powerful the social logic of private affluence becomes. But the loss of common endeavour is an inevitable consequence of economies that feed, almost literally, on privatizing our lives. A different kind of economy is essential for a different kind of prosperity.

Cinderella at the ball?

Let's forget for a moment about growth. Let's concentrate instead on summarizing what we want the economy to deliver. Surprisingly it boils down to a few obvious things. Capabilities for flourishing. The means to a livelihood, perhaps through paid employment. Participation in the life of society. A degree of security. A sense of belonging. The ability to share in a common endeavour and yet to pursue our potential as individual human beings.

It sounds simple enough! But of course, delivering these goals is a huge challenge. Ultimately, that task lies beyond the scope of any single book. Indeed, as Sandel points out in the quote at the start of this chapter, a new citizenship requires a 'robust public discourse'. Opening out that discourse has been one of the key aims of this book.

At the same time, we already know something of what's involved here (Figure 12.1). Some of the issues have already been explored in depth. And some of the conditions for this new economy have been identified. We know for example that resilience matters. Economies which collapse under perturbation directly threaten flourishing. We know that equality matters. Unequal societies drive unproductive status competition and undermine well-being not only directly but also by eroding our sense of shared citizenship. Work still matters in this new economy.[7] It's vital for all sorts of reasons. Apart from the obvious contribution of paid employment to people's livelihoods, work is a part of our participation in the life of society. Through work we create and recreate the social world and find a credible place in it.[8]

We know too that the economy must remain within ecological limits. The limits on economic activity are established in part by

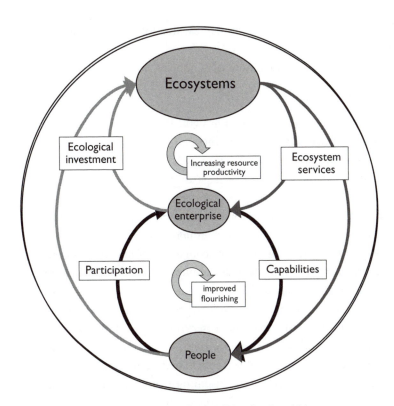

Figure 12.1 A bounded economy of capabilities for flourishing

Source: Author.

the ecology of the planet and in part by the scale of the global population. Together these factors determine equitable levels of resource use and ecological space per person. And within any given economy, these levels indicate the limits of sustainable economic activity.[9]

Such limits need to be coded directly into the organization and working principles of the economy. The identification and valuation of ecosystem services, the greening of the national accounts, the identification of an ecologically-bounded production function:

all of these are likely to be essential to the development of a sustainable economic framework.

Crucially we also know quite a lot about the nature of productive activities in such an economy. In the first place, they have to satisfy three clear operational principles:

- positive contribution to flourishing;
- provision of decent livelihoods;
- low material and energy throughput.

Note that it isn't just the outputs from these activities that must make a positive contribution to flourishing. It's the form and organization of our systems of provision as well. Economic organization needs to work with the grain of community and the long-term social good, rather than against it.

Chapter 8 identified a primitive blueprint for this kind of activity. Community-based 'ecological' enterprises engaged in delivering local services: food, health, public transport, community education, maintenance and repair, recreation; these activities contribute to flourishing, are embedded in community and have the potential to provide meaningful work with a low-carbon footprint.[10]

This Cinderella economy is problematic in conventional terms because its potential for productivity growth is almost negligible. There are very good reasons for this. Human interaction lies at the heart of the 'value proposition' for many such social enterprises. Reducing the labour content makes no sense at all here. In a conventional growth-based economy, this is potentially disastrous. In an economy geared towards providing capabilities for flourishing (including decent work), it is a considerable bonus.

Supporting and expanding this kind of activity doesn't of course mean that this is all the economy is doing. There will still be a role for many of the traditional economic sectors. The resource extraction sectors will diminish in importance as fewer materials are used and more are recycled. But manufacturing, construction, food and agriculture, and more conventional service-based activities such as retail, communication and financial intermediation, will still be important.

Critically though, these sectors will look rather different from the way they do right now. Manufacturing will need to pay more attention to durability and repairability. Construction must prioritize refurbishment of existing buildings and the design of new sustainable and repairable infrastructures. Agriculture will have to pay more attention to the integrity of land and the welfare of livestock. Financial intermediation will depend less on monetary expansion and more on prudent long-term stable investment.

Investment is absolutely vital to the new economy. But the nature of investment will change. From its traditional role as a stimulus to productivity growth, investment will be geared much more towards ecological transformation: increased energy and resource efficiency, renewable and low-carbon technologies and infrastructures, public assets, climate adaptation, ecological enhancement.

Ecological investment calls up a different 'investment ecology'. Capital productivity will probably fall. Returns will be lower and delivered over longer timeframes. Though vital for ecological integrity, some investments may not generate returns in conventional monetary terms. Profitability – in the traditional sense – will be diminished. In a growth-based economy, this is deeply problematic. For an economy concerned with flourishing it needn't matter at all.[11]

The end of capitalism?

Does the Cinderella economy spell the end of capitalism? It's a question that's inevitably been raised many times during the writing of this book and in the responses to the report on which it is based.

For some people, growth and capitalism go together. Growth is functional for capitalism. It's a necessary condition for a capitalistic economy. And for this reason, the idea of doing without growth is seen as tantamount to doing away with capitalism.

Interestingly, we've already seen that this presumption is false in general. As William Baumol and his colleagues have pointed out, not all varieties of capitalism are equal in terms of growth. Admittedly, the ones that don't grow are 'bad' in Baumol's eyes. But the point is that capitalist economies that don't grow can and do exist. Equally there are non-capitalist economies which do grow. Russia, as a case in point, illustrates both these counter-intuitive trends at different times in its chequered history.[12]

So both questions are worth asking. But it's probably a good idea to separate out the question of growth from the question of capitalism. What can we conclude about growth in the new economy? And is it still a capitalist economy?

Taking the growth question first, it's clear that three distinct features of the new economy would tend to slow down growth. The first is the imposition of ecological limits. Of course it depends how firmly these limits are imposed. But if the spirit of this condition were taken seriously, the impact on growth could be substantial.

To see this, let's consider an illustrative scenario in which economic activity is constrained by an allowable carbon budget. The most recent scientific evidence (see Chapter 1) suggests that the scale of this budget between now and 2050 amounts to only 670 billion tonnes of CO_2 or an average emission limit of approximately 18 billion tonnes a year.

Next suppose that this budget was allocated on an equal per capita basis as suggested by the principle of contraction and convergence. This would mean constraining annual CO_2 emissions in the developed economies to around 3 billion tonnes a year. At today's carbon intensity, the allowable GDP would be a little over a quarter of the current GDP of the advanced nations.[13]

Of course higher levels of GDP could be allowable as the carbon intensity of economic activity falls. Even so, this condition represents a serious curtailment of the possibilities for continued growth in the absence of dramatic improvements in carbon intensity. And there is a case to suggest that growth should not even be contemplated until the carbon intensity has improved at least fourfold over its current level if this particular ecological limit is to be achieved.

The second downward pressure on growth in the new economy is exerted by the structural transition to particular kinds of service-based activity. The inherent labour intensity of these sectors suggests that historical rates of productivity growth are simply not sustainable. This means a substantial restriction on the growth potential of the economy.

Finally, the allocation of significant resources to ecological investment would slow down economic growth. By diverting income from consumption to savings and channelling those savings into investments that are less 'productive' in conventional terms, the potential for long-run growth is once again constrained.

It's worth noting that these last two effects – the shift to low labour productivity and the increase in ecological investment are achieved by structural changes in the economy, whereas the first is an externally-imposed constraint on the level of economic activity. Suppose that the structural changes failed to reduce economic activity below the allocated carbon budget. We would then need some other mechanism for slowing down economic output if we wanted to remain within the ecological limit.

This would have to be achieved by reducing other 'factor inputs' to the economy. The most important of these is labour. Reducing overall working hours would reduce the economic output. It would also improve the work-life balance. But crucially if this strategy is not to lead to unemployment (which would go against the all-important condition of fairness), then it would mean sharing out the available work through appropriate working time and employment policies.

In short, the three key macro-economic interventions needed to achieve ecological and economic stability in the new economy are quite specific:

- structural transition to service-based activities;
- investment in ecological assets; and
- working time policy as a stabilizing mechanism.

Conversely, of course, if the structural interventions were effective on their own in reducing carbon emissions below the required threshold, then we could potentially grow the economy (for instance by increasing working hours), provided that overall activity remained within the allowable carbon budget. The way things look right now, that doesn't seem very likely. The growth potential is virtually non-existent. But it could potentially happen.

Turning now to the question of capitalism, we have to settle on a useable definition of the term. Not easy in the first place. But let's start with Baumol's assumption that capitalistic economies are those where ownership and control of the means of production lies in private hands, rather than with the state.

In general terms, this suggests there's a likelihood that the new economy is going to be 'less capitalistic'. To see why, we have to return to the investment ecology called up by the particular needs of ecological transition.

As Chapter 8 reveals, this new investment ecology is likely to change the balance between private and public investment. Longer-term, less productive investments will be essential for sustainability but less attractive to private capital. So the role of the state in protecting these assets is going to be vital. Financing this investment without increasing public sector debt can only be achieved through higher taxation or through the public sector taking some ownership stake in productive assets.

Interestingly, the fairness argument for a larger public stake in ownership was already been rehearsed explicitly during the financial crisis. Why should the taxpayer bear all the risk and reap none of the benefits of underwriting the financial sector?[14]

This same principle is valid when asking about state investment in ecological assets. Not all of these are productive in the conventional sense. But some of them are. Forestry, renewable technologies, local amenities, natural resources: all of these can be revenue-generating. In broader terms, the whole economy is underpinned by the revenue generation potential of ecological services. Public sector investment in these assets should, as a point of principle, seek returns from their productive capabilities.

This looks at first glance like the end of capitalism pure and simple – at least on the definition we identified above. But even Baumol and his colleagues accept that capitalistic economies often have some element of public ownership and control in the means of production.

On closer inspection, it turns out that the whole debate is far too polarized. The reality is that pure state ownership and pure private ownership are just two variants in a quite wide spectrum of possibilities. Perhaps most interesting here are the various models of 'distributed' ownership and control which have a surprisingly long pedigree and are beginning to see something of a resurgence.

Employee ownership, for example, of both small and large enterprises has shown some notable success in recent years, particularly in situations where more traditional capitalism has failed. Likewise there are much more distributed models of public sector control. These examples erode the clear distinctions between capitalism and socialism even under a fairly conventional definition of these terms.[15]

Exploring these options in detail is beyond the scope of this book. The point here is much simpler. The demands of the new economy call on us to revisit and reframe the concepts of productivity, profitability, asset ownership, and control over the distribution of surpluses.

Wherever we end up from this exploration, two things are clear: investment in capital assets remains critically important; and the ecology of this investment looks very different from the way that capital markets work today. In the light of their culpability for the current economic crisis, that may be no bad thing.

Is it still capitalism? Does it really matter? For those for whom it does matter, perhaps we could just paraphrase Star Trek's Spock and agree that it's 'capitalism, Jim. But not as we know it'.

It's about time . . .

The analysis in this book makes much of the potentially disruptive power of relentless consumer novelty. We've seen how the production and consumption of novelty drives the growth economy. Novelty both reinforces and is reinforced by the social logic of consumerism.

We've also seen how this dynamic has been deliberately reinforced by government, because of its role as a driver of growth. The fetishization of novelty is on a par with the fetishization of productivity. Indeed the two things are closely related.

Rejecting this obsession with novelty carries a risk: that novelty itself is demonized, while tradition or conservation – the opposite dimension in the Schwartz values scale (Figure 10.1) – is lionized for its own sake instead. It should be clear that this would be a serious mistake, for exactly the same reasons that it is a mistake to lionize novelty at the expense of tradition.

The tension between these two things exists for a reason. Innovation confers advantages in evolutionary adaptation – allowing us to respond flexibly to a changing environment. This ability is more critical now than ever. But tradition and conservation also serve our long-term interests. In evolutionary terms they allowed us to plan for security by establishing a meaningful sense of connection – both to the past and to the future.

The point is not to reject novelty and embrace tradition. Rather it is to seek a proper balance between these vital dimensions of what it means to be human. A balance that has been lost in our lives, in our institutions and in our economy.[16]

The same point can be made about the concerns over hyper-individualism. To reassert the crucial importance of shared endeavour is not to demonize individual needs or personal dreams. The point is to redress the balance between the self and society – in a way that re-establishes the importance of public goods in working for the benefit of us all.

It's telling that our obsession with novelty bears such a key responsibility for undermining sustainability. Because the fundamental point about sustainability is that it's about time. Relentless novelty undermines our sense of a common endeavour embedded over time. And the social institutions that might correct for this have themselves been undermined by growth.[17]

In short, the cultural drift that reinforces individualism at the expense of society, and supports innovation at the expense of tradition, is a distortion of what it means to be human.

This drift serves and is served by the pursuit of growth. But those who hope that growth will lead to a materialistic Utopia are destined for disappointment. We simply don't have the ecological capacity to fulfil this dream. By the end of the century, our children and grandchildren will face a hostile climate, depleted resources, the destruction of habitats, the decimation of species, food scarcities, mass migrations and almost inevitably war.

So our only real choice is to work for change. To transform the structures and institutions that shape the social world. To articulate a more credible vision for a lasting prosperity.

The dimensions of this task are both personal and societal. The potential for personal – or community-based – action is clear.

Change can be expressed through the way we live, the things we buy, how we travel, where we invest our money, how we spend our leisure time. It can be achieved through our work. It can be influenced by the way we vote and the democratic pressure we exercise on our leaders. It can be expressed through grass-roots activism and community engagement. The pursuit of an individual frugality, a voluntary simplicity, is considerable.

At the same time, the constraints on this possibility as a wide-scale mechanism for social change are abundantly clear. Structural change is essential at the societal level. This book has highlighted three specific dimensions of that task. In the first place, we have to establish ecological bounds on human activity. Secondly, there is an urgent need to fix the illiterate economics of relentless growth. Finally, we must transform the damaging social logic of consumerism.

We've seen how a faulty economics drives and is driven by a distorted social logic. But we've also seen that a different economics is achievable. A better and fairer social logic lies within our grasp. Neither ecological limits nor human nature constrain the possibilities here: only our capacity to believe in and work for change.

Appendix 1
The SDC Redefining Prosperity Project

This book represents the culmination of an extensive inquiry by the UK Sustainable Development Commission into the relationship between sustainability and economic growth. That inquiry was launched in 2003, when the Commission published its landmark report – *Redefining Prosperity* – which challenged government 'fundamentally to rethink the dominance of economic growth as the driving force in the modern political economy, and to be far more rigorous in distinguishing between the kind of economic growth that is compatible with the transition to a genuinely sustainable society and the kind that absolutely isn't'.[1]

The earlier report (itself drawing on a commissioned think-piece[2]) summarized evidence of a 'mismatch' between economic growth, environmental sustainability and human well-being, and called on politicians, policy experts, commentators, business people, religious leaders and NGOs to 'put these issues on their must-get-to-grips-with agenda, rather than defer them endlessly as tomorrow's issues'. The Commission itself kick-started that process with a series of stakeholder workshops (held during the latter part of 2003) to discuss the report's findings.

During 2004 and early 2005, SDC worked closely with government to renew the UK Sustainable Development Strategy. In particular, the Commission itself led the engagement process that resulted in the five Sustainable Development 'principles'. A key element in these principles is the recognition that rather than being an end in itself a 'sustainable economy' should be regarded as the means to reaching the more fundamental goal of a 'strong, healthy and just society' that is 'living within environmental limits'.[3]

Following the launch of the new Strategy, the Commission helped government meet its commitment in *Securing the Future* to explore the concept of well-being and develop new well-being indicators for the UK. In particular, SDC convened a web-based consultation involving several hundred respondents to explore people's perceptions of the relationship between well-being and economic progress.[4]

A key finding from the consultation was that the conventional measure of economic output – the GDP – is widely regarded as an inadequate measure of sustainable well-being, and that there is a need to 'open out political space' within which to address the shortcomings of conventional approaches to prosperity.

In the spirit of 'opening out space', SDC launched a new programme of work on prosperity during 2007 which led to the publication of SDC's report Prosperity without Growth? in early 2009. The programme involved a series of workshops held between November 2007 and April 2008. The workshops entailed intensive discussions based around invited 'think-pieces' on different aspects of prosperity from senior academics, policy-makers, business and NGOs. The essays and the workshops were organized around four related themes.

- **Visions of Prosperity**: identified a variety of different perspectives (historical, economic, psychological, religious) on the meaning and interpretation of prosperity.
- **Economy 'Lite'**: examined international evidence concerning the feasibility of 'decoupling' economic progress from material throughput and environmental impact.

- **Confronting Structure**: addressed the structural drivers associated with continued economic growth and explored the impediments to a 'stationary state economy'.
- **Living Well**: explored the links between the prosperity, economic progress and the recent surge of policy and media interest in happiness and well-being.

It is intended to publish the seminar contributions as an edited collection.[5] In the meantime, draft versions of these papers can be found on the *Redefining Prosperity* website at www.sd-commission.org.uk/pages/redefining-prosperity.html. Together with 'background' reports prepared by SDC staff (and interns) and the extensive literature on growth and sustainability, these essays provide a part of the 'evidence base' from which this study has drawn.

However, this book, which draws extensively on SDC's report, is not intended to be a commentary on the *Redefining Prosperity* workshops. Nor can it really do justice to the wealth of input and advice that we received from those who attended the workshops and contributed think-pieces to them. Rather, *Prosperity without Growth* aims to convey a coherent position on questions of sustainability and economic growth; and to offer some clear recommendations to policy-makers struggling to take concrete steps towards a sustainable economy.

Appendix 2
Towards an Ecological Macro-economics

This annex addresses the broad goal of developing an ecological macro-economics (Chapter 8). Explicitly, it sets out some of the features of a potential macro-economic simulation model that would be capable of testing the relationship between the economy and the demands of sustainability. Specific aims of such a model would be:

- to test the stability of different macro-economies under exogenously defined carbon emission and energy resource constraints;
- to explore the potential for macro-economies with high investment to consumption ratios;
- to explore the potential for macro-economies with high public sector expenditure and investment;
- to explore the stability of macro-economies with low or no consumption growth;
- to explore the stability of macro-economies with low or no aggregate demand growth.

The rationale for exploring different investment-to-consumption ratios and different public-to-private ratios follows from the discussion in Chapter 8. In the first case, it is assumed that changes in investment structure are a pre-requisite for sustainability. In particular, there will be a need to shift investment substantially towards resource productivity, energy efficiency and low-carbon (for example renewable) technologies. Secondly, some of this investment may need to be led by the public sector because of the nature of the required projects. This requirement is discussed in more detail below.

Model development

A simple approach to developing a macro-economic simulation for a national economy would be to take a broadly Keynesian model in which aggregate demand or expenditure (E) given by:

$$E \equiv C + G + I + \bar{X} \qquad (1)$$

(where C = private consumption, G = government expenditure, I = investment and $\bar{X}$ = net exports) is coupled with some form of production function. The simplest (and commonest) such production function is a two-factor Cobb–Douglas function of the form:

$$Y \equiv Y(K, L) = a.K^{\alpha}.L^{(1-\alpha)} \qquad (2)$$

where Y is the aggregate supply (or output), K is capital, L is labour, a is an efficiency factor and $0 < \times < 1$. The fundamental macro-economic identity is then given by the equation:[1]

$$Y(K, L) = C + G + I + \bar{X} \qquad (3)$$

This form of production function has been subject to two main criticisms by ecological economists: firstly that it includes no explicit reference to material resources, and secondly that it assumes perfect substitutability between factors. For these reasons, we may want to adopt a production function that has explicit reference to (say) energy resources (E):

$$Y \equiv Y (K, E, L) \tag{4}$$

where the energy variable accounts separately for fossil resources F and renewable resources R, and the level of renewable resources R in any given year is a function of investment in renewables capacity.

$$R_t \equiv R_t (R_{t-1}, I^R_{t-1}) \tag{5}$$

We may also want to use a production function where the elasticity of substitution is constant but less than 1. The general form of three factor constant elasticity of substitution (CES) production function is given by:

$$Y = a.(\alpha K^\rho + \beta L^\rho + \gamma E^\rho)^{1/\rho} \tag{6}$$

where a is an efficiency factor, $\alpha + \beta + \gamma = 1$ and $\rho = (s - 1) / s$ where s is the elasticity of substitution.

Finally, we might want the production function to be able to 'pick out' improvements in resource productivity, separately from total factor productivity. Our initial requirements for a suitable production function are therefore as follows:

- includes explicit account of energy resources;
- allows for incomplete substitutability between factors;
- accounts for resource productivity improvements.

Additionally, we will probably want our model to reflect the more detailed account of investment structure that lies at the heart of our exploration of alternative macro-economic structures. In fact, this feature of our model could be regarded as the single most important innovation over conventional macro-economic models and is worth setting out in more detail here.

Specifically, we want to distinguish between different forms of investment in two distinct 'dimensions':

- the *target* for investment; and
- the *conditions* of investment.

Firstly, we will probably want to identify different technological targets for investment. For instance, we might want to separate investment dedicated to reducing the demand for resources from conventional business investments aimed at the recapitalization of productive capacity. Energy demand-reducing investments themselves could be of two main types: some devoted to improvements in energy efficiency, some devoted to substitution of renewables (say) for fossil-fuelled technologies. We may also want to consider investments dedicated to improving ecosystem functioning; or investments targeted at climate adaptation.

Our second 'dimension' of investment structure follows on from this consideration of investment demands in different categories. In particular, we need to identify different conditions of investment. For example, investment focused on technological efficiency might well be viewed straightforwardly as a conventional business sector investment. However, investment in ecosystem function or adaptation might more realistically be envisaged as requiring significant public investment. Somewhere between these extremes we might want to consider categories of infrastructure investment which typically require some public sector involvement. The Severn Tidal Barrage may be one potential investment in this category.[2]

Perhaps the most significant difference between different investment conditions is the required rate (and period) of financial return. Whereas typically models of this kind would assume a single rate of return consistent with current commercial conditions, a part of the hypothetical exercise set out here would be to explore the potential for different kinds of investment conditions, which might be more suited to the long-term public sector investments needed to mitigate or adapt to climate change or to restore ecosystem integrity. Taken together, these two dimensions suggest a 'matrix' of investment types, something like the following:[3]

Table A2.1 Potential investment dimensions in the model

	Business sector: commercial rate of return	Public sector: quasi commercial	Public sector: social rate of return
Energy efficiency	I_B^E	I_P^E	I_S^E
Renewable supply	I_B^R	I_P^R	I_S^R
Other capacity	I_B^O	I_P^O	I_S^O
Climate adaptation	I_B^A	I_P^A	I_S^A
Ecosystem maintenance	I_B^M	I_P^M	I_S^M

Source: Author.

The next consideration in developing a model along the lines outlined here would be to connect these different investment types to the production function. In principle, investments should add to capital stocks and the augmented capital stocks will then lead – via the production function – to increased output. In practice, however, connections between our different types of investment and the production function might be of different kinds. For example, energy efficiency investments might lead specifically to changes in the efficiency factor in the production function.

On the one hand, investments in ecosystem maintenance may have no direct impact on the production function at all. They are 'non-productive' in conventional economic terms – whatever their importance for sustainability. On the other hand, they 'soak up' income and have to be included in the model.

Investments in renewable energy (as indicated above) might contribute directly to the E factor in the production function. Some may be less productive (in conventional terms) than others. The Tidal Barrage is an example of such an investment: its value is difficult to capture at commercial rates of return, in part because of the longevity of the investment.

This is not to denigrate these relatively 'unproductive' investments. They may be essential to reduce carbon emissions, to protect ecosystems or to guarantee long-term energy security. The point is that we need to be able to distinguish different categories of investment in terms of three key parameters:

- their contribution to emission limits or resource caps;
- their contribution to aggregate demand; and
- their impact on the productive capacity of the economy.

While 1 and 2 are relatively straightforward to handle exogenously, 3 requires us to establish (within the model) a relationship between the schedule of investments determined by Table A2.1 and the production function.

At the moment, it isn't entirely clear how this is to be achieved. Several possibilities exist. One would be to assume that different forms of investment augment different categories of capital, each of which has a different productivity factor. Another would be to separate out (energy) resources specifically in the production function and relate investment to changes in the availability of those resources. A further avenue would be to aggregate capital into (say) two categories in the production function with different productivity assumptions associated with each.

Broadly speaking, the development of an appropriate production function emerges as one of the key tasks inherent in taking this work forward. One of the difficulties in achieving this lies in the calibration of the model. It isn't clear whether we have enough econometric data, for example, to estimate productivities separately for each of the capital stocks implied by Table A2.1. This may not necessarily matter for a simulation model, but at some level we will want to ensure that business as usual can be calibrated consistently with current trends.

A further aspect that would need to be developed in the model is the ability to map the carbon emission and/or resource implications of different levels and compositions of aggregate demand. The most immediate way to take this forward would be to expand or disaggregate the subcategories of the aggregate demand function (C, G, I, X) and to use an Environmental Input-Output (EIO) model[4] to attribute the carbon emissions and/or energy resource requirements associated with the different demand categories using known carbon intensities. In principle, this attribution exercise could also be used to develop different scenarios with different carbon/resource implications, subject to some obvious caveats about the limitations of the underlying EIO data.[5]

In summary, this brief overview serves to establish the outlines for a macro-economic model that could be used to explore further some of the arguments made in this study. In particular, the enhanced capability to explore different targets of and conditions for investment is key. It will be essential in understanding how to build a different kind of macro-economics, one in which stability is no longer predicated on increasing consumption growth, but emerges through strategic investment in jobs, social infrastructures, sustainable technologies and the maintenance and protection of ecosystems.

List of Figures, Tables and Boxes

Figures

Tables

Boxes

List of Acronyms and Abbreviations

ARRA   American Recovery and Reinvestment Act
CMEPSP   Commission on the Measurement of Economic
           Performance and Social Progress
DMC   Direct Material Consumption
GDP   Gross Domestic Product
GEF   Global Environment Facility
EIO   Environmental Input-Output
IEA   International Energy Agency
IFS   Institute for Fiscal Studies
IMF   International Monetary Fund
IPCC   Intergovernmental Panel on Climate Change
ITPOES   Industry Taskforce on Peak Oil and Energy Security
MEA   Millennium Ecosystem Assessment
NCC   National Consumer Council
NGO   non-government organization
OECD   Organisation for Economic Co-operation and
           Development
PPM   Parts Per Million
RESOLVE   Research group on Lifestyles, Values and
           Environment
SDC   Sustainable Development Commission
SDRN   Development Research Network
SELMA   Surrey Environmental Lifestyle MApping
TARP   Troubled Assets Relief Program

UNDP   United Nations Development Programme
UNEP   United Nations Environment Programme
UNFCCC   United Nations Framework Convention on Climate
          Change
WPA   Works Progress Administration
WRI   World Resources Institute

Notes

1 Prosperity Lost

1   From a speech at Cooper Union, New York, 27 March 2008, online at www.barack-obama.com/2008/03/27/remarks_of_senator_barack_obam_54.php. Accessed 17 July 2009.

2   From the Latin pro- (in accordance with) speres (hopes, expectations).

3   9.2 billion people is the mid-range projection for global population by 2050 according to the United Nations Department of Economic and Social Affairs latest projections (UN 2007). The lower end of the range is 7.8 billion, while the higher end is 11.1 billion.

4   As we discuss in Chapter 6, the GDP is basically an accounting identity that provides a rough measure of 'economic activity' in a region. It can be thought of as simultaneously measuring the sum of all economic output (gross value added), the sum of all incomes (wages and dividends/profits) and the sum of all expenditures (consumption and investment).

5   It's worth pointing out here that a rising GDP will only lead to rising income (per capita GDP) if the economy grows faster than the population does. Indeed an increasing population may in and of itself be regarded as a driver of economic growth. If the population expands but the GDP remains constant, then income levels will fall. GDP must rise at least as fast as population just to conserve people's standard of living in this view.

6   UNDP 2005.

7   This evocative phrase comes from the Indian ecologist Madhav Gadjil (Gadjil and Guha 1995).

8   'Be moderate in prosperity, prudent in adversity', advised Periander, the ruler of Corinth in 600BC; 'Prosperity tries the fortunate; adversity the great', claimed Rose Kennedy, mother of JFK and RFK.

9   On income inequality in developed nations see OECD 2008; on global disparities see UNDP 2005. On the effects of income inequality see Marmot 2005, Wilkinson 2005, Marmot and Wilkinson 2006, Wilkinson and Pickett 2009.

10 See for example: Layard 2005, **nef** 2006, Haidt 2007, Norman et al 2007, Abdallah et al 2008. On 'social recession' see Rutherford 2008. On well-being and inequality see Jackson 2008a.

11 Peak oil is the term used to describe the point at which global oil output reaches a peak, before entering a terminal decline.

12 For fuller discussion of Malthus' *Essay* and its relevance to sustainable development see Jackson 2002, 2003 and references therein.

13   Maddison 2008.

14   See Chapter 5 for more details.

15   Meadows et al 1972; Meadows et al 2004.

16   The G20 group warned of the threat of rising oil prices to global economic stability as early as 2005 (www.independent.co.uk/news/business/news/g20-warns-of-oil-price-threat-to-global-economic-stability-511293.html). The fears peaked in July 2008 when oil prices reached $147 a barrel. Though they fell sharply in the following months, the long term concern is widely acknowledged. See for example the IEA's World Energy Outlook (IEA 2008) and the report of the Industry Taskforce on Peak Oil and Energy Security (ITPOES 2008).

17   Source data are from *The Economist* dollar-based Commodity Price Index (accessed at www.economist.com).

18   On mineral reserves and extraction rates see Turner et al 2007, especially Tables 1–3. See also Cohen 2007.

19   McKibben 2007, p18. On sources v. sinks see for example Common and Stagl 2006, Pearce and Turner 1990, Turner et al 2007.

20   Stern 2007, p xv. The widely cited conclusion was that 'if we don't act, the overall costs of and risks of climate change will be equivalent to losing at least 5% [and perhaps as high as 20%] of global GDP each year, now and forever'. By contrast, the report suggested, 'the costs of action can be limited to around 1% of GDP each year'. We'll return to this conclusion in Chapter 5.

21   Strictly speaking this target should be expressed as 550 ppm CO_2e (carbon dioxide equivalent). Climate change is caused by a variety of greenhouse gases including carbon dioxide, methane, nitrous oxide and various other industrial gases. The most important greenhouse gas is carbon dioxide and greenhouse gas concentrations and emissions are often converted to carbon dioxide equivalents (CO_2e).

22   A 2°C temperature rise may not sound very much. But this is a global annual average and already implies much higher local and seasonal increases and significant climate change impacts. But 2°C is the threshold agreed by the EU as defining the difference between acceptable and dangerous climate change. Some observers – including the Alliance of Small Island States – are calling for a lower threshold of 1.5°C.

23   This 85 per cent target comes from the IPCC's Fourth Assessment Report (2007). In Chapter 5 we'll use this target to work out exactly how much technological improvement is necessary for different levels of economic growth and find out just how demanding stabilizing climate change could be.

24   See Allen et al 2009; Meinshausen et al 2009. Of the existing stabilization scenarios, James Hansen's 350 ppm target offers the best hope of preventing dangerous climate change because it's based on a lower emissions budget.

25   For useful summaries of these impacts see for example Brown 2008 (Chapter 2–6), McKibben 2007 Victor 2008a, (Chapter 1), Monbiot 2006, Northcott 2007, Porritt 2005 (Chapter 3), Booth 2004 (Chapters 4 & 5), GND 2008, IEA 2008, ITPOES 2008, Lynas 2004, Stern 2007, amongst many others, including of course the Sustainable Development Commission's own report on *Redefining Prosperity* (SDC 2003) and the very useful Millennium Ecosystem Assessment (MEA 2005).

26   MEA 2005, TEEB 2008.

27   The average annual growth in global GDP in the last 50 years is just over 3 per cent per year. If the economy grows at the same rate over the next 91 years, it will be $(1.031)91 = 16.1$ times bigger than it is today.

28   This is the UN's mid-range population estimate for 2050 (see note 2).

29   Typical EU income in 2007 was $27,000 per capita (in $2000) dollars. At 2 per cent average growth per annum, this reaches $63,000 by 2050. For 9 billion people to

achieve this income, the global economy must be $573 trillion dollars. In 2007 it was $39 trillion. This means that the economy in 2050 is 570/39 = 14.6 times the size it is today. Assuming that population is stabilized by 2050 and that any further growth is due to income growth at the same 2 per cent average rate, then by 2100 the economy is (1.02)50 = 2.7 times bigger than it is in 2050, that is, around 2.7 x 15 = 40 times bigger than it is today.

2 The Age of Irresponsibility

1   Taken from a speech by the British Prime Minister to the United Nations in New York, Friday 26 September 2008, see: www.ft.com/cms/s/0/42cc6040-8bea-11dd-8a4c-0000779fd18c.html. Accessed 17 July 2009.

2   Soros 2008, p159.

3   On IMF prediction, see World Economic Outlook (IMF 2008), p *xiv*; for OECD see http://news.bbc.co.uk/1/hi/business/7430616.stm; on 'financial markets' see Soros 2008; on 'stagflation' see http://news.bbc.co.uk/1/hi/business/127516.stm; on food riots see (for example) http://news.bbc.co.uk/1/hi/world/7384701.stm.

4   Robert Peston, 'The £5,000 billion bailout', BBC Online: www.bbc.co.uk/blogs/thereporters/robertpeston/2008/10/the_5000bn_bailout.html. Meeting in London in April 2009, the G20 nations agreed an additional $1.1 trillion support through the international financial institutions.

5   The London G20 statement can be found online at http://news.bbc.co.uk/go/pr/fr/-/1/hi/business/7979606.stm.

6   See for example: www.guardian.co.uk/business/2008/dec/17/goldmansachs-executivesalaries.

7   See Hall and Soskice 2001. The authors also identified a group of countries which clustered together in a form they called Mediterranean capitalism.

8   Most recent statistics on UK consumer debt taken from 'Debt Facts and Figures – Compiled 1 February 2009' published by Credit Action, online at www.creditaction.org.uk/debt-statistics.html.

9   Source data are from the Office for National Statistics (accessed at www.statistics.gov.uk).

10 Formally known as the public sector net debt, the national debt measures the 'financial liabilities issued by the public sector less its holdings of liquid financial assets, such as bank deposits' (see for example the ONS factsheet on Government and Public Sector Debt Measures, online at www.statistics.gov.uk/about/methodology_by_theme/public_sector_accounts/downloads/debt_history.pdf.

11 On rising inequality and increasing relative poverty in the UK – and in other developed nations – see OECD 2008. The report notes that 'The gap between rich and poor and the number of people below the poverty line have both grown over the past two decades. The increase is widespread, affecting three-quarters of OECD countries. The scale of the change is moderate but significant.' In the first five years of the 21st century, however, the report reveals that income inequality fell in the UK.

12 On military spending see Harrison 1988, Table 3. Note that the measure of national income used here is the Net National Product which differs slightly from the GDP. On US government debt see Mankiw 2007, p433.

13 See the CIA World Factbook, online at www.cia.gov/library/publications/the-world-factbook/rankorder/2079rank.html. See also IMF data available online at www.statistics.gov.uk/IMF.

14 See *The Economist*, Race to the Bottom, 13 February 2009, online at www.economist.com/daily/news/displaystory.cfm?story_id=13129949.

15 Soros 2008, p81 et seq.

16 See Greenspan 2008.

17 In particular, Greenspan himself and several other free-market economists believed that self-interest would restrain financial institutions from taking risks!

18 *The Economist*, 'A short history of modern finance', 18 October 2008, p98.

19 Barack Obama (amongst others) has offered a convincing historical perspective on this trend. See, for example, the speech at Coopers Union, New York on 27 March 2008, online at www.barackobama.com/2008/03/27/remarks_of_senator_barack_obama_54.php.

20 Citibank quote is from the *Financial Times*, 10 July 2007.

21 Citigroup had to be rescued by the US government on 23 November 2008, with an injection of $20 billion and the underwriting of more than $300 billion in risky assets.

22 *Financial Times*, 28 October 2008, 'World Will Struggle to Meet Oil Demand', online at www.ft.com/cms/s/0/e5e78778-a53f-11dd-b4f5-000077b07658.html.

3 Redefining Prosperity

1 From Zia Sardar's 'think-piece' for the Sustainable Development Commission (Sardar 2007).

2 A survey of these different visions of prosperity was one of the aims of the SDC's *Redefining Prosperity* project (Appendix 1).

3 See in particular the 'think-piece' contributions to the SDC project from Tim Kasser (2007), Avner Offer (2007), John O'Neill (2008), Hilde Rapp (2007), Zia Sardar (2007) and Kate Soper (2008), online at www.sd-commission.org.uk/pages/redefining-prosperity.html.

4 There are strong resonances here with Mary Douglas' (2006 (1976)) understanding of consumers as attempting to 'create the social world and find a creditable place in it'; and also with Peter Townsend's groundbreaking analysis of poverty, in which he argued that people can be said to be poor when their resources are 'so seriously below those commanded by the average individual or family that they are in effect, excluded from ordinary living patterns, customs and activities' (Townsend 1979, p31). Rather than being about money or material possessions as such, Townsend claimed, poverty is about the inability to participate actively in society.

5 Sardar 2007.

6 Brown and Garver 2008.

7 See for example Dolan et al 2006 & 2008, Layard 2005, Jackson 2008a.

8 From a poll undertaken for the BBC by GfK NOP during October 2005. Results available at: http://news.bbc.co.uk/nol/shared/bsp/hi/pdfs/29_03_06_happiness_gfkpoll.pdf.

9 'The living standard' (Sen 1984) was originally published in Oxford Economic Papers, an economics journal, but is usefully reproduced (Sen 1998) along with excerpts from some of Sen's later essays on the subject in Crocker and Linden (1998). See also Sen 1985, 1999.

10 Actually there is some disagreement as to whether the concept of utility is about the 'satisfactions' received from commodities or the desires for them (Sen 1998, p290), but this distinction need not concern us here.

11 This distinction led the economist Kelvin Lancaster (1966) to develop a sophisticated theory of 'attributes' which attempted to get round the difficulty that commodities are not the same as satisfactions. There is also an extensive and useful discussion of the relationship between satisfaction and material commodities in modern needs theories; see

for example: Doyal and Gough 1991, Ekins and Max Neef 1992, Jackson et al 2004, Max Neef 1991.

12   For a discussion of trends over time in the UK see Jackson and Marks 1999, Jackson and Papathanasopoulou 2008.

13   See Anderson 1991 for a concise analysis of the limitations of GDP and a discussion of alternative economic indicators. See for example Jackson and McBride 2005 for a survey of the literature on adjusted economic indicators – or green GDP. More recently, this issue has been addressed in depth by the Sen/Stiglitz Commission on the Measurement of Economic Performance and Social Progress set up by President Sarkozy and due to report shortly (Stiglitz 2008).

14   Defensive expenditures are those incurred as a result of the need to 'defend' against activity elsewhere in the economy. The costs of car accidents and cleaning up oil spills have this character. Positional expenditures can be seen as a special case, in which expenditures – on positional goods – are necessary mainly to defend our social position. Though these expenditures make sense at an individual level it is perverse to count them cumulatively as an addition to well-being.

15   Data on each of these countries can be found in Ruut Veenhoven's 'World Happiness Database' available on the web at: www2.eur.nl/fsw/research/happiness.

16   Worldwatch Institute, State of the World 2008, Fig 4.1. Redrawn from data in Inglehart and Klingemann 2000.

17   This was pointed out in two of the think-piece contributions to the SDC's *Redefining Prosperity* project (O'Neill 2008; Ormerod 2008).

18   Kahnemann and Sugden 2005.

19   Statisticians say the two scales have different 'orders of integration'. For a more detailed discussion of this issue see Ormerod 2008.

20   Offer 2006, 2007.

21   Although this insight into a particular human frailty does have interesting lessons for government policy which I shall return to later.

22   Sen 1998, p295.

23   And also with Townsend's (1979) concept of poverty.

24   In *Development as Freedom* (Sen 1999) for example, he argues explicitly that freedom is both the means and the end of development.

25   Robeyns and van der Veen 2007.

26   Nussbaum 2006.

4 The Dilemma of Growth

1   Baumol et al 2007, p 23.

2   For more insight on the symbolic role of consumer goods see for example: Baudrillard 1970, (1976) (1998); Bauman 2007; Douglas and Isherwood 1996; Dittmar 1992; McCracken 1990. On its relevance for sustainable consumption see Jackson in particular 2005a & 2005b, 2006b, 2008b.

3   Berger 1969.

4   Belk et al 2003.

5   Douglas 2006, (1976).

6   For a more detailed exploration of Indian attitudes to the environment, see for example Mawdsley 2004.

7   As anthropologist Grant McCracken (1990) describes it.

8   Support for the relevance of income as a factor in well-being also emerged from Defra's recent well-being survey (Defra 2007). Though not the most important influence, income clearly emerged as a contributing factor in the survey.

9   Evidence of the importance of relative income was first highlighted by Richard Easterlin (1972). For more recent confirmation see Dolan et al 2006 and Dolan et al 2008, Easterlin 1995,.

10 Offer 2006.

11 Data from the Health Survey for England, Madhavi Bajekal, National Centre for Social Research, cited in Marmot 2005. See also Marmot and Wilkinson 2005, Wilkinson 2006.

12 The most notable exception to the rule that higher social grades show higher satisfaction is in the domain of community, where the lower social grades profess themselves more satisfied on average than the higher grades.

13 Offer 2006. Some have used this argument to explain the life-satisfaction paradox mentioned in Chapter 3.

14 See for example James 2007, Layard 2005, **nef** 2006.

15 Wilkinson and Pickett 2009.

16 Data are taken from statistics compiled for the Human Development Report, available online at the UNDP website: http://hdr.undp.org/en/statistics/.

17 There are some notable recent attempts to develop this field of study, in particular Hans Rosling's interactive GAPMINDER project, online at www.gapminder.org.

18 There is a strong correlation (the R2 value on the graph) between per capita GDP and life expectancy; but a relatively weak dependency (the x-coefficient) on income growth.

19 Franco et al 2007, p1374.

20 In the conventional model, resources are often excluded from the equation and the main dependencies are thought to be on labour, capital and technological innovation.

21 For more detail on (and critique of) this underlying model see for example: Ayres 2008, Booth 2004, Common and Stagl 2006, Victor 2008b.

22 IFS 2009.

23 It's important to qualify this claim with the recognition that short-run fluctuations in the growth rate are an expected feature of growth-based economies and there are some feedback mechanisms which do bring the economy back into equilibrium. For instance, as unemployment rises, wages fall and labour becomes cheaper. This encourages employees to employ more people and increases output again. But increasing labour productivity without increasing output doesn't have this characteristic.

24 The terminology of 'de-growth' (*décroissance* in French) emerged in France in 2006. As a technical term it refers to (planned) reductions in economic output. As a social movement it seems to have convened a wider array of interests around political and social change (see for example Baycan 2007, Fournier 2008, Latouche 2007, Sippel 2009).

5 The Myth of Decoupling

1   From a speech by Jean-Claude Trichet, President of the European Central Bank to a conference in Barcelona, in June 2008; as reported in *The Times*, online at http://business.timesonline.co.uk/tol/business/columnists/article4092764.ece.

2   IPCC 2007, Table SPM.6.

3   IPCC 2007, p4.

4   See Figure 25 in EIA 2008.

5   Data from Table E1G in the *International Energy Annual 2006* (EIA 2008).

6   Data from Table E1G in the *International Energy Annual 2006* (EIA 2008).

7   Measured as Direct Material Consumption (DMC) per unit of GDP, indexed to 1975. Data for Austria, Germany, Japan and the Netherlands taken from WRI 2000, Annex 2. Points for 1997–2000 estimated using linear extrapolations (over the period 1975–1996). Data for the UK from Sheerin 2002. DMC takes domestically extracted

resources, adds in resource imports and subtracts resource exports. It doesn't account for the resources 'embedded' in finished and semi-finished goods.

8 Source data for individual nations taken from EIA 2008, Table H1GCO$_2$, 'World Carbon Dioxide Emissions from the Combustion and Flaring of Fossil Fuels per Thousand Dollars of Gross Domestic Product Using Market Exchange Rates'. World carbon intensity is calculated using total emissions data in Table H1CO2 in the EIA database and world GDP data (at constant 2000 prices, market exchange rates) taken from IMF (2008), online at www.imf.org/external/pubs/ft/weo/2008/02/weodata/index.aspx.

9 Source data for the period 1980–2006 for fossil fuels taken from EIA 2008, Table 1.8; data for 2007 estimated using linear extrapolation over the period 2000–2006. Data for CO$_2$ emissions taken from EIA 2008, Table H1CO2.

10 Source data as for Figure 5.1, note 7, except that linear extrapolations for Germany are based on a shorter period: 1991–1996.

11 These numbers are taken from Druckman and Jackson 2008, based on results from the Surrey Environmental Lifestyle Mapping (SELMA) framework. Similar results for the UK have been reported from other studies including Carbon Trust 2006, Defra 2008, Helm 2008a, Jackson et al 2006, Jackson et al 2007.

12 Source data from the US Geological Survey Statistical Summaries. Online since 2000 at http://minerals.usgs.gov/minerals/pubs/commodity/statistical_summary/index.html#myb. Available from the US Bureau of Mines data archive for earlier years: http://minerals.usgs.gov/minerals/pubs/usbmmyb.html.

13 See for example: 'Digging for victory', *The Economist*, 15 November 2008, p69.

14 It's also true that efficiency (technological progress) is itself a driver of economic growth. The problem of 'rebound' is discussed further in Chapter 6.

15 This relationship is sometimes called the Environmental Kuznets Curve after the economist Simon Kuznets who proposed that a similar inverted U-shaped relationship exists between incomes and income inequality. Evidence of the income Kuznets curve is also difficult to find (OECD 2008). For more discussion of the Environmental Kuznets Curve hypothesis, see for example Grossman and Krueger 1995, Jackson 1996, Rothman 1998.

16 Booth 2004, p73 et seq.

17 Ayres 2008, p292.

18 See Ehrlich 1995 (1968).

19 See for example: APPG 2007.

20 It follows from the IPAT equation that the average annual growth in emissions r_i over any given period satisfies the equation: $1+r_i = (1+r_p) \times (1+r_a) \times (1+r_t)$, where r_p is the average population growth rate, r_a is the average growth in per capita income and r_t is the average growth (or decline) in carbon intensity. Multiplying out the factors on the right hand side of the equation gives the approximate 'rule of thumb': $r_i \approx r_p + r_a + r_t$. This approximation works very well for small percentage changes (a few per cent per annum). It needs more care in application when the rates of change exceed this. It can also be shown that when per capita income and population rates are positive, the estimated technology improvement rate is always slightly higher than the actual rate. So the rule of thumb provides a robust indication of a sufficient rate of improvement to achieve target reductions.

21 The error term in calculating the technological improvement rate using the rule of thumb is less than 0.001 per cent. Rates of change for r_a were calculated using world GDP data (at constant 2000 prices, market exchange rates) taken from IMF (2008), available online at www.imf.org/external/pubs/ft/weo/2008/02/weodata/index.aspx.

22 IPCC estimates (Table SPM.6) that to stabilize atmospheric carbon at between 445 and 490 ppm (resulting in an estimated global temperature 2 to 2.4°C above the pre-indus-

trial average) emissions would need to peak before 2015, with 50–85 per cent reductions on 2000 levels by 2050. The equivalent (pro-rata) target range for carbon dioxide emissions in 2050 would be somewhere between 3560 and 11,880 $MtCO_2$. Here it is assumed that global emissions today are around 30,000 $MtCO_2$ and that we would want to achieve something towards the lower end of that range, say 4000 $MtCO_2$ – partly because the target is to get down to the lower end of the range of atmospheric concentrations, and partly because we might need reductions in CO_2 to do more work, particularly at the margin, than reductions in other greenhouse gases.

23   The UN low, middle and high estimates for population in 2050 are 7.8 billion, 9.2 billion and 10.8 billion (UN 2007).

24   The rule of thumb here gives: 4.9 + 0.7 + 3.6 = 9.2 per cent, but the error term is slightly larger (0.4 per cent). The actual value is a little over 8.8 per cent.

25   Calculations for this study, using data from EIA 2008, IMF 2008, UN 2007 and targets from IPCC 2007.

26   Though the numbers here refer to carbon emissions, the same basic arithmetic applies when considering finite resource throughputs, scarce forestry resources or biodiversity impacts.

27   IEA 2008. Executive summary available online at www.iea.org/WEO2008.

28   Nuclear power could certainly be added to this theoretical list. But even if the issues around waste disposal and decommissioning could adequately be addressed, its contribution would be severely limited by resource constraints in the context of a continually expanding global demand (SDC 2006b).

29   Ekins 2008. See also Ekins 2000, Jackson 1996, von Weizsacker et al 1998.

30   Stern 2007, pxvi.

31   On Stern's revised estimate see: 'Cost of tackling global climate change doubles, warns Stern', *The Guardian* 26 June 2008, online at www.guardian.co.uk/environment/ 2008/jun/26/climatechange.scienceofclimatechange. For PwC estimate see 'Time for deeds not words', *The Guardian*, 3 July 2008, online at www.guardian.co.uk/ environment/2008/jul/03/carbonemissions.climatechange. See also the Climate Change Committee's first report (CCC 2008) which has costs broadly in line with the original Stern estimate.

32   Stern 2007, Table 9.3, p262.

33   Helm 2009.

34   Helm 2008b, 225–228. See also Nordhaus 2007.

35   A critical issue here is the extent to which climate change investments do or do not enhance economic productivity. While investments which improve resource productivity (for example) may offer positive returns, and investments in renewables could be cost-saving, particularly as fossil fuel costs rise, enhanced early investments in renewables, in carbon capture and storage (CCS) and in ecosystem protection may not always be productive in a narrow economic sense (see Chapter 8 and Appendix 1).

6 The 'Iron Cage' of Consumerism

1   Extract from 'Pack behaviour' an article about the vulnerability of banking giant Santander, *The Economist*, 15 November 2008, p96.

2   Numerous commentators over the course of the last century or more have picked up on this anxiety, both as an epidemiological fact and as a systemic aspect of modern life. Notable contributions include: Alain de Botton 2004, Emile Durkheim 1903, Fred Hirsch 1977, Oliver James 1998, 2007, Kierkegaard 1844, Jonathon Rutherford 2008, Tibor Scitovski 1976.

3   The term 'iron cage' was first coined by Max Weber (1958) in *The Protestant Ethic and the Spirit of Capitalism* to refer to the bureaucracy that he saw emerging as a constraint on individual freedoms in capitalism. But there are also elements in Weber's work where he uses the same concept to characterize consumerism itself as the following quote shows: 'In Baxter's view, the care for external goods should only lie on the shoulders of the "saint like a light cloak, which can be thrown aside at any moment". But fate decreed that the cloak should become an iron cage.' (Weber 1958, p181). This theme has been picked up and applied to consumerism more explicitly by sociologist George Ritzer (2004).

4   Hall and Soskice 2001.

5   More specifically, the categories are: 'state-guided capitalism, in which government tries to guide the market most often by supporting particular industries that it expects to become "winners"; oligarchic capitalism, in which the bulk of the power and wealth is held by a small group of individuals and families; big firm capitalism, in which the most significant economic activities are carried out by established giant enterprises; entrepreneurial capitalism, in which a significant role is played by small, innovative firms.' Baumol et al 2007, p60 et seq.

6   Ibid.

7   Oddly for a system which borrows its name from it, the term 'capital' is confusing in the sheer variety of meanings given to it within that system. Buildings and machinery are 'capital goods' sometimes called physical capital. Financial capital is used to refer to reserves of money (savings for instance), which of course can be used to invest in capital goods. And confusingly the term 'capital' is also used to refer to the accumulation of wealth or assets – which include both financial and physical capital. In simple terms, capital simply means a stock of something. This broader meaning has been taken (for example Porritt 2005) as the basis for arguing that there are things called natural capital (stocks of resources, say), human capital (stocks of skills) and social capital (stocks of community).

8   For a more formal exposition of the basic economics here see for example Anderton 2000, Begg et al 2003, Hall and Papell 2005. For its relevance to the environment see Booth 2004, Daly 1996, Jacobs 1991, Victor 2008b.

9   This is probably the one place where the standard economic model pays any attention to the physical reality of keeping activity going. The gradual degradation of capital goods is foreseen explicitly by the laws of thermodynamics.

10   It's important to note that capital is not the only requirement here. Management practice, organizational changes and training are also critical in increasing productivity in the firm (for example Freeman and Shaw 2009).

11   The most common way to increase capital productivity has been to increase the capital utilization factor, making sure that machinery and buildings are fully utilized, for example through continuous batch processing and other process design changes (see for example Lientz and Rea 2001, Reay et al 2008).

12   For an exploration of national trends in labour productivity and their impact on growth see Maddison 2007, p304 et seq, Timmer et al 2007. For a discussion on productivity at firm level see Freeman and Shaw (2009) and for UK firms see Oulton 1996.

13   Data on labour productivities and growth rates are taken from the EU KLEMS project (for example Timmer et al 2007). Interestingly, the productivity growth in the second period would have been much lower (1.4 per cent per year) if not for the ten new accession states.

14   Timmer et al 2007, pp6–7. The difference is 'almost' entirely due to changes in productivity because capital productivity also had some impact. Multi-factor productivity in Figure 6.2 is a combination of both.

15 The EU 15 countries are: Austria, Belgium, Denmark, Finland, France, Germany, Greece, Ireland, Italy, Luxembourg, the Netherlands, Portugal, Spain, Sweden and the UK.

16 The hypothesis that technological change is a key driver of growth is a key component of the so-called Solow–Swan growth model. Production output depends on three so-called 'factors of production': labour, capital and materials. Early growth theories suggested that growth could be predicted mainly on the basis of how much labour and capital was available. But these models failed to account for the 'residual' growth after expansions in capital and labour had been factored in. In 1956, economists Robert Solow and Trevor Swan independently argued that this residual could be explained by technological progress (Solow 1956, Swan 1956).

17 See Sorrell 2007 for an in-depth discussion of the rebound effect.

18 See Jackson 1996, Chapter 1, for a more detailed discussion of this point; see also Georgescu-Roegen 1972; Daly 1996.

19 See Schumpeter 2008 (1934), 1994 (1950), (1954). For more detailed discussion of the relevance of Schumpeter's work in this debate see Booth 2004, Bouder 2008, Rutherford 2008, Wall 2008.

20 Carlota Perez describes how creative destruction has given rise to successive 'epochs of capitalism'. Each technological revolution 'brings with it, not only a full revamping of the productive structure, but eventually a transformation of the institutions of governance, of society, and even of ideology and culture' (Perez 2002, p25).

21 For an extensive recent treatment of creative innovation as the 'origin of wealth' see Beinhocker 2007.

22 For example Lewis and Bridger 2001.

23 For more empirical evidence see for example Csikszentmihalyi and Rochberg-Halton 1981.

24 Belk 1988.

25 Dichter 1964.

26 See for example Belk et al 1989, Armstrong and Jackson 2008; Arndt et al 2004, Jackson and Pepper 2009.

27 Veblen 1998 (1898); Hirsch 1977. See also Baudrillard 1998 (1970); Bourdieu 1984.

28 Campbell 2004, 2005.

29 McCracken 1990, Chapter 7.

30 Cushman 1990, p599.

31 Booth 2004, Chapter 2.

7 Keynesianism and the 'Green New Deal'

1 Achim Steiner, Executive Director of UNEP commenting on the launch of UNEP's Green Economy Initiative in the *Independent on Sunday*, 12 October 2008.

2 'The green lining to this chaos', leading article in the *Independent on Sunday*, 12 October 2008.

3 See for example Mankiw 2007, Chapter 11, for a formal explanation of this process.

4 This is why the UK government opted for a reduction in VAT rather than in income tax in the fiscal stimulus package set out in the 2008 Pre-Budget Report (HMT 2008). Increases in income tax are more likely to be put away as savings than reductions in tax on consumables. Even so, the Treasury estimated that up to a half of the £12.5 billion stimulus through reduced VAT might end up as a reduction in credit card bills rather than an increase in spending.

5 In a definitive study of 1930s fiscal policy, US economist Cary Brown argues that this

was largely because the federal public spending stimulus was undermined by spending cuts and tax hikes at local and state level.

6   Paul Krugman, 'Franklin Delano Obama?', *New York Times*, 10 November 2008.

7   'Finding a way out of the Economic Crisis', 14 November 2008. BBC reporter Nick Robinson's newslog and interview with Paul Krugman is online at www.bbc.co.uk/blogs/nickrobinson/2008/11/finding_a_way_out_of_the_economic_crisis.html.

8   Cited in 'Global Green New Deal – UNEP Green Economy Initiative'. Press Release at London Launch, 22 October 2008, online at www.unep.org/ Documents. Multilingual/Default.asp?DocumentID=548&ArticleID=5957&l=en.

9   Globally, environmental industries are worth $4 trillion dollars already and are likely to expand by at least 50 per cent in the next decade.

10   GND 2008, p3.

11   In a paper published in 1997, ecological economists Robert Costanza and his colleagues estimated that the value of global ecosystem services amounted to around $33 trillion per year. At the time, the global GDP was only $18 trillion per year (Costanza et al 1997).

12   World Energy Outlook 2008 (www.iea.org/Textbase/npsum/WEO2008SUM.pdf). Reference scenario (business as usual) investment is $26 trillion. Achieving a 550 ppm stabilization would cost $4.1 trillion more than this, and achieving a 450 ppm stabilization would add another $5.1 trillion to this cost.

13   Nicholas Stern's (2007) review on the economics of climate change famously argued that for as little as 1 per cent of GDP we could save ourselves costs as high as 25 per cent of GDP later on.

14   DB 2008, p4.

15   PERI 2008, p10.

16   See Gough 1979, Chapter 6 and Appendix A.2.

17   See for example *The Guardian*, 30 December 2008, online at www.guardian.co.uk/business/2008/dec/30/general-motors-gmac.

18   'US Porn Industry seeks multi-billion dollar bailout'. *Daily Telegraph*, 8 January 2009, online at www.telegraph.co.uk/news/newstopics/howaboutthat/4165049/US-porn-industry-seeks-multi-billion-dollar-bailout.html.

19   The American Recovery and Reinvestment Act of 2009 – Discussion Draft, online at http://appropriations.house.gov/pdf/RecoveryReport01-15-09.pdf.

20   Both the US and the UK car industry support packages have elements of this. £1 billion of the UK package is for investment in the development of green vehicles. See for example: http://news.bbc.co.uk/1/hi/uk_politics/7853149.stm.

21   HSBC 2009. *A Climate for Recovery*[81] – *The Colour of Stimulus Goes Green*[81], HSBC Global Research.

22   Online at http://english.mosf.go.kr/issues/policyissues/economic_view.php?sect=laws_policies&pmode=&cat=&sn=6280&page=1&SK=ALL&SW#4.

23   The American Recovery and Reinvestment Act of 2009 – Discussion Draft, online at http://appropriations.house.gov/pdf/RecoveryReport01-15-09.pdf.

24   Some commitments are over shorter periods of 1–2 years but others – including the large US commitments – are over a considerably longer timeframe.

25   Bowen et al 2009; SDC 2009b.

26   For example, a reduction in the VAT charged on consumer goods was the single biggest element in the UK stimulus package announced in November 2008 (HMT 2008).

27   The Keynesian multiplier effect states that for each dollar of government spending, a greater amount – typically 2 to 3 times the amount of government spending – is added to incomes. The formula to calculate the government spending multiplier is m = (1-

MPC)-1, where MPC is the marginal propensity to consume. When MPC is 0.6, then the multiplier is given by m = 1/(1-0.6) = 1/0.4 = 2.5. For a derivation of the formula see for example Mankiw 2007, p284. Note however that the result only holds as long as taxes are held constant. So additional government purchases have to be funded – at least initially – through increased debt.

28 The external debt refers to debts held overseas, see Chapter 2, Box 2.1.

29 On 25 March 2009, a 'gilt' auction failed in the UK for only the fourth time since 1986. Though not in itself an indication of a collapse, this failure was a worrying indication of increasing difficulty (and cost) in funding UK public debt.

30 'I will if you will', Report of the UK Sustainable Consumption Roundtable (Sustainable Development Commission (2006).

31 OECD 2008.

32 Though most people associate Keynes's name with using public sector money to stimulate economic demand in times of crisis, his influence on today's macro-economics runs much deeper than that and provides the basis for the idea that high-street spending is the key to economic stability. As James Ahiakpor (2001) points out: 'Fundamental to Keynes's development of the multiplier concept is the view that insufficient consumption spending is the principal limitation on the growth of aggregate demand, hence, income and employment creation.'

33 GND 2008, p27.

8 Ecological Macro-economics

1   Booth 2004, p153.

2   Macro-economics is, quite simply, the study of the economy as a whole. In conventional economics it's distinguished from micro-economics, which studies individual markets and or individual decision-makers.

3   Mill 1857, cited in Daly 1996, Chapter 1; Keynes 1930.

4   Daly 1972.

5   These 'final' expenditures exclude intermediate flows between firms as this would result in double counting of the overall level of activity. Net exports are the sum of exports minus imports. These are included in order to make the three accounts balance properly.

6   Some wages are paid by government. In a capitalistic economy, where government doesn't own productive assets, these wages are paid from taxes levied either on businesses or on households.

7   The national accounts (where GDP is computed annually) tend to 'force' an equilibrium between aggregate supply and aggregate demand by making adjustments for stocks and inventories held by firms. This is also of course the practical means by which supply and demand are balanced. If demand falls below supply in a given year, companies hold more in stocks and set these off against future demand. If demand rises above supply they draw down stocks and build them up next year.

8   These kinds of costs are called 'externalities' in the economic jargon.

9   This is one of the reasons why it was so easy not to see the financial crisis of 2008 coming. Growth in the GDP was stronger than forecast for 2006 and 2007.

10 See Common and Stagl 2005, Costanza 1991, Daly 1996, Ekins 2000, Lawn 1999. For an overview see Jackson and McBride 2005. See also the interim report of President Sarkozy's newly established Commission on the Measurement of Economic Performance and Social Progress (CMEPSP 2008).

11 And also on the expected costs of borrowing and the expected rewards from saving.

12   This form of production function is called a Cobb–Douglas production function.
13   A further criticism is that this form of production function carries an implicit assumption that it's possible to substitute different factors of production indefinitely.
14   The d'Alessandro model discussed later in the chapter has this form. For other attempts see Ayres and van den Bergh 2005, Common and Stagl 2006, Chapters 6 and 7.
15   Ayres 2008, p292.
16   BERR 2008. See also Jackson 1996.
17   In fact, the biggest contributor to growth over the last decade, across the EU as a whole was the IT sector. Of the EU 15, only the UK placed its emphasis more firmly in the financial and business sector (see Figure 8.1). This underlines the fact that there are different versions of capitalism even within the advanced economies. But none of them has so far achieved significant progress in relation to 'de-materialized services'.
18   When accounted for using a consumption-based perspective: see, Druckman and Jackson 2008, 2009; Jackson et al 2007, Tukker and Jansen 2006.
19   After all we know that it is these services – thermal comfort, lighting, communication and so on – that people want rather than coal or gas or even electricity for its own sake. The idea of energy services has a long pedigree (see for example Jackson 1992, 1997, Jackson and Jacobs 1991, Patterson 2007). It was the motivation for the UK government's call (in a 2006 Energy White paper) for a 'Supplier Obligation' – a mechanism for capping carbon emissions associated with sales from energy suppliers.
20   See Jackson 1996; Stahel and Jackson 1993.
21   Actually there's another fundamental question here which is, even if you can, should you make money from all these things? Does the increasing commercialization of the simpler, more creative bits of our lives change the nature of the activities themselves for the worse? There are certainly some who argue that it does. Jonathan Rutherford's (2008) think-piece for the Sustainable Development Commission cites Paulo Virno's argument that post–Fordist economic activity is focused on the 'life of the mind'.
22   Daly 1972, p119.
23   Bill McKibben (2007) makes a passionate case for exactly this kind of community-based social enterprise in his book *Deep Economy*.
24   I'm profoundly grateful to Brian Davey at Feasta (The Foundation for the Economics of Sustainability) for suggesting this terminology – and indeed for underlining to me the relevance of this informal economy to the arguments here.
25   Manu = Manufacturing; Oth Goods = Other Goods; Dist = Distribution and Retail; Finbus = Financial and Business services; Pers = Personal and Social Services; EleCom = Electronics and Communication; Reallo = Reallocation.
26   See Timmer et al 2007, Table 1.
27   As I've already indicated we have to be a little bit careful with this assertion. Local community-based services aren't automatically low carbon or materially light. But there's evidence that some subsectors within personal and social services have considerably lower carbon intensity. Results from the Surrey Environmental Lifestyle Mapping model suggest that the carbon intensity of social work activities (0.31 $tCO_2e/£$), membership organizations (0.31), health services (0.39), recreational services (0.43) and other service activities (0.40) were around half the average carbon intensity of UK economic activities (0.69 $tCO_2e/£$) when measured from a consumption-based perspective (Druckman and Jackson 2009).
28   Perhaps surprisingly, this fact has been recognized by economists for decades. It even has a name. It's called Baumol's disease. Yes, the same Baumol who believes that *Good Capitalism* is the one that delivers as much growth as possible!
29   Notice that this is sometimes a difficult call to make. The quality of the working experience is itself affected by how 'productive' working time is supposed to be.

30 The model is described in more detail in a think-piece he prepared for the SDC's *Redefining Prosperity* project (Victor 2008b) and in his recent book (Victor 2008a). As with any model, it has some limitations. Principal amongst these is the absence of a monetary sector. 'For simplicity it is assumed that the Bank of Canada, Canada's central bank regulates the money supply to keep inflation at or near the target level of 2 per cent per year.' Victor (2008b, p3).

31 Poverty is tracked using the United Nation's Human Poverty Index. The model simulates the ability to affect this index through redistributive policies and through health spending. The model also contains a forestry sub-model, which looks at changes in forestation. Since this is less relevant for the UK, it is not discussed further here.

32 The Toronto Agreement signed in 1989 was an informal precursor to the Kyoto Protocol. It set a target for reducing carbon emissions in developed countries by 20 per cent before 2005. Not a single signatory achieved the target.

33 Over the 30 years of the scenario, the average working week declines by 14 per cent. The annual working hours fall from 1737 hours in 2005 to 1492 in 2035. 'This compares with levels already approached or surpassed in Sweden (1587), France (1546), Germany (1437), the Netherlands (1367) and Norway (1360)' (Victor 2008b, p12).

34 See for example Bosch 2002, Hayden 1999, Golden and Figart 2000.

35 For example Gorz 1999; Lord 2003.

36 Bosch 2002, p185.

37 See d'Alessandro et al 2008. A key feature of this model is the use of a production function which includes explicit reference to both energy resources and the capital stock. It also assumes non-substitutability between these two.

38 The main limitation of the study is that it is not calibrated against historical data. For this reason, the exact size of the 'sustainability window' is difficult to ascertain.

39 Note, though, that this conclusion might change if the value of ecosystem services were included in the calculation – and perhaps also in the production function.

40 Interestingly, this problem has the same basic structure as the problem of funding public sector spending in a welfare economy. Investment in social goods may be less productive in the short-term and makes no direct contribution in a conventional production function (except perhaps in maintaining the labour supply), but is nonetheless essential for social welfare and indeed for the long-term sustainability of the economy (Gough 1979, see especially Chapter 6 and Appendix A.2).

41 See Costanza et al 1997, Defra 2007, UNEP 2008.

9 Flourishing – Within Limits

1 Ben Okri, 'Our false oracles have failed. We need a new vision to live by.' *The Times*, 30 October 2008.

2 Putnam 2001.

3 Rutherford 2008; Norman et al 2007. Jonathan Rutherford is from the leftwing think-tank Compass, Jesse Norman from the rightwing think-tank Centre Forum.

4 Strictly, speaking this is an index of 'aloneness' rather than 'loneliness'. But as an indicator of the degree of fragmentation of communities it is a useful tool.

5 See **nef** 2009.

6 Dorling et al 2008. Mark Easton's BBC report (including Professor Dorling's quote) is at http://news.bbc.co.uk/1/hi/uk/7755641.stm. The index measures a weighted average of the numbers of non-married adults, one-person households, recent inhabitants (people who have moved to their current address within the last year) and people renting privately.

7   Increased divorce rates have themselves been linked to declining social integration. See for example Shelton 1987.

8   On mobility and labour productivity, see: 'Lack of labour mobility hurts EU productivity', *New Europe* 697, 30 September 2006, online at www.neurope.eu/articles/ 65450.php.

9   Smith 1937 (1776) p821.

10 Sen 1998, p298.

11 See for example the groundbreaking work of the Young Foundation's Local Well-being project, online at www.youngfoundation.org.uk/home/themes/local-wellbeing.

12 Soper 2008.

13 See also Bunting 2005 on the work-life balance.

14 Kasser 2002, 2007.

15 See Hamilton 2003.

16 On downshifting and voluntary simplicity see Elgin (1991 (1981)), Etzioni (2006 (1998)), Hamilton (2003), Schor (1998), Wachtel (1983) amongst many others; for a detailed examination of the pros and cons of the idea of living better by consuming less see Jackson (2005b); for social psychological evidence see Kasser (2002, 2007).

17 Richard Gregg (Ghandi's student) originally published his paper on 'Voluntary Simplicity'(1936) in the Indian Journal *Visva Bharati Quarterly.*

18 Elgin 1991 (1981).

19 Csikszentmihalyi 1990, 2000, 2003.

20 See the Findhorn Foundation 2006 Vision in Action. Annual Report 2006 available online at www.findhorn.org/about_us/annualreport06.pdf.

21 On Plum Village see www.plumvillage.org/.

22 On the Simplicity Forum, see www.simplicityforum.org/index.html; on Downshifting Downunder see: http://downshifting.naturalinnovation.org/index.html.

23 Australian data from Hamilton and Mail 2003. US data from the Merck Family Fund poll (1995); See also Huneke 2005; Hamilton 2003; Schor 1998.

24 See Brown and Kasser 2005; Kasser 2007; Gatersleben et al 2008.

25 See for example: Armstrong and Jackson 2008; Bedford 2007; Evans and Abrahamse 2008; Hobson 2006; Pepper et al 2009.

26 Jackson 2005b; SDC 2006c.

27 On wage disparities see, for example Bradley 2006. On discounted long-term costs see Stern 2007. On signalling status see Schor 1998, Bunting 2005. On the 'shopping generation' see NCC 2006.

28 'Enormous shopping complex opens', BBC news, 30 September 2008, online at http://news.bbc.co.uk/1/hi/england/london/7699209.stm.

29 Of course it is difficult for government to do this, while economic stability relies on increasing consumption! Government itself is deeply conflicted here and can only resolve this by addressing the macro-economics of sustainability. I return to this question in Chapter 10.

30 James 2007, Appendices 1 and 2.

31 The index of 'health and social problems' on the y-axis in Figure 9.2 includes life expectancy, literacy, infant mortality, homicide, imprisonment, teenage births, trust, obesity, mental illness (including alcohol and drug addiction) and social mobility (Wilkinson and Pickett, 2009).

10 Governance for Prosperity

1   From an article for the Huffington Post by Peter Hall, Professor of European Studies at Harvard and co-author of *Varieties of Capitalism*, online at www.huffington post.com/2008/10/13/global-economic-crisis-li_n_134393.html.

2   This question was evident for example in the clash during one of the *Redefining Prosperity* workshops between Jonathan Rutherford (from the political left) arguing for more state and Jesse Norman (from the political right) arguing for less state. For a useful – and still relevant – discussion of the ambivalent political economy of the welfare state see Gough 1979.

3   'Redesigning global finance', *The Economist* leader, 15 November 2008, p13.

4   For background on the evolution of social behaviours see Axelrod 2006 (1984), Sober and Wilson 1998, Wright 1994.

5   The idea of the social contract was first articulated in Hobbes' *Leviathan* in 1651, and developed further by John Locke and Jean-Jacques Rousseau in the late 17th and 18th centuries. For further discussion on the relevance of the social contract to modern environmental debates see: Hayward and O'Brien 2010, Jackson 2008a, O'Brien et al 2009.

6   See Offer 2006.

7   On parenthood, see Offer 2006, Chapter 14; on savings rates see 'Saving in the World: Stylized Facts', Washington DC: World Bank, available online at www.worldbank.org/ research/projects/savings/savinwld.htm. On consumer debt, see: Credit Card Industry Facts and Personal Debt Statistics (2006–2007), online at www.creditcards.com/ statistics/credit-card-industry-facts-and-personal-debt-statistics.php.

8   Dawkins 2001.

9   Schwartz 2006, 1999.

10 It also strikes the balance between novelty and tradition differently.

11 This finding was first demonstrated formally by the game theorist Robert Axelrod 2006 (1984).

12 Wilkinson and Pickett 2009.

13 Absolute levels of unemployment in Germany are considerably higher than in the UK and have been since German re-unification, although they have been coming down steadily over the last decade.

14 Data for USA, Germany and Denmark from the International Labour Organization (ILO) online statistical database at: http://laborsta.ilo.org/. The UK data on the ILO database (as in several other international databases) is woefully out of date. Trends for the UK are calculated using Labour Force Statistics. Online at: http://www.statistics. gov.uk/STATBASE.

15 See for example Culpepper 2001; Estevez-Abe et al 2001.

16 See Kasser's presentation to a RESOLVE seminar at the University of Surrey, November 2007, online at www.surrey.ac.uk/RESOLVE.

17 For example, the unemployment rate in Canada (a liberalized market economy) has fallen slightly, while unemployment in Sweden (a coordinated market economy) has risen by almost a quarter.

18 Online at www.huffingtonpost.com/2008/10/13/global-economic-crisis-li_n_ 134393.html.

19 This tension is what the historian Polanyi (2002 (1942)) called the 'double movement' of society.

20 'People power vital to climate deal', *The Guardian*, 8 December 2008, online at www.guardian.co.uk/environment/2008/dec/08/ed-miliband-climate-politics-environment.

21 See for example, Doyal and Gough 1991, Helliwell 2003, Layard 2005.

11 The Transition to a Sustainable Economy

1 From a speech on 'shared prosperity' that Obama made in Janesville, Wisconsin, 13 February 2008, online at www.barackobama.com/2008/02/13/remarks_of_senator_barack_obam_50.php.

2 See for example CCC 2008, IPCC 2007.

3 Contraction and convergence (C&C) refers to an approach originally proposed by the Global Commons Institute but now widely agreed to represent a fair and meaningful way of achieving stabilization targets. Overall emissions 'contract' to a level compatible with the stabilization target, and per capita emissions 'converge' towards an equal per capita share of the overall emissions budget. Very simply, C&C is a way of transparently structuring future negotiations on the understanding that prosperity is governed by ecological limits on the one hand and fair shares on the other. For more information on the approach see for example Meyer 2004. See also briefings by the Global Commons Institute, online at: http://www.gci.org.uk/briefings/ICE.pdf and at http://www.tangentfilms.com/GCIjul6.pdf.

4 See for example Pearce et al 1989.

5 Tietenberg (1990) demonstrates a formal equivalence between carbon taxes and carbon permits sold under auction. But in practice the two mechanisms have very different architectures and policy implications and these differences have tended to divide the policy community. More important than these divisions is the need to make decent progress towards internalizing the social cost of carbon and other environmental impacts.

6 See for example Dresner et al 2006; von Weizsäcker and Jesinghaus 1992.

7 The GEF was established under the terms of the UN Framework Convention on Climate Change to fund technology transfer to non-Annex 1 (developing) countries. For further information see www.gefweb.org.

8 See 'Decoupling 2.0', *The Economist* leader, 23 May 2009, p13.

9 This call is made explicitly by Helm 2009 (for instance). It is also inherent in legislative initiatives such as Obama's (failed) 2007 Global Poverty Act (S2433). A revised version of the bill (HR 2639) is now in Congress.

10 This mechanism was suggested for example by Guy Liu (2008) in his think-piece for the Sustainable Development Commission's *Redefining Prosperity* project.

11 See for example Timmer et al 2007.

12 TEEB 2008.

13 Notable exceptions are the work of Peter Victor (2008a and 2008b) cited in Chapter 8, Cambridge Econometrics (www.camecon.com/suite_economic_models/mdme3.htm) and the burgeoning literature on the economics of climate change (for example Stern 2007 and references cited therein).

14 For further discussion of this whole area see Chapter 7 and the references cited there, in particular Deutsche Bank 2008, GND 2008, SDC 2009b, UNEP 2008.

15 See for example the statement from G20 leaders at the April 2009 London Summit, online at http://news.bbc.co.uk/go/pr/fr/-/1/hi/business/7979606.stm.

16 Supporters of the idea have included the multi-billionaire George Soros who proposed a version of the Tobin Tax called Special Drawing Rights (to support development) and former UK Development Secretary Claire Short. See for example www.independent.co.uk/news/uk/politics/tories-attack-shorts-support-of-tobin-tax-682801.html.

17 Herman Daly (2008) calls for a 100 per cent reserve in his SDC think-piece. See also the American Money Institute (www.monetary.org) and the work of James Robertson in the UK (www.jamesrobertson.com/newsletter.htm).

18 On Adjusted Net Savings see for example Sears and Ruta 2007; for a summary of the Index of Sustainable Economic Welfare see Jackson and McBride 2005. The OECD *Beyond GDP* initiative can be found at http://europe.beyondgdp.eu. See also the interim report from the Sarkozy Commission (CMEPSP 2008).

19 'Loi relative a la réduction du temps de travail', Law n. 2000-37, 19 January 2000. See Ministry of the Economy 'Les dispositions successives sur la durée du travail', online at http://industrie.gouv.fr/sessi/cpci/cpci2003/CPCI2003_10_fiche35A.pdf.

20 See for example Schor 1992.

21 See for instance: TUC Seminar report, online at www.tuc.org.uk/the_tuc/tuc-15673-f0.cfm?regional=8/.

22 See Defra 2007, Diener and Seligman 2004, Robeyns and van der Veen 2007, nef 2009.

23 See for example www.internationalresilience.org; www.youngfoundation.org/localwell-being; www.transitiontowns.org.

24 In the UK an early report from the Prime Minister's Strategy Unit on Social Capital proved influential in government (Halpern 2005). More recent work has been carried out on the concept of mental capital and well-being (Foresight 2008).

25 On advertising see for example 'Sweden Pushes its Ban on Children's Ads', *Wall Street Journal*, 29 May 2001; 'The Norwegian Action Plan to Reduce Commercial Pressure on Children and Young People', Ministry of Children and Equality, online at www.regjeringen.no/en. On São Paolo's *Lei Limpa Cuidade*, see: 'São Paulo: A City Without Ads', David Evan Harris, Adbusters, September–October 2007.

12 A Lasting Prosperity

1 From Michael Sandel's first Reith Lecture (Sandel 2009).

2 It would be wrong to dismiss entirely the potential for technological breakthroughs. The fact is we already have at our disposal a range of options that could begin to deliver effective change: renewable, resource-efficient, low-carbon technologies capable of weaning us from our dangerous dependence on fossil fuels. These options have to provide the technological platform for the transition to a sustainable economy. But the idea that they will emerge spontaneously by giving free reign to the competitive market is patently false.

3 See for example Bauman 1998, 2007, Campbell 2005.

4 Eyres 2009.

5 Burningham and Thrush 2001.

6 It's telling that the most common experience of shared public space in the consumer society is the shopping mall. The commercialized and individualized nature of activities in that space works directly against a sense of shared endeavour.

7 And not just paid employment.

8 To paraphrase Mary Douglas 2006 (1976).

9 Addressing population growth is clearly relevant here – as we saw in Chapter 5. But in recent years affluence (income level) has been a bigger influence on environmental impact than population, particularly in the advanced nations. So the main relevance of population for the discussion of growth in advanced nations is that it establishes the allowable (equitable) per capita allocation of resources, emissions and ecological space at a global level.

10 As we noted in Chapter 8, there are some provisos here. Not all of these activities necessarily have a low carbon footprint. Much depends on their precise form and nature.

11 Two key provisos emerge here. One is around competitiveness. We saw in Chapter 8 how maintaining a healthy trade balance relies on supporting the competitiveness of

key export sectors. The second proviso concerns the question of public revenues. Again we've looked at this issue a number of times. Financing public investment requires either higher taxation rates, increasing debts or some form of public ownership of revenue-generating assets.

12   See Figure 4.5, Chapter 4, for evidence of this. See Baumol et al 2007. Note also here that Peter Victor's work demonstrates explicitly that it's possible in principle to 'stabilize' a fairly conventional capitalist economy (Victor 2008a and 2008b).

13   Assume a total carbon dioxide budget of 700 billion tonnes between now and 2050 (see Chapter 1 and Allen et al 2009, Meinshausen et al 2009). So the average annual global allowable CO_2 budget is about 17.5 billion tonnes. Assuming an equal per capita allocation of carbon, the allowable average annual CO_2 budget in developed nations (population around 1.2 billion out of a global population of 6.7 billion) is just over 3 billion tonnes per year. At an average carbon intensity of 0.35 $kgCO_2$/\$, the allowable economic activity would be around \$9 trillion. The actual GDP in the OECD nations in 2007 was around \$33 trillion in 2000 dollars at purchasing power parity.

14   This argument was made explicitly by the UK Treasury in the financial sector bailouts of November 2008.

15   On employee ownership, see for example Abrams 2008; Erdal 2008.

16   This idea is close to what Ziauddin Sardar (2007) has called transmodernity.

17   John O'Neil (2008) and Avner Offer (2007) make this point in different ways.

Appendix 1 The SDC Redefining Prosperity Project

1   *Redefining Prosperity* (SDC 2003) is available on the Sustainable Development Commission website: www.sd-commission.org.uk.

2   Levett et al 2003.

3   *Securing the Future* (Defra 2005) is available on the government's sustainable development website: www.sustainable_development.gov.uk.

4   A report on this work – *Redefining Progress* (SDC 2006a) – is also available on the SDC website: www.sd-commission.org.uk.

5   Jackson and Anderson 2009.

Appendix 2 Towards an Ecological Macro-economics

1   This is similar to the basic form of the macro-economic model in Peter Victor's (2008a) study of the Canadian economy, although he does not constrain the production function indices to sum to 1.

2   For more information, see SDC 2007 'Turning the Tide – tidal power' in the UK.

3   Investment is shown in the table in each target and condition dimension. In practice, it is most likely that some targets (for example ecosystem maintenance) will only be undertaken under specific conditions (for example public sector, social).

4   For example, the Surrey Environmental Lifestyle Mapping (SELMA) framework is an environmental input-output model that can be used to attribute the carbon emissions (and/or resources) associated with different final demand categories (Druckman et al 2008, Druckman and Jackson 2008, Jackson et al 2007).

5   The paucity of basic UK IO statistics is now well-known. Official analytical tables for the UK have not been produced since 1995, in spite of a commitment by the Labour

government to produce them annually from 2000, and a requirement in EU legislation to submit updated analytical tables to Eurostat on at least a five yearly basis. Like the absence of up-to-date unemployment statistics in the ILO database, this failure of the UK government to take essential social and environmental indicators seriously is positively embarrassing given its claims for international leadership in sustainability.

References

Abdallah, Saamah, Sam Thompson and Nic Marks (2008) 'Estimating worldwide life satisfaction'. *Ecological Economics* 65 (1), 35–47.

Abrams, John (2008) *Companies We Keep: employee ownership and the business of community and place*. White River Junction, VT: Chelsea Green Publishing Company.

Ahiakpor, James (2001) 'On the mythology of the Keynesian multiplier', *American Journal of Economics and Sociology* 60, 745–773.

Allen, Myles, David Frame, Chris Huntingford, Chris Jones, Jason Lowe, Malte Meinshausen and Nicolai Meinshausen (2009) 'Warming caused by cumulative carbon emissions towards the trillionth tonne'. *Nature* 458, 1163–1166.

Anderson, Victor (1991) *Alternative Economic Indicators*. London: Routledge.

Anderton, Alain (2000) *Economics* (3rd Edition). Ormskirk: Causeway Press.

APPG (2007) 'Return of the population growth factor – its impact on millennium development goals'. Report of Hearings by the All Party Parliamentary Group on Population, Development and Reproductive Health. London: Population Sustainability Network.

Armstrong, Alison and Tim Jackson (2008) 'Tied up in 'nots': an exploration of the link between consumption and spirituality'. Paper presented to the European Sociological Association conference in Helsinki, August 2008.

Arndt, Jamie, Sheldon Solomon, Tim Kasser and Kay Sheldon (2004) 'The urge to splurge: a terror management account of materialism and consumer behaviour'. *Journal of Consumer Psychology* 14 (3), 198–212.

Axelrod, Robert (1984) (reprinted 2006) *The Evolution of Cooperation*. London: Basic Books.

Ayres, Robert (2008) 'Sustainability economics: Where do we stand'. *Ecological Economics* 67, 281–310.

Ayres, Robert and Jeroen van den Bergh (2005) 'A theory of economic growth with material/energy resources and dematerialisation: Interaction of three growth mechanisms'. *Ecological Economics* 55, 96–118.

Baudrillard, Jean (1970) (reprinted 1998) *The Consumer Society – myths and structures*. London: Sage Publications.

Bauman, Zygmunt (1998) *Work, Consumerism and the New Poor*. Buckingham: Open University Press.

Bauman, Zygmunt (2007) *Consuming Life*. Cambridge: Polity Press.

Baumol, William, Robert Litan and Carl Schramm (2007) *Good Capitalism, Bad Capitalism, and the Economics of Growth and Prosperity*. Newhaven and London: Yale University Press.

Baycan, Baris Gencer (2007) 'From limits to growth to degrowth within French green politics'. *Environmental Politics* 16 (3), 513–517.

Bedford, Tracey (2007) 'Ethical consumerism: Everyday negotiations in the construction of an ethical self'. Seminar Presentation, RESOLVE, University of Surrey, 15 February 2007, available at www.surrey.ac.uk/resolve/seminars/Tracey%20Bedford%20Slides.pdf.

Begg, David, Stanley Fischer and Rudiger Dornbusch (2003) *Economics* (7th Edition), Maidenhead: McGraw-Hill.

Beinhocker, Eric (2007) *The Origin of Wealth: Evolution, Complexity, and the Radical Remaking of Economics.* London: Random House.

Belk, Russell (1988) 'Possessions and the extended self'. *Journal of Consumer Research* 15, 139–168.

Belk, Russell, Melanie Wallendorf and John F. Sherry (1989) 'The sacred and the profane in consumer behavior: Theodicy on the Odyssey'. *Journal of Consumer Research* 16, 1–38.

Belk, Russ, Guliz Ger and Søren Askegaard (2003) 'The fire of desire – a multi-sited inquiry into consumer passion'. *Journal of Consumer Research* 30, 325–351.

Berger, Peter (1969) *The Sacred Canopy – elements of a sociological theory of religion.* New York: Anchor Books.

BERR (2008) 'Smart Business – sustainable solutions for changing times'. Report of the UK Government's Business Taskforce on Sustainable Consumption and Production. London: Department for Business, Enterprise and Regulatory Reform.

Booth, Douglas (2004) *Hooked on Growth – economic addictions and the environment.* New York: Rowman and Littlefield.

Bosch, Gerhard (2002) 'Working time reductions, employment consequences and lessons from Europe'. In Golden, L. and D. Figart (eds) (2002) *Working Time: international trends, theory and policy perspectives.* London and New York: Routledge.

Bouder, Frederic (2008) 'Can decoupling work?' Think-piece contributed to the SDC Workshop 'Economy Lite – can decoupling work?' February 2008. London: Sustainable Development Commission. Online at www.sd-commission.org.uk/pages/redefining-prosperity.html.

Bourdieu, Pierre (1984) *Distinction – A social critique of the judgement of taste.* London: Routledge and Kegan Paul.

Bowen, Alex, Nick Stern, Sam Fankhauser and Dimitri Zenghelis (2009) *An Outline of the Case for a Green Stimulus.* London: Grantham Institute.

Bradley, S. (2006) *In Greed we Trust: Capitalism gone wrong.* Victoria, BC: Trafford.

Brown, Kirk and Tim Kasser (2005) 'Are psychological and ecological well-being compatible? The role of values, mindfulness, and lifestyle'. *Social Indicators Research* 74 (2), 349–368.

Brown, Lester (2008) *Plan B 3.0 – mobilizing to save civilization.* New York: W.W. Norton & Co.

Brown, Peter and Geoffrey Garver (2008) *Right Relationship – building a whole earth economy.* San Francisco: Berrett-Koehler Publishers Inc.

Bunting, Madeleine (2005) *Willing Slaves: How the overwork culture is ruining our lives.* London: Harper.

Burningham, Kate and Diana Thrush (2001) *Rainforests Are a Long Way from Here: The environmental concerns of disadvantaged groups.* York: York Publishing Services Ltd.

Campbell, Colin (2004) 'I shop therefore (I know that) I am. The metaphysical foundations of modern consumerism'. In Ekstrom, K. and H. Brembeck (eds) (2004) *Elusive Consumption.* Oxford: Berg.

Campbell, Colin (2005) *The Romantic Ethic and the Spirit of Modern Consumerism.* Oxford: Basil Blackwell.

Carbon Trust (2006) *The Carbon Emissions in All that We Consume.* London: Carbon Trust.

CCC (2008) 'Building a low-carbon economy – the UK's contribution to tackling climate change'. 1st Report of the Climate Change Committee. London: TSO.

Cohen, D. (2007) 'Earth's natural wealth: an audit'. *New Scientist*, 23 May 2007.

Common, Michael and Sigrid Stagl (2006) *Ecological Economics – an introduction*. Cambridge: Cambridge University Press.

Costanza, Robert (ed) (1991) *Ecological Economics – the science and management of sustainability*. New York: Columbia University Press.

Costanza, Robert, Ralph d'Arge, Rudolph de Groot, Stephen Farber, Monica Grasso, Bruce Hannon, Karin Limburg, Shahid Naeem, Robert V. O'Neill, Jose Paruelo, Robert G. Raskin, Paul Sutton and Marjan van den Belt (1997) 'The value of the world's ecosystem services and natural capital'. *Nature* 387, 256, Table 2.

Crocker, David and Toby Linden (eds) (1998) *The Ethics of Consumption*, New York: Rowman and Littlefield.

Csikszentmihalyi, Mihalyi (1990) *Flow: The psychology of optimal experience*. New York: Harper and Row.

Csikszentmihalyi, Mihalyi (2000) 'The costs and benefits of consuming'. *Journal of Consumer Research* 27 (2), 262–272. Reprinted as Chapter 24 in Jackson 2006a.

Csikszentmihalyi, Mihalyi (2003) 'Materialism and the evolution of consciousness'. In Kasser, T. and A. Kanner (eds) *Psychology and Consumer Culture – the struggle for a good life in a material world*. Washington DC: American Psychological Association, Chapter 6.

Csikszentmihalyi, Mihaly and Eugene Rochberg-Halton (1981) *The Meaning of Things – domestic symbols and the self*, Cambridge and New York: Cambridge University Press.

Culpepper, Pepper (2001) 'Employers, public policy and the politics of decentralised cooperation in France and Germany'. In Hall, P. and D. Soskice (eds) (2001) *Varieties of Capitalism: The institutional foundations of competitive advantage*. Oxford: Oxford University Press, Chapter 8.

Cushman, Philip (1990) 'Why the self is empty: Toward a historically situated psychology'. *American Psychologist* 45, 599–611.

D'Alessandro, Simone, Tommaso Luzzati and Mario Morroni (2008) 'Feasible transition paths towards a renewable energy economy: Investment composition, consumption and growth'. Think-piece presented to the SDC Seminar: 'Confronting Structure'. April 2008. London: Sustainable Development Commission. Online at www.sd-commission.org.uk/pages/redefining-prosperity.html.

Daly, Herman (1972) *The Steady State Economy*. London: W.H. Freeman and Co. Ltd.

Daly, Herman (1996) *Beyond Growth*. Washington DC: Beacon Press.

Daly, Herman (2008) 'A steady-state economy'. Think-piece for the SDC workshop 'Confronting Structure'. April 2008. London: Sustainable Development Commission. Online at www.sd-commission.org.uk/pages/redefining-prosperity.html.

Dawkins, R. (2001) 'Sustainability does not come naturally – a Darwinian perspective on values'. *The Values Platform for Sustainability Inaugural Lecture at the Royal Institution*, 14 November 2001. Fishguard: Environment Foundation.

De Botton, Alain (2004) *Status Anxiety*. Oxford: Oxford University Press.

Defra (2005) 'Securing the future'. UK Sustainable Development Strategy. London: Department for Environment, Food and Rural Affairs.

Defra (2007) 'Sustainable development indicators in your pocket'. London: TSO.

Defra (2008) 'Development of an embedded emissions indicator'. Report to the Department for the Environment, Food and Rural Affairs by the Stockholm Environment Institute and University of Sydney. London: Defra. Online at http://randd.defra.gov.uk/Document.aspx?Document=EV02033_7331_FRP.pdf.

Deutsche Bank (2008) 'Economic stimulus: The case for "green" infrastructure, energy security and "green" jobs'. Deutsche Bank Advisors. New York: Deutsche Bank.

Dichter, Ernst (1964) *The Handbook of Consumer Motivations: The psychology of consumption*. New York: McGraw-Hill.

Diener, Ed and Marty Seligman (2004) 'Beyond money – towards an economy of wellbeing'. *Psychological Science in the Public Interest* 5 (1), 1–31.

Dittmar, Helga (1992) *The Social Psychology of Material Possessions – to have is to be.* New York: St Martin's Press.

Dolan, Paul, Tessa Peasgood and Matthew White (2006) 'Review of research on the influences on personal well-being and application to policy making'. Report to Defra. London: Defra.

Dolan, Paul, Tessa Peasgood and Matthew White (2008) 'Do we really know what makes us happy? A review of the economic literature on the factors associated with subjective well-being'. *Journal of Economic Psychology* 29, 94–122.

Dorling, Danny, Dan Vickers, Bethan Thomas, John Pritchard and Dimitris Ballas (2008) *Changing UK: The way we live now.* Sheffield: University of Sheffield. Online at: http://sasi.group.shef.ac.uk/research/changingUK.html.

Douglas, Mary (1976) (reprinted 2006). 'Relative poverty, relative communication'. In Halsey, A. (ed), *Traditions of Social Policy,* Oxford: Basil Blackwell; reprinted as Chapter 21 in Jackson (2006a) *Earthscan Reader in Sustainable Consumption.* London: Earthscan.

Douglas, Mary and Baron Isherwood (1996) *The World of Goods.* 2nd Edition. London: Routledge.

Doyal, Len and Ian Gough (1991) *A Theory of Human Needs.* Basingstoke: Palgrave Macmillan.

Dresner, Simon, Louise Dunne and Tim Jackson (2006) 'Social and political responses to ecological tax reform in Europe'. *Energy Policy,* 34 (8): 895–970.

Druckman, Angela and Tim Jackson (2008) 'The Surrey Environmental Lifestyle Mapping (SELMA) Framework – development and key results to date'. RESOLVE Working Paper 08–08. Guildford: University of Surrey. Online at http://www.surrey.ac.uk/resolve/Docs/WorkingPapers/RESOLVE_WP_08-08.pdf.

Druckman, Angela and Tim Jackson (2009) 'The carbon footprint of UK households 1990–2004: A socio-economically disaggregated, quasi-multi-regional input-output model'. *Ecological Economics* [forthcoming].

Druckman, Angela, Pete Bradley, Eleni Papathanasopoulou and Tim Jackson (2008) 'Measuring progress towards carbon reduction in the UK'. *Ecological Economics* 66 (4), 594–604.

Durkheim, Emile (1903) *Suicide.* Reprinted 2002 in Routledge Classics. London: Routledge.

Easterlin, Richard (1972) 'Does economic growth improve the human lot? Some empirical evidence'. In David, D. and M. Reder (eds) (1972) *Nations and Households in Economic Growth.* Stanford: Stanford University Press.

Easterlin, Richard (1995) 'Will raising the incomes of all increase the happiness of all?' *Journal of Economic Behaviour and Organization* 27, 35–47.

Ehrlich, Paul (1968) (reprinted 1995) *The Population Bomb.* New York: Buccaneer Books.

EIA (2008) *International Energy Annual 2006.* Washington DC: Energy Information Administration. Online at www.eia.doe.gov/emeu/iea.

Ekins, Paul (2000) *Economic Growth and Environmental Sustainability.* London: Routledge.

Ekins, Paul (2008) 'Policies for decoupling'. Think-piece contributed to the SDC workshop 'Decoupling Lite – can decoupling work?' February 2008. London: Sustainable Development Commission. Online at www.sd-commission.org.uk/pages/redefining-prosperity.html.

Ekins, Paul and Manfred Max Neef (eds) (1992) *Real-life Economics: Understanding wealth creation.* London: Routledge.

Elgin, Duane (1981) (reprinted 1993) *Voluntary Simplicity – towards a way of life that is outwardly simple, inwardly rich.* New York: William Morrow.

Erdal, David (2008) *Local Heroes: How loch fyne oysters embraced employee ownership and business success*. London: Viking.

Estevez-Abe, Margarita, Torben Ivesen and David Soskice (2001) 'Social protection and the formation of skills'. In Hall, P. and D. Soskice (eds) (2001) *Varieties of Capitalism: The institutional foundations of competitive advantage*. Oxford: Oxford University Press, Chapter 4.

Etzioni, Amitai (1998) 'Voluntary simplicity: Characterisation, select psychological implications and societal consequences'. *Journal of Economic Psychology* 19 (5), 619–643. Reprinted as Chapter 12 in Jackson 2006a.

Evans, David and Wokje Abrahamse (2008) 'Beyond rhetoric: The possibilities of and for "sustainable lifestyles"'. RESOLVE Working Paper Series 06–08. Guildford: University of Surrey.

Eyres, Harry (2009) 'The sour smell of excess'. *Financial Times*. Saturday 23 May 2009.

Foresight (2008) 'Mental Capital and Wellbeing Project', Final Project report – Executive summary. London: The Government Office for Science.

Fournier, Valérie (2008) 'Escaping from the economy: the politics of degrowth'. *International Journal of Sociology and Social Policy* 28 (11/12), 528–545.

Franco, Manuel, Pedro Orduñez, Benjamín Caballero, José A. Tapia Granados, Mariana Lazo, José Luís Bernal, Eliseo Guallar and Richard S. Cooper (2007) 'Impact of energy intake, physical activity, and population-wide weight loss on cardiovascular disease and diabetes mortality in Cuba, 1980–2005'. *Journal of Epidemiology* 166, 1374–1380.

Freeman, Richard and Kathryn Shaw (2009) 'International differences in the business practices and productivity of firms'. Proceedings of a conference held at the National Bureau of Economic Research 2006. Chicago: University of Chicago Press. Online at www.nber.org/books/free07-1.

Gadjil, Madhav and Ramachandra Guha (1995) *Ecology and Equity – the use and abuse of nature in contemporary India*. New York: Routledge, 35.

Gatersleben, Birgitta, Jesse Meadows, Wokje Abrahamse and Tim Jackson (2008) 'Materialistic and environmental values of young volunteers in nature conservation projects'. RESOLVE Working Paper Series 07–08. Guildford: University of Surrey.

Georgescu-Roegen, Nicholas (1972) *The Entropy Law and the Economic Process*. Cambridge, Mass: Harvard University Press.

GND (2008) 'A Green New Deal: Joined up policies to solve the triple crunch of the credit crisis, climate change and high oil prices'. The first report of the Green New Deal Group. London: nef.

Golden, Lonnie and Deborah Figart (2002) *Working Time: International trends, theory and policy perspectives*. London and New York: Routledge.

Gorz, André (1999) *Reclaiming Work – beyond the wage-based society*. London: Polity Press.

Gough, Ian (1979) *The Political Economy of the Welfare State*. Basingstoke: Palgrave Macmillan.

Greenspan, Alan (2008) *The Age of Turbulence: Adventures in a new world*. London: Penguin.

Gregg, Richard (1936) 'Voluntary Simplicity'. *Visva-Bharati Quarterly*, August. Reprinted 1974 in *Manas, 27 (September), 36–37*.

Grossman, Gene and Alan Krueger (1995) 'Economic growth and the environment'. *Quarterly Journal of Economics* 110, 353–378.

Haidt, Jonathan (2007) *The Happiness Hypothesis – finding modern truth in ancient wisdom*. New York: Basic Books.

Hall, Peter and David Soskice (eds) (2001) *Varieties of Capitalism: The institutional foundations of competitive advantage*. Oxford: Oxford University Press.

Hall, Robert and David Papell (2005) *Macroeconomics: Economic growth, fluctuations and policy*. New York: W.W. Norton 7 Co.

Halpern, David (2005) *Social Capital*. Cambridge: Polity Press.

Hamilton, Clive (2003) 'Downshifting in Britain: A sea-change in the pursuit of happiness'. Discussion Paper No. 58. Canberra: The Australia Institute.

Hamilton, Clive and L. Mail (2003) 'Downshifting in Australia: A sea-change in the pursuit of happiness'. Discussion Paper No. 50. Canberra: The Australia Institute.

Harrison, Mark (1988) 'Resource mobilization for World War II: The USA, UK, USSR and Germany, 1938–1945'. *Economic History Review* 41 (2), 171–192.

Hayden, Anders (1999) *Sharing the Work, Sparing the Planet – work time, consumption and ecology*. London: Zed Books.

Hayward, Bronwyn and Karen O'Brien (2010) 'Security of what for whom? Rethinking social contracts in a changing climate'. In O' Brien, K.L., A. St. Clair and B. Kristoffersen (eds), *Climate Change, Ethics, and Human Security*. Cambridge: Cambridge University Press [forthcoming].

Helliwell, John (2003) 'How's life? Combining individual and national variables to explain subjective wellbeing'. *Economic Modelling* 20 (2), 331–360.

Helm, Dieter (2008a) 'Too good to be true'. Online at www.dieterhelm.co.uk.

Helm, Dieter (2008b) 'Climate-change policy: Why has so little been achieved?' *Oxford Review of Economic Policy* 24 (20), 211–238.

Helm, Dieter (2009) 'Environmental challenges in a warming world: Consumption, costs and responsibilities'. Tanner Lecture. New College, Oxford. 21 February 2009.

Hirsch, Fred (1977) *Social Limits to Growth*. Revised edition (1995) London and New York: Routledge.

HMT (2008) 'Facing global challenges: Supporting people through difficult times'. PreBudget Report 2008. London: HM Treasury.

Hobson, K. (2006) 'Competing discourses of sustainable consumption: Does the rationalisation of lifestyles make sense?' In Jackson 2006a, 305–327.

HSBC (2009) *A Climate for Recovery – 6een*. HSBC Global Research. London: HSBC.

Huneke, M. (2005) 'The face of the un-consumer: An empirical examination of the practice of voluntary simplicity in the United States'. *Psychology and Marketing* 22 (7), 527–550.

IEA (2008) 'World Energy Outlook 2008'. Paris: International Energy Agency.

IFS (2009) 'The IFS Green Budget January 2009'. London: Institute for Fiscal Studies.

IMF (2008) 'World Economic Outlook 2008'. Washington DC: International Monetary Fund.

Inglehart, Ronald and Klingemann, H.-D. (2000) *Genes, Culture and Happiness*. Boston: MIT Press.

IPCC (2007) 'Climate change 2007: Mitigation. Contribution of Working Group III to the Fourth Assessment Report of the Intergovernmental Panel on Climate Change'. Cambridge: Cambridge University Press.

ITPOES (2008) 'The oil crunch: Securing the UK's energy future'. 1st report of the Industry Taskforce on Peak Oil and Energy Security. London: ITPOES.

Jackson, Tim (1992) *Efficiency without Tears – no regrets energy policy to combat climate change*. London: Friends of the Earth.

Jackson, Tim (1996) *Material Concerns: Pollution, profit and quality of life*. London: Routledge.

Jackson, Tim (1997) *Power in Balance – energy challenges for the 21st Century*. London: Friends of the Earth.

Jackson, Tim (2002) 'Consumer culture as a failure in theodicy'. in T. Cooper (ed), *Consumption, Christianity and Creation*, Proceedings of an Academic Seminar, 5th July, Sheffield Hallam University, Sheffield.

Jackson, Tim (2003) 'Sustainability and the "Struggle for Existence": The critical role of metaphor in society's metabolism', *Environmental Values*, 12 (3), 289–316.

Jackson, Tim (2005a) 'Motivating sustainable consumption – a review of evidence on consumer behaviour and behavioural change'. London: SDRN.

Jackson, Tim (2005b) 'Live better by consuming less? Is there a double dividend in sustainable consumption?' *Journal of Industrial Ecology* 9 (1–2), 19–36.

Jackson, Tim (ed) (2006a) *Earthscan Reader in Sustainable Consumption*. London: Earthscan.

Jackson, Tim (2006b) 'Consuming paradise? Towards a social and cultural psychology of sustainable consumption'. Chapter 25 in Jackson (ed) (2006a) *Earthscan Reader in Sustainable Consumption*. London: Earthscan.

Jackson, Tim (2008a) 'Where is the wellbeing dividend? Nature, structure and consumption inequalities'. *Local Environment* 13 (8), 703–723.

Jackson, Tim (2008b) 'The challenge of sustainable lifestyles'. In Gardner, G. and T. Pugh (eds) 2008, *State of the World 2008 – innovations for a sustainable economy*. Washington DC: WorldWatch Institute, Chapter 4.

Jackson, Tim and Michael Jacobs (1991) 'Carbon taxes and the assumptions of environmental economics'. In Barker, T. (ed) (1991) *Green Futures for Economic Growth*. Cambridge: Cambridge Econometrics, 49–68.

Jackson, Tim and Nic Marks (1999) 'Consumption, sustainable welfare and human needs – with reference to UK expenditure patterns 1954–1994'. *Ecological Economics* 28 (3), 421–442.

Jackson, Tim, Wander Jager and Sigrid Stagl (2004) 'Beyond insatiability – needs theory and sustainable consumption'. In Reisch, L. and I. Røpke (eds) (2004) *Consumption – perspectives from ecological economics*. Cheltenham: Edward Elgar.

Jackson, Tim and N. McBride (2005) 'Measuring progress? A review of adjusted measures of economic welfare in Europe'. Report for the European Environment Agency. Guildford: University of Surrey.

Jackson, Tim, Eleni Papathanasopoulou, Pete Bradley and Angela Druckman (2006) 'Attributing carbon emissions to functional household needs: A pilot framework for the UK'. International Conference on Regional and Urban Modelling, Brussels, Belgium. 1–2 June 2006.

Jackson, Tim, Eleni Papathanasopoulou, Pete Bradley and Angela Druckman (2007) 'Attributing UK carbon emissions to functional consumer needs: Methodology and pilot results'. RESOLVE Working Paper 01–07, University of Surrey. Online at www.surrey.ac.uk/resolve/Docs/WorkingPapers/RESOLVE_WP_01-07.pdf.

Jackson, Tim and Eleni Papathanasopoulou (2008) 'Luxury or lock-in? – an exploration of unsustainable consumption in the UK 1968–2000'. *Ecological Economics* 68, 80–95.

Jackson, Tim and Victor Anderson (2009) *Redefining Prosperity – essays in pursuit of a sustainable economy.* London: Earthscan/SDC.

Jackson, Tim and Miriam Pepper (2009) 'Consumerism as theodicy: An exploration of secular and religious meaning functions in consumer society'. In Thomas, L. (2009) *Consumerism: Religious and secular perspectives*. London: Palgrave.

Jacobs, Michael (1991) *The Green Economy*. London: Pluto Press.

James, Oliver (1998) *Britain on the Couch: Why we're unhappier compared to 1950 despite being richer*. London: Arrow Books.

James, Oliver (2007) *Affluenza*. London: Vermillion.

Kahneman, Daniel and Robert Sugden (2005) 'Experienced utility as a standard of policy evaluation'. *Environmental & Resource Economics* 32, 161–181.

Kasser, Tim (2002) *The High Price of Materialism*. Cambridge, Mass: MIT Press.

Kasser, Tim (2007) 'A vision of prosperity'. Think-piece for the SDC's *Redefining Prosperity* project. London: Sustainable Development Commission.

Keynes, John Maynard (1930). *Economic Possibilities for our Grandchildren. Essays in persuasion*. New York: W.W. Norton & Co.

Kierkegaard, Søren (1844) *The Concept of Anxiety: A simple psychologically orienting deliberation on the dogmatic issue of hereditary sin.* Reprinted (1980) as Volume VIII, Kierkegaard's Writings. Princeton: Princeton University Press.

Lancaster, Kelvin (1966) 'A new approach to consumer theory'. *Journal of Political Economy* 174, 132–157.

Latouche, Serge (2007) 'De-growth: An electoral stake?' *The International Journal of Inclusive Democracy* 3 (1), January 2007. Online at www.inclusivedemocracy.org/journal/vol3/vol3_no1_Latouche_degrowth.htm.

Lawn, Philip (2003) 'A theoretical foundation to support the index of sustainable economic welfare (ISEW), Genuine Progress Indicator (GPI0 and other measures'. *Ecological Economics* 44 (1), 105–118.

Layard, Richard (2005) *Happiness.* London: Penguin.

Levett, Roger, Ian Christie, Michael Jacobs and Riki Therivel (2003) *A Better Choice of Choice – quality of life, consumption and economic growth.* London: Fabian Society.

Lewis, David and Darren Bridger (2001) *The Soul of the New Consumer: Authenticity – what we buy and why in the new economy.* London: Nicholas Brealey.

Lientz, Bennet and Kathryn Rea (2001) *The 2001 Professional's Guide to Process Improvement: Maximizing profit, efficiency, and growth.* Colorado: Aspen Publishers Inc.

Liu, Guy (2008) Think-piece contributed to the SDC workshop 'Decoupling Lite – can decoupling work?' February 2008. London: Sustainable Development Commission. Online at www.sd-commission.org.uk/pages/redefining-prosperity.html.

Lord, Clive (2003) *A Citizen's Income – a foundation for a sustainable world.* Charlbury, Oxford: Jon Carpenter Publishing.

Lynas Mark (2004) *High Tide.* London: Flamingo.

Maddison, Angus (2007) *Contours of the World Economy 1 – 2030: Essays in macro-economic history.* Oxford: Oxford University Press.

Maddison, Angus (2008) 'Historical statistics for the world economy'. Online at www.ggdc.net/maddison/.

Mankiw, Gregory (2007) *Macroeconomics.* 6th Edition. New York: Worth Publishers.

Marmot, Michael (2005) *Status Syndrome – how your social standing directly affects your health.* London: Bloomsbury.

Marmot, Michael and Richard Wilkinson (eds) (2006) *Social Determinants of Health.* 2nd Edition. Oxford: Oxford University Press.

Mawdesley, Emma (2004) 'India's middle classes and the environment'. *Development and Change* 35 (1), 79–103.

Max Neef, Manfred (1992) *Human-scale Development: Conception, application and further reflection.* London: Apex Press.

McCracken, Grant (1990) *Culture and Consumption.* Bloomington and Indianapolis, Indiana University Press.

McKibben, Bill (2007) *Deep Economy – the wealth of communities and the durable future.* New York: Henry Holt & Co.

MEA (2005) *Ecosystems and Human Wellbeing: Current states and trends.* Washington DC: Island Press.

Meadows, Donella, Dennis, Meadows, Jørgen Randers and William W. Behrens III (1972) *The Limits to Growth.* A report to the Club of Rome. New York: Universe Books.

Meadows, Donella, Jørgen Randers and Dennis Meadows (2004) *Limits to Growth – the 30 year update.* London: Earthscan.

Meinshausen, Malte, Nicolai Meinshausen, William Hare, Sarah Raper, Katja Frieler, Reto Knutti, David Frame and Myles Allen (2009) 'Greenhouse-gas emission targets for limiting global warming to 2°C'. *Nature* 458, 1158–1162.

Merck Family Fund (1995). The Harwood Group *Yearning for Balance: Views of Americans on consumption, materialism and the environment*. Takoma Park, MD: Merck Family Fund.

Meyer, Aubrey (2004) 'Briefing: Contraction and convergence'. *Engineering Sustainability* 157 (4), 189–192.

Mill, John Stuart (1848) (reprinted 2004) *Principles of Political Economy*. Great Minds Series. New York: Prometheus Books.

Monbiot, George (2006) *Heat – how we can stop the planet burning*. London: Penguin.

NCC (2006) 'Shopping generation'. London: National Consumer Council.

nef (2006) 'A wellbeing manifesto'. London: New Economics Foundation.

nef (2009) 'National accounts of wellbeing – bringing real wealth into the balance sheet'. London: New Economics Foundation.

Nordhaus, William (2007) 'A review of "The Stern review on the economics of climate change"'. *Journal of Economic Literature* 45(3), September.

Norman, Jesse, Kitty Ussher and Danny Alexander (2007) 'From here to fraternity: Perspectives on social responsibility'. London: CentreForum.

Northcott, Michael (2007) *A Moral Climate – the ethics of global warming*. London: Darton, Longman and Todd.

Nussbaum, Martha (2006) *Frontiers of Justice: Disability, nationality and policy design*. Cambridge: Cambridge University Press.

OECD (2002) 'Towards sustainable consumption: An economic conceptual framework'. Paris: Organisation for Economic Co-operation and Development.

OECD (2006) 'International comparisons of labour productivity levels'. Paris: Organisation for Economic Co-operation and Development. Online at www.oecd.org/dataoecd/31/7/29880166.pdf.

OECD (2007) 'Beyond GDP – measuring progress, true wealth and the wellbeing of nations'. Summary Notes from the Conference. Online at www.beyond-gdp.eu/download/bgdp-summary-notes.pdf (accessed 12th July 2009).

OECD (2008) 'Growing unequal? Income inequality and poverty in OECD countries'. Paris: Organisation for Economic Co-operation and Development.

Offer, Avner (2006) *The Challenge of Affluence*. Oxford: Oxford University Press.

Offer, Avner (2007) 'A vision of prosperity'. Think-piece for the SDC workshop Visions of Prosperity. November 2007. London: Sustainable Development Commission. Online at www.sd-commission.org.uk/pages/redefining-prosperity.html.

O'Brien, Karen, Bronwyn Hayward and Berkes, F. (2009) 'Rethinking social contracts: Building resilience in a changing climate'. *Ecology and Society* [forthcoming].

O'Neill, John (2008) 'Living Well – within limits: Wellbeing, time and sustainability'. Think-piece for the SDC seminar 'Living Well – within limits', April 2008. London: Sustainable Development Commission. Online at www.sd-commission.org.uk/pages/redefining-prosperity.html.

Ormerod, Paul (2008) 'Is the concept of "wellbeing" useful for policy making?' Think-piece for the SDC seminar 'Living Well – Within Limits'. April 2008. London: Sustainable Development Commission. Online at www.sd-commission.org.uk/pages/redefining-prosperity.html.

Oulton, Nicholas (1996) 'Competition and the dispersion of labour productivity amongst UK companies'. NIESR Paper No 103. London: National Institute of Economic and Social Research.

Patterson, Walt (2007) *Keeping the Lights On: Towards sustainable electricity*. London: Chatham House/Earthscan.

Pearce, David, Anil Markandya and Ed Barbier (1989) *Blueprint for a Green Economy*. London: Earthscan.

Pearce, David and Kerry Turner (1990) *Economics of Natural Resources and the Environment*. Baltimore, MD: John Hopkins University Press.

Pepper, Miriam, Tim Jackson and David Uzzell (2009) 'Values and sustainable consumer behaviours'. *International Journal of Consumer Studies*. Special issue on Sustainable Consumption [forthcoming].

Perez, Carlota (2002) *Technological Revolutions and Financial Capital, the Dynamics of Bubbles and Golden Ages*. Cheltenham: Edward Elgar.

PERI (2008) 'Green recovery: A program to create good jobs and start building a low-carbon economy'. Report by the Political Economy Research Institute, University of Massachusetts, Amherst, September 2008. Washington DC: Center for American Progress.

Polanyi, Karl (1942) (reprinted 2002) *Great Transformation – the political and economic origins of our time*. Uckfield: Beacon Press.

Porritt, Jonathon (2005) *Capitalism – as if the world matters*. London: Earthscan.

Putnam, Robert (2001) *Bowling Alone: The collapse and revival of American community*. New York: Simon and Schuster.

Rapp, Hilde (2007) 'Fulfillment and prosperity: A neo-Gandhian vision'. Think-piece for the SDC seminar 'Visions of Prosperity', November 2007. London: Sustainable Development Commission. Online at www.sd-commission.org.uk/pages/redefining-prosperity.html.

Reay, David, Colin Ramshaw and Adam Harvey (2008) *Process Intensification: Engineering for efficiency, sustainability and flexibility*. Oxford: Butterworth-Heinemann.

Ritzer, George (2004) *The McDonaldization of Society*. New York: Pine Forge Press.

Robeyns, Ingrid and Robert van der Veen (2007) 'Sustainable quality of life – conceptual analysis for a policy-relevant empirical specification'. MNP report 550031006/2007. Bilthoven: Netherlands Environmental Assessment Agency.

Rothman, Dale (1998) 'Environmental Kuznets curves – real progress or passing the buck? A case for consumption-based approaches'. *Ecological Economics* 25 (2), 177–194.

Rutherford, Jonathan (2008) 'Wellbeing, economic growth and recession'. Think-piece for the SDC workshop 'Living Well – Within limits'. March 2008. London: Sustainable Development Commission. Online at www.sd-commission.org.uk/pages/redefining-prosperity.html.

Sandel, Michael (2009) 'The new citizenship', 2009 Reith Lectures. London: BBC. Online at www.bbc.co.uk/worldservice/specialreports/2009/06/090612_reith_lectures_2009.shtml.

Sardar, Ziauddin (2007) 'Prosperity: A transmodern analysis'. Think-piece for the SDC seminar 'Visions of Prosperity', November 2007. London: Sustainable Development Commission. Online at www.sd-commission.org.uk/pages/redefining-prosperity.html.

Schor, Juliet (1992) *The Overworked American – the unexpected decline in leisure*. New York: Basic Books.

Schor, Juliet (1998) *The Overspent American: Upscaling, downshifting and the new consumer*. New York: Basic Books.

Schumpeter, Joseph (1934) (reprinted 2008) *The Theory of Economic Development*. London: Transaction Publishers.

Schumpeter, Joseph (1950) (reprinted 1994) *Capitalism, Socialism and Democracy*. London: Routledge.

Schumpeter, Joseph (1954) (reprinted 1994) *History of Economic Analysis*. London: Routledge.

Schwartz, Shalom (1994) 'Are there universal aspects in the structure and contents of human values?'. *Journal of Social Issues* 50, 19–45.

Schwartz, Shalom (1999) 'A theory of cultural values and some implications for work'. *Applied Psychology* 48 (1), 23–47.

Schwartz, Shalom (2006) 'Value orientations: Measurement, antecedents and consequences across nations'. In Jowell, R., C. Roberts, R. Fitzgerald and G. Eva (eds) *Measuring Attitudes Cross-nationally –lessons from the European Social Survey*. London: Sage.

Scitovski, Tibor (1976) *The Joyless Economy*. Oxford: Oxford University Press.

SDC (2003) 'Redefining prosperity: Resource productivity, economic growth and sustainable development'. London: Sustainable Development Commission. Online at http://tinyurl.com/ckuurl.

SDC (2006a) 'Redefining progress. Report of the SD panel consultation on Progress'. London: Sustainable Development Commission. Online at www.sd-commission.org.uk/publications/downloads/RedefiningProgressv2.pdf.

SDC (2006b) 'The role of nuclear power in a low-carbon economy'. London: Sustainable Development Commission.

SDC (2006c) 'I will if you will'. Report of the UK Sustainable Consumption Round Table. London: Sustainable Development Commission/National Consumer Council.

SDC (2007) 'Turning the Tide – tidal power in the UK'. London: Sustainable Development Commission.

SDC (2009a) *Prosperity without Growth? The transition to a sustainable economy*. London: Sustainable Development Commission.

SDC (2009b) *A Sustainable New Deal – a stimulus package for economic, social and ecological recovery*. London: Sustainable Development Commission.

Sears, Alexandra and Giovanni Ruta (2007) 'Adjusted Net Saving (ANS) as percentage of GNI'. Contribution to Beyond GDP: measuring progress, true wealth and the wellbeing of nations. World Bank: Washington DC.

Sen, Amartya (1984) 'The living standard'. *Oxford Economic Papers* 36, 74–90.

Sen, Amartya (1985) *Commodities and Capabilities*. Amsterdam: Elsevier.

Sen, Amartya (1998) 'The living standard'. Chapter 16 in Crocker, D. and T. Linden (eds) (1998) *The Ethics of Consumption*. New York: Rowman and Littlefield, 287–311.

Sen, Amartya (1999) *Development as Freedom*. Oxford: Oxford University Press.

Sheerin, Caroline (2002) 'UK material flow accounting'. *Economic Trends* 583 June 2002, 53–61.

Shelton, Beth Anne (1987) 'Variations in divorce rate by community size: A test of the social integration explanation'. *Journal of Marriage and the Family* 49, 827–832.

Sippel, Alexandra (2009) 'Back to the future: Today's and tomorrow's politics of degrowth economics (décroissance) in light of the debate over luxury among eighteenth and early nineteenth century Utopists'. *International Labor and Working-Class History* 75, 13–29.

Smith, Adam (1776) (reprinted 1937) *An Inquiry into the Nature and Causes of the Wealth of Nations*. New York: Modern Library.

Sober, E. and D. Wilson (1998) *Unto Others – The evolution and psychology of unselfish behaviour*. Cambridge, Mass: Harvard University Press.

Solow, Robert (1956) 'A contribution to the theory of economic growth'. *Quarterly Journal of Economics* 70(1), 65–94.

Soper, Kate (2008) 'Exploring the relationship between growth and wellbeing'. Think-piece for the SDC Seminar 'Living Well – Within Limits'. February 2008. London: Sustainable Development Commission. Online at www.sd-commission.org.uk/pages/redefining-prosperity.html.

Soros, George (2008) *The New Paradigm for Financial Markets. The credit crisis of 2008 and what it means*. London: PublicAffairs.

Sorrell, Steve (2007) 'The rebound effect: An assessment of the evidence for economy-wide energy savings from improved energy efficiency'. Report by the Sussex Energy Group for the UK Energy Research Centre. London: UK Energy Research Group.

Stahel, Walter and Tim Jackson (1993) 'Optimal utilisation and durability: Towards a new definition of the service economy', Chapter 14 in Jackson, T. (ed) *Clean Production Strategies: Developing preventive environmental management in the industrial economy.* Boca Raton, Fl. Lewis, 261–294.

Stern, Nicholas (2007) *The Economics of Climate Change: The Stern Review.* Cambridge: Cambridge University Press.

Stiglitz, Joseph, Amartya Sen and Jean-Paul Fitoussi (2008). CMEPSP Issues Paper, 25 July 2008. Commission on the Measurement of Economic Performance and Social Progress. Paris: CMEPSP.

Swan, Alan (1956) 'Economic growth and capital accumulation'. *Economic Record* 32, 344–361.

TEEB (2008) 'The economics of ecosystems and biodiversity'. Interim Report. Brussels: European Commission.

Tietenberg, Tom (1990) 'Economic Instruments for environmental regulation'. *Oxford Review of Economic Policy* 6 (1), 17–33.

Timmer, Marcel, Mary O'Mahony and Bart van Ark (2007) 'EU KLEMS Growth and Productivity Accounts: Overview November 2007 Release'. Groningen: University of Groningen. Online at www.euklems.net/data/overview_07ii.pdf (accessed 10th July 2009).

Townsend, Peter (1979) *Poverty in the United Kingdom – a survey of household resources and standards of living.* London: Penguin.

Tukker, Arnold and Birt Jansen (2006) 'Environmental impacts of products: A detailed review of studies'. *Journal of Industrial Ecology* 10 (3), 159.

Turner, Kerry, Sian Morse-Jones and Brendan Fisher (2007) 'Perspectives on the "Environmental Limits" concept'. Research report completed for the Department for Environment, Food and Rural Affairs. London: Defra.

UN (2007) 'World population prospects: The 2006 revision, highlights'. Working Paper No. ESA/P/WP 202. UN Department of Economic and Social Affairs. New York: United Nations. Online at www.un.org/esa/population/publications/wpp2006/WPP2006_Highlights_rev.pdf.

UNDP (2005) *Human Development Report.* Oxford: Oxford University Press.

UNEP (2008) 'Global Green New Deal – UNEP Green Economy Initiative'. Press Release at London Launch, 22nd October 2008. Online at: www.unep.org/Documents.Multilingual/Default.asp?DocumentID=548&ArticleID=5957&l=en (accessed 11th July 2009).

Veblen, Thorstein (1898) (reprinted 1998) *The Theory of the Leisure Class.* Great Minds Series. London: Prometheus Books.

Victor, Peter (2008a) *Managing without Growth – slower by design not disaster.* Cheltenham: Edward Elgar.

Victor, Peter (2008b) 'Managing without growth'. Think-piece for the SDC workshop 'Confronting Structure'. April 2008. London: Sustainable Development Commission. Online at www.sd-commission.org.uk/pages/redefining-prosperity.html.

von Weizsäcker, Ernst and Jochen Jesinghaus (1992) *Ecological Tax Reform. A policy proposal for sustainable development.* London: Zed Books.

von Weizsäcker, Ernst, Amory Lovins, L. Hunter Lovins (1998) *Factor Four: Halving resource use, doubling wealth.* London: Earthscan.

Wachtel, Paul (1983) *The Poverty of Affluence – a psychological portrait of the American Way of Life.* New York: The Free Press.

Wall, Derek (2008) 'Prosperity without growth'. Think-piece for the SDC workshop: 'Confronting Structure'. April 2008. London: Sustainable Development Commission. Online at www.sd-commission.org.uk/pages/redefining-prosperity.html.

Weber, Max (1958) *The Protestant Ethic and the Spirit of Capitalism* (translated by Talcott Parsons). New York: Charles Scribner's Sons.

WHO (2004) 'Prevalence, severity and unmet need for treatment of mental disorders'. *Journal of the American Medical Association* 291, 2581–2589.

Wilkinson, Richard (2005) *The Impact of Inequality: How to make sick societies healthier.* London: Routledge.

Wilkinson, Richard and Kate Pickett (2009) *The Spirit Level – why more equal societies almost always do better.* London: Penguin.

Williams, Tennessee (1955) (reprinted 2001) *Cat on a Hot Tin Roof and Other Plays.* Penguin Modern Classics. London: Penguin.

WRI (2000) *The Weight of Nations – material outflows from industrial economies.* Washington DC: World Resources Institute.

Wright, Robert (1994) *The Moral Animal – why we are the way we are.* London: Abacus.

Index